DATE DUE

DE 7 '95			
NV 17			
NO 6'00			
MR 15 '05			
JE 28 '05			
5 06			
OC 7 08			

DEMCO 38-296

HOPE IS THE LAST TO DIE

HOPE IS THE LAST TO DIE

A COMING OF AGE UNDER NAZI TERROR

A CLASSIC OF HOLOCAUST LITERATURE

EXPANDED WITH A NEW POSTSCRIPT

HALINA BIRENBAUM

Translated from the Polish by
David Welsh

M.E. Sharpe
Armonk, New York
London, England

)k may be reproduced in any form
e publisher, M. E. Sharpe, Inc.,
nonk, New York 10504.

title *Nadzieja umiera ostatnia*
arsaw, 1967.
sonal Documentation of Nazi Terror, published
, New York, 1971.
y Hakibutz Hameuhad, Tel Aviv, 1983.
German editions, *Die Hoffnung Stirbt Zuletzt,* published by Rainer Padligur Verlag, Hagen, 1989,
and Fischer Taschenbuch Verlag, Frankfurt am Main, 1995.
Auschwitz editions published by Publishing House of the State Museum, Auschwitz, 1993 (German,
Die Hoffnung Stirbt Zuletzt), 1994 (English, *Hope Is the Last to Die*), and 1996
(with Parol Publishing, Polish, *Nadzieja umiera ostatnia*).

Hope Dies Last, in Polish with English subtitles, an oral record of the events in this book,
was produced by Film Production, Studio WIR, Warsaw, Poland. © 1992 by Studio WIR.
Related films in which Mrs. Birenbaum has appeared are *Contre l'Oubli* [Against forgetting],
produced by France 2–Taxi Productions, Paris, France, 1995; *La Mort en Face* [Facing death],
produced by Planette–Cable–France 2–Taxi Productions, Paris, France, 1995;
and *Because of That War,* produced by Israeli Film Service, Jerusalem, Israel, 1988.

Library of Congress Cataloging-in-Publication Data

Birenbaum, Halina, 1929–
[Nadzieja umiera ostatnia. English]
Hope is the last to die : a coming of age under Nazi terror /
Halina Birenbaum.—A new, expanded ed.
p. cm.
ISBN 1-56324-746-1 (hardcover : alk. paper).—
ISBN 1-56324-747-X (paperback : alk. paper)
1. Jews—Poland—Warsaw—Persecutions.
2. Holocaust, Jewish (1939–1945)—Poland—Personal narratives.
3. Birenbaum, Halina, 1929– .
4. Warsaw (Poland)—Ethnic relations.
5. Holocaust survivors—Israel—Travel—Poland.
I. Title.
DS135.P62W256313   1996
940.54'7243—dc20
95-49342
CIP

Printed in the United States of America

The paper used in this publication meets the minimum requirements of
American National Standard for Information Sciences—
Permanence of Paper for Printed Library Materials,
ANSI Z 39.48-1984.

EB (c)   10   9   8   7   6   5   4   3   2   1
EB (p)   10   9   8   7   6   5   4   3   2   1

Introduction

I received a copy of *Hope Is the Last to Die* in June 1995 with the question: would I be willing to publish a new English-language edition? After a brief correspondence with Halina Birenbaum the matter was arranged. In September I met the author in New York. We spent several hours discussing changes that she wanted to make to bring an otherwise excellent translation closer to the meaning that she intended to convey in the original Polish. During that time, I had an opportunity to form an impression. She is as she writes: direct and open; and her conversation makes the same impression as her writing: that of a woman who saw so much death that she marvels at life.

We know about the Holocaust because we have read about it and we don't know about it because we weren't there. Here is a book that takes us as close as we will ever get. It burns with an urgency and an immediacy that forces us to see, hear, smell, taste, and feel the Holocaust as the author did from the time that she was ten in occupied Warsaw until she was fifteen in the concentration camp at Neustadt-Glewe from which she was liberated. We feel endless terror—the terror of occupation; the terror of rifle shots, falling bombs, and smoking rubble; the terror of being hunted like an animal to be exterminated. And the terror of the "selections" in the concentration camps: the "strong" go to the right and live; the "weak" go to the left and die. Through the eyes of a young girl we see everything shattered—her family, Warsaw, Poland, humanity, even the idea of a merciful God who presides over the universe. Everything shattered except her will to live and hope despite the unfathomable evil that surrounded her.

More than half a century has passed since the end of the Holocaust. Most people alive today were either children or were yet unborn. What do these seemingly remote events mean now? What will they mean in the future? I entered into a correspondence with Halina Birenbaum and asked her questions.

"What can you say to new readers?" She replied:

> I show through my book that people today *can* understand and identify with our suffering and struggle for life in the Holocaust. We were ordinary human beings with normal human feelings. After the Holocaust people used to say that the truth about this tragedy was impossible to describe, it could not be understood by those who were not there. I am happy that I have been able to refute this false theory and to prove the opposite. Everything that a human being experiences can be described—life, death, love, hate, longing, fear. For many years people were afraid to hear what happened and didn't want to know the whole naked truth. They lost the chance to learn how strong hope is, the real value of life and human feeling—their power even in the worst circumstances, in hell.

I wrote back with these questions: "What do you tell people when they ask why we should remember the Holocaust? And how, in what way, should we remember it?"

> We learn about historical events and pass the knowledge from generation to generation over the centuries. What happened during the Holocaust is something that mankind never experienced before, could not even imagine. Daily murder, the worst evil that human beings ever faced, became normal, legal. It was no longer important who was a doctor, who was a professor, who had an even higher rank—the prominence that we today admire so much and strive for ourselves—all this was ridiculous, banal. All we wanted was a little air to breathe, a little place to put our bodies—something to put in

our mouths besides the smoke of the crematorium burning thousands of people who only moments before got out of boxcars hugging their children.

We have to remember the Holocaust because of the people who didn't survive. They wanted to stay alive to tell the world all that I have told, their last dream was to be remembered. We all, the whole of humanity, owe them that. When I speak about those who did not survive, describe them, I am trying to give them another hour of life so they can live on in the minds and hearts of those who hear me. The murderers, the Nazis, didn't want anybody to know what they did to us. If we do not remember today—forever—we do what *they* wanted!

Remembering is not for the purpose of hate, not for vengeance, but to learn what hate brings. Remember so as to preserve your humanity, to be proud of your human feelings. Remember so as to learn what we must not be.

This was my last question: "Which members of your family, besides yourself and your brother Marek, survived?"

As to my family before the Nazis came, we had both grandparents from my mother's and father's sides and my mother had two grandmothers from her father's and mother's sides. We had many uncles, aunts, cousins, and my brother Hilek. Aside from Marek and me [Marek, or Mark, now lives near Cleveland], only one cousin survived, Rachelka, whom I met in Majdanek.

I would like to repeat a proverb that appeared on the dust jacket of the first English-language edition. It is said in the Jewish tradition that it would be enough if a book merely recorded the events witnessed. When the record is enhanced by vivid words, the document becomes all the more precious. Perhaps the unknown writer of the proverb would not object if we added a third category. When an author records events, records them in vivid words, and speaks for six million who cannot speak for themselves, her document is transformed. It is no longer simply a document but a testament.

How long will it be before we are ready for it?

M. E. Sharpe
February 1996

Preface

I was aged ten in 1939. I lived through the war and occupation in the Warsaw ghetto, and in the concentration camps at Majdanek, Auschwitz, Ravensbrück and Neustadt-Glewe. In the ghetto and later in Auschwitz I often noted down my impressions and observations of those terrible times. In Auschwitz I used to write on scraps of empty cement sacks. But I was not able to keep these notes until liberation came. In any case, I did not make notes with the idea of using them later; they simply helped me in some way to survive.

Hope Is the Last to Die consists of recollections from 1939 to 1945; it is my first extensive work.

In June 1945, after the Soviet army liberated our camp, I went back to Warsaw, where I almost immediately began studying at night school. In 1947 I emigrated to Israel with a group of young people from a Jewish association. I worked in a kibbutz until my marriage in 1950.

When I arrived in Israel, at the beginning of the War of Independence in 1947, everyone was struggling for his very existence and that of the State which had just been established. There was no time to talk about still fresh memories. There was also no one interested in listening. There was no lack of burning issues of the moment, and a great desire to provide us with new experiences and values—different ones, the ones of Israel.

I accepted this. I dealt with the needs and obligations of the present. I lived then as if I had known no other reality—as if everything had begun only from then. And in this way I suppressed a great part of myself deep within me. I ignored myself to a great extent.

The Eichmann trial proved a great turning point in my life. From the time that the uplifting voice of the prosecutor, Mr. Gideon Hausner, was heard over the air waves I sat glued to the radio. I left my housework. I neglected the children. I did only the minimum things necessary—and I listened to the trial. I *lived* the trial. Everything awakened in me anew with a great intensity. I saw clearly all the scenes from the past as if I held them in the palm of my hand. I returned to my true self. I was now complete. I belonged—to the past *and* to the present.

Practically the entire country listened to the testimony of the trial. My life and my roots were no longer hidden, rejected and unknown. I *also* came from somewhere. I *also* was born someone even though no trace of my past life remained. For me in many ways it was like returning home, feeling that I *was* home. But in many of the witnesses' shocking statements that were heard at the trial I felt something was missing, something very familiar to me—the unceasing feeling of terror that existed in living among all those horrors. I lived that feeling during the six years of that dreadful war—years where every hour was like eternity or like the hour before your last.

For days and nights on end I described all this to my husband until one day he exclaimed, "Write it all down in a book!" I was stunned and terrified at the very idea. Me? How? How could one include it all? So many facts and events, so much suffering and desperate hope! Six years of days, nights, and feelings . . .

It gave me no rest. I felt pangs of conscience—as if I wanted to evade a heavy and compulsory obligation.

When I finished writing I didn't fall asleep till the morning. I lay awake all night, eyes open wide. I felt wonderful—I had done everything demanded of me in my lifetime. It was really what I was obliged to do in this world—and I had accomplished it! Here was the end, the summit of my journey.

My dear ones—all their past, and my past together with them, their lives and their deaths—were no longer locked away inside me. It was as if they were living once again beside me. Anyone could know them, could know *about* them—anyone who was close to me today and anyone who was interested.

Through this book I reached the hearts of many people. I was privileged to gain friends in many countries—children and adults, Jews and people of other lands. They identified with me. They showed deep understanding and appreciation. I don't have enough words to acknowledge them. I was moved to tears to discover the wonderful feeling for me from people far away, people I had never known. I realized that everywhere there are people who are prepared to listen, to sympathize. When you open your heart sincerely and tell the whole truth with love and faith, it will be accepted, however difficult and painful it may be. And it seems it will awaken within them hope in life.

One of my fondest dreams, that this, my life's story, be published in my country, in the mother tongue of my children, that they, their friends and my friends in Israel might read it, came true with the Hebrew translation of the book in 1983.

Now another of my greatest wishes, that my book be made available again in the most widely read language in the world, has been granted. I want to thank from the bottom of my heart all those who have helped in realizing the mission of my life.

(translated from the Hebrew by Elaine Morton)

HOPE IS THE LAST TO DIE

I was born and raised in Warsaw.

We lived on Nowiniarska Street—my mother, father and two elder brothers. My father, who came from Biala Podlaska in Eastern Poland, was in business in a small way. My mother took care of our home, and supplemented our modest finances by sewing. She came from Zelechow (Warsaw province). She was remarkably courageous and wise, and I loved and respected her more than I did the other members of my family. Both my brothers were still studying: Marek was a medical student in France, Hilek attended a trade school.

When September 1939 came, I was just ten and about to enter the third year of elementary school.

Overhearing what the grown-ups were saying that summer, I realized that Poland was threatened by a war far worse than the previous war, to be waged by great numbers of airplanes, explosive bombs and gas, and that it would be a war especially terrible for us, the Jewish people. I could not imagine what it would be like, but a persistent sensation of fear haunted me. I was obscurely afraid of something, and expected my mother to reassure me. But her uneasiness and unhappiness said more to me than any words of comfort . . . The oppressive atmosphere in Warsaw, the groups of anxious people in the streets nervously discussing political events, radio news . . . It all boded no good.

Then the war broke out! Our evil forebodings became a reality and a nightmare.

Squadrons of *Messerschmitts* and the glow of conflagrations veiled the Warsaw sky. Alarm sirens wailed, whistling and exploding bombs fell everywhere, bringing misery and death.

During the early days of the siege of Warsaw and the incessant air-raids, we took refuge downstairs in the hallway, believing that the thick walls and structure of the staircase would protect us from shells. As we crouched together, listening to the ominous rumblings, we prayed to God for help.

But the uproar had evidently deafened God Himself. Houses collapsed in ruins, burying people underneath; fires broke out. Death had its hands full.

On Yom Kippur, the holiest of Jewish holidays, the Nazis bombed the Jewish districts with particular force and accuracy. Our street and others went up in flames that same night.

Our house was burned out.

It was as light as day in the yard, but nobody was putting the fires out. There was no water, no food, no strength left.

We fled from the burning house, taking anything we could carry; we managed to reach Swietojerska Street, where a colleague of my brother's lived. There we found shelter in a crowded cellar. A terrible stench prevailed, it was hard even to breathe, but at least the bursting of bombs and roar of aircraft were not so loud, and that in itself seemed happiness to me . . .

After three weeks a strange hush set in. We thought the worst was over. The end of the air raids! How naive! It was not until the Occupation that the enemy revealed its true face.

Warsaw surrendered. Columns of German troops marched into the burning, ruined city. To me they looked invincible, self-assured, powerful. Pale, weary crowds of people thronged the streets, emerging from shelters and cellars, with bundles on their backs, seeking a corner in the houses that still stood. Here and there the Nazis distributed bread and soup from kettles. The famished people of Warsaw stood in lines from which the Nazis at once dragged out any Jews and beat them mercilessly.

For right at the beginning, they separated their victims into "better" and "worse" categories, Aryans and Semites, Poles and Jews—so as then to ill-treat, loot and murder like with like. They set up districts for Germans only, with separate districts for Poles and yet others for Jews. To simplify the differentiation of Jews from other nationalities, they forced Jews to wear a special armband bearing the Star of David; this made it easier to ill-treat them, for the armband served as an identification mark.

My parents found a room on Muranowska Street in an apartment building with a Jewish lady dentist. In the five-room apartment there were already four other families living (people were sleeping in the kitchen too). All our furniture and possessions had been burned in Nowiniarska Street. The few rescued things were kept in a box; my mother arranged for us to sleep on the floor on mattresses saved from the fire. A small clay stove, set up in one corner of the room, enabled us to cook, and in winter it served to warm the room. It was crowded and stuffy in this kitchen of ours, which was also a bedroom, a dining room, a wash and laundry room. Five of us lived there two years—until the deportation.

In the streets assaults and roundups raged. The Nazis seized Jews for slave labor within the city and outside it. Men had to clear away ruins, clean houses for the Germans, and carry about the furniture they looted. Many never returned from this labor, for they were shot or beaten to death. Those who came back— witnesses or victims of the terrible sadism of the Nazis—caused indescribable terror by their reports. The mere sight of the roundups was horrifying. I frequently watched them from the window. Trucks would suddenly appear in a crowded street; passersby took to their heels. With the shout "Halt!" or a gesture, the Germans stopped men and loaded them into the trucks, herding and beating them savagely. While this was going on, they fired into the scattering crowd, at the children who sold candy, cigarettes or armbands in the streets, and who disappeared with their "wares" as fast as they could run. The Nazis also fired into the windows of houses.

The coarse abuse and curses of the Nazi soldiery mingled with the shrieks and cries of the wounded, and the panic-stricken clatter of feet running away. The street and sidewalks were covered with bodies and blood. Finally the loaded trucks would move off, taking their living loot with them.

Then people crept out of their holes and corners again, the traders and beggars reappeared in their earlier positions—everything apparently went back to its previous rhythm, until once again the cry "Germans!" resounded from the depths of a street, paralyzing everyone with fright.

Life was like this for many weeks and months. New victims, new orders and regulations daily restricted our right to live, move and even breathe.

The Nazis established the ghetto in the fall of 1940.

They concentrated Jewish refugees from other towns and all the Jews of Warsaw within an area of a few streets. The ghetto separated them with a high wall from what were known as "Aryan districts," while German gendarmes, and Polish and Jewish police were stationed at the exits.

The Nazis made the *Judenrat* (Jewish Community Committee) responsible for the ghetto. This committee was totally subservient to the Nazis, and together with the Jewish police it blindly carried out their criminal orders. The committee contributed greatly to the sufferings and destruction of the unfortunate inhabitants of the ghetto.

All financial contributions, deliveries of supplies and of human beings for slave labor—later also for extermination and the gas chambers—were obtained by the Nazis from the *Judenrat,* although the wealthy usually bought themselves out, and the poor, being unable to buy themselves out, were taken away at the hands of their fellows and the invaders.

This regrouping of people encouraged the false hope that extermination would not include all Jews, and that anyone with sufficient funds would survive the war—this belief made some people insensitive to the misery of others.

Muranowska Street was within the ghetto area, and this "fortunate" circumstance spared us the sufferings of the thousands who
lived outside the area allotted to the Jews. They were forced to
leave their homes within an hour on pain of being shot, and they
could only take with them what they could carry—so they
pushed their household goods in handcarts or prams. Many had
no place to go. They literally camped in the streets, yards and
hallways, crowds died of starvation, filth, epidemics—because of
the lack of the most primitive facilities.

Hunger did not beset us during the first period of the ghetto,
since Poles with whom my father had worked before the war
used to send us food and help in other ways. A Polish engineer,
Mr. Stanislaw Strojwas, one of my father's acquaintances, gave
us constant help until we left the ghetto.

My elder brother was working as a student in a Jewish hospital, and he also gave injections in private homes. The younger
became an electrician in the ghetto—and so we managed somehow.

Obviously such foodstuffs as meat, sugar, eggs or milk were
not to be had in the ghetto, so we filled our bellies with potatoes,
grits and bread full of chaff and dirt. I gained weight on this diet,
and it proved advantageous to me later on, for I looked a great
deal more serious and was able to deceive the executioners by
concealing my real age from them—according to the Nazi law,
death was the lot of children.

The hard, gloomy days passed, each worse and harder than
those preceding. Incidents and events followed each other so
rapidly that I could scarcely grasp and understand them. Until so
recently we had had everything we needed, and I kept bothering
my mother with questions whether the rumors of war were "really true." My mother had assured me they were not, and asked
me not to listen to "such nonsense." Then, during the air raids,
she had held me close, sheltering me with her own body, telling
me fervently that it would soon be over . . .

When the Nazis occupied Warsaw, and when the bestial terror
began—our only reality—my mother used to calm me with the

assurance that the Nazis' defeat was inevitable and close at hand, that I was not to be afraid, I must gather together all my strength and survive . . .

My mother listened with terror but also with distrust to news spread by refugees from the ghetto in the city of Lodz, of the inhuman cruelty and mass executions of local Jews. "They could not do that in Warsaw, they could not imprison and destroy a half-million Jews!"

That was how my mother reasoned at first, and our neighbors thought the same. Doubting the truth of the nightmarish news, they comforted and encouraged each other, seeking refuge from a tragic and hopeless future.

The streets of the Warsaw ghetto swarmed with beggars in lice-infested, dirty rags. Whole families, swollen with famine, camped in hallways, gates and streets; dead bodies lay there, covered by newspapers or by snow in winter.

An epidemic of typhus broke out, accompanied by indescribable famine. The death rate was so high that it was impossible to keep up with taking the dead bodies away, and carting them to common graves in a cemetery.

Such were the conditions under which I grew up and learned to understand the world. I eyed the beggars, the starving urchins, the dead bodies in the streets, the carts moving through the ghetto carrying boxes into which they piled ten or more dead bodies at a time, so that the lids would not shut . . .

I slowly stopped believing in my mother's assurances.

Although I myself had not yet starved, my heart bled at the sight of the hunger of others, my girlfriend Elusia and her family, the children of the dentist we lived with, who was paralyzed after a nervous breakdown which afflicted her during the bombing of Warsaw in September 1939 . . . Day and night, for many months and despite the curfew, groans and cries resounded in the yards and streets and under our windows *"A shtykele broit, a shtykele broit!"* (A piece of bread, a piece of bread!). I often stole bread or potatoes from home and took them out into the street, but there were so many starving people, so very many—

how could I help them all? I reproached my mother for not letting me give food to the beggars or to Elusia . . . I did not understand that we ourselves did not have too much food, that my mother was sick with apprehension at the thought that tomorrow or the next day we too should want for bread.

There were many things I did not understand. For instance, I could not understand why the misfortune that was Hitler had come upon us, and what it was he wanted from us Jews. I did not understand why the rest of the world watched but said nothing. I wanted to live, and hoped none of my family or friends would perish. I longed for it all to come to an end as soon as possible: the war, the terror, the hunger, the suffering and the constantly circulating rumors that gas chambers and crematoria were being built to exterminate and burn Jews. The eyes of the starving reduced me to despair. I recall how I first learned to read them.

One of my younger brother's friends, a very handsome 18-year-old boy, tall and fair-haired, with blue eyes and an intelligent, noble expression, used to sell bread from door to door. He could not buy the bread for himself . . . He appeared at our house, and when he was taking money from my mother, he glanced at the bread with so much tragic yearning in his eyes that they appeared ready to jump out; his protruding Adam's apple moved rapidly, uneasily . . .

At the time I was eleven years old. I suddenly realized the inhuman anguish of hunger, its humiliation, its helplessness. I felt as though something had burst within me. Yet it was not pity! It was something more than ordinary pity. The boy's glance penetrated the depths of my being, it fastened on to me like a leech, and for some time I could not eat the bread he had sold us. I also lost the desire to play, to do anything at all. For long afterwards I could not regain my mental balance, or shake off my depression.

In later years I was more than once visited by a feeling of helplessness, of despair, at seeing the sufferings of those I loved, and this feeling was usually a hundred times worse than my own sufferings.

Those who did not believe at first that the Nazis would estab-

lish a ghetto and murder the Jews in and around Warsaw—as
they were doing in other smaller towns—finally realized that
they had not reckoned with the bestial intentions and murderous
extent of the Nazis' plans. But even when the ghetto was established, and the murderous aims of the Nazis became known,
many Jews still deluded themselves (and the *Judenrat* tried as
best they could to foster the perilous illusion) into believing that
by maintaining far-reaching caution and obedience towards their
executioners, most Jews could avoid death. These people, mainly
the officials of the *Judenrat,* stated and warned us that any kind
of resistance or (Heaven forbid!) struggle against the Nazis
would immediately bring down a disaster on all Jewry.

Such views, disseminated among the inhabitants of the ghetto,
gave rise to shameful collaboration between the *Judenrat* and the
Jewish police with the Nazis. Collaboration with and blind obedience to the Nazis' savage orders struck hard at the ghetto community.

The more I heard of such things at home from my parents and
their friends, the more indignant I became, and I hated those
traitors.

We found that people can live under even the most inhuman
conditions. People adapt, cope and fight as best they can for existence, trusting that the morrow will be better. We were helped by
our belief that the final defeat of fascism was close at hand.

Soup kitchens were organized in the ghetto for the poor, refugees, homeless people and orphaned children. Dozens of house
committees were formed, as well as a hospital. The assistance the
committees provided was negligible (stealing and corruption occurred here too) since there were more people who needed help
than people able to give it.

Conditions in the hospital were dreadful, for the patients (and
sometimes the dead) lay three to a bed, food was short, and so were

medicines, dressings and everything else. There were hundreds of people wounded and tortured by the Nazis—the hospital could not accommodate them all; these unfortunates increased in number daily.

Study courses were secretly organized in some private homes, attended by a certain number of young people. Jewish patriots gathered together the best individuals in the ghetto with the idea of fighting the Nazi invaders. I was a child, so the existence of a secret organization and the newspaper it published remained concealed from me, but I guessed the truth since my brother Hilek belonged to the *"Hashomer Hatzair."** We had a typewriter at home, so I often saw Hilek using it to copy various materials for the resistance movement. My father opposed this, and kept telling Hilek that the Nazis would take us all to Auschwitz, to our deaths, on account of his illegal scribblings. Even before the war, my father refused to let Hilek go to meetings, and was furious when he came home late from them in the evenings. Now there was no end to the shouting and quarreling. But Hilek dismissed the pleas and demands in silence and went on with his business. Sometimes when he damaged the typewriter in his haste, we would tell Father that I had been playing with it, that it was my fault . . . Father forgave me more easily.

The yard on Muranowska Street was my world of games and daydreams. In the ghetto these yards served children as garden, school, reading room, playing field . . . I played at hide-and-seek, tag, hopscotch with a group of children my own age. Here we told each other of books we read, boasted of our progress in study at the secret courses, for some of us studied despite everything. We told each other scraps of news we gleaned from the grown-ups. The news was of Nazi cruelty, murders and robbery, of shameful acts and bribery by Jewish traitors belonging to the *Judenrat* or the police.

---

*A scouting organization for young people, formed by extreme left-wing Zionists. One of its leaders, Mordecai Anielewicz (1920–1943) became commander in chief of the Jewish Military Organization during the Warsaw Ghetto Uprising.—Ed.

We daydreamed aloud of the good food, fruit and candy that had existed before the war, and which we now yearned for. We talked of distant forests, sweet-smelling meadows and rivers, now accessible to us only in books and from our elders' tales. We enjoyed wondering what things would be like after the war. We joyfully greeted every scrap of news, true or invented, about the German defeats on the Eastern front.

Our chattering, games and play in the yard were often interrupted by the sudden appearance of Storm Troopers (SS). At the sound of the words "Here come the Germans!" we first froze with terror, then rushed as fast as our legs would carry us to our homes and our mothers.

Two years passed in this way.

I studied at home, and although conditions were very hard I worked through the syllabus from the third grade of elementary school to the first grade of secondary school, first under the direction of my elder brother, and later with Mrs. Estera, a private teacher. (She had taught Polish before the war in a Warsaw secondary school; in the ghetto she starved to death.*) Marek paid special attention to my education and regarded it as something essential, despite the terrible proportions of general misery prevailing, and our difficult living conditions.

I liked studying. But I liked reading still better. I would sit over my books until late at night, by a smelly carbide lamp, or a candle, or the little gas flame that often provided the only light in our room. My mother would urge me to bed, but I would find an excuse and say, "In a minute," or "Coming!" or "A little longer"—until in the end my mother, discouraged by vainly scolding me,

---

*I went to her funeral. That was when we still had funerals. Later that was all part of a better past—having a proper burial, in a cemetery, with mourners. Later you just died, were wiped out. No time for a look back, for a few tears. People just turned to stone.

would fall asleep with the rest of the family while I, often stiff with cold, did not go to bed until I had finished my reading.

Studying and reading in those terrible times took me into another world, a world free of Nazis, ghettos and murder.

I believed I would wake up one morning to find no more Germans left in Warsaw, that they would vanish, disappear forever like figures in a nightmare.

Nor was I the only person to have such dreams, for they were the dreams of thousands of oppressed people in the ghetto. But the immediate future proved vastly different.

Towards the end of July 1942, notices were posted on walls in the Warsaw ghetto announcing in Polish and German that all the Jews were to be deported to the East to work there. Anyone who volunteered to go would be given bread and a kilogram of jam; those who resisted would be shot.

Panic seized the ghetto. Adam Czerniakow, president of the *Judenrat,* committed suicide on July 24, 1942.* Czerniakow protested in this way against the deportations, and the news reinforced the terrible suspicion that the Nazi authorities were "tactfully" and cautiously planning mass exterminations.

The despairing people read these notices in a stupor; they speculated in groups in the streets and houses as to what should be done, where and how they might seek help. All food immediately vanished from the stores and stalls, and famine threatened the entire ghetto. There was now no chance of help or escape. All that remained was an unequal fight for an hour of life with a powerful and merciless oppressor. Few were prepared to wage this fight at the time. Generally people were afraid even to think of it.

For years, up to the time of the extensive "campaigns" of deporting thousands of people to the extermination camp at Treblinka, the *Judenrat* kept suppressing the spirit of resistance and fighting in our community. The *Judenrat* was feeble and

---

*Two days later the Nazi authorities started the mass deportations of Jews from the ghetto to the death camp at Treblinka.—Ed.

subservient to the orders of the German Nazis, deaf to our cries
and insensible to people's tears. Its members only wanted to
please their executioners and to save their own skins, the lives of
their families, relatives and friends, and those who could repay
them well for help—in exchange for obedience.

We left our room in the apartment of the sick dentist on
Muranowska Street, took the possessions we considered most
useful, and also warm clothing, in case we were caught and deported to the East . . .

In our hearts we cherished the hope that soon the situation
would clear up, that our panic and fear would prove exaggerated
or groundless, and life would once again proceed in the previous
"calm" rhythm of the ghetto. Saying goodbye to our neighbors,
we wished each other a happy return home and to conditions we
had already become accustomed to enduring in the hard years of
war, occupation and the ghetto. We did not suppose at the time
that we would never see the house or the neighbors again. The
entire street was burned down and later utterly wiped out—our
friends, neighbors and all my playmates were murdered.

As my mother wanted to be with her younger sister Fela, the
best-loved of her entire family, at this crucial time, we moved to
her apartment.

My uncle had already died. During the occupation he had
helped transfer Jews by rail from the Warsaw ghetto to localities
where other Jewish communities were gathered. The procuring
of special passes for them from the Nazi authorities required a
great deal of money, pleas and solicitations for patronage by
middlemen in the *Judenrat.* The Nazis caught my uncle on a train
in 1941 and shot him, along with the members of the group he
was leading.

My aunt's 20-year-old son, Kuba, had been deported to forced
labor in Ostrowiec, from where he gave no sign of life.

My aunt Fela and her daughter, who was two years older than I, lived on the fifth floor of an apartment house on Nalewki Street.

At the time this apartment seemed to be the safest refuge possible—at this height, on the fifth floor (we thought) no one would come looking for us. For we were determined not to let ourselves be deported at any price.

Fierce manhunts for Jews now started. Allegedly, the intention was to send us to work in the East—but in reality, it was a matter of mass extermination in Treblinka, though we knew nothing of this at first, and which was still very hard to believe.

These Nazi manhunts, called "campaigns," began at eight in the morning and continued until evening. Cattle cars were brought daily to the *Umschlagplatz.** The devotees of the Nazi "New Order" used the boxcars to deport Jews to the gas chambers. First they deported those who volunteered to go out of hunger for the bread and jam; next it was the turn of beggars lying in the streets, the refugees swollen with famine, and homeless orphaned children.

Thus they cleared the ghetto streets of the obvious signs of misery, dirt and spreading epidemics. The desperate appeals for pity, for a crust of bread now died away . . .

They—the poorest—were the first victims of the deportations. Those who remained did not have to wait much longer; every day some ten to fifteen thousand people were taken away to meet their death. We knew by the number of freight cars drawn up at the *Umschlag* whether the "campaign" on any particular day would be severe or less severe. Now people spoke of nothing but the "boxcars" and the "campaigns." The Nazis brought in Lithuanian and Ukrainian Nazis for the purpose, while the Jewish and Polish police also roamed the streets of the ghetto, smashing into yards and apartments, dragging people out by force. They broke

---

*A neutral zone between the Aryan and Jewish districts, literally a "loading place," at first used for this purpose. After 1941 Jews brought from the ghetto were loaded into the railroad trains drawn up here and shipped to Treblinka and other extermination camps.—Ed.

down doors with iron bars, penetrated to the darkest corners and hiding places on all floors. They smashed their way in with rifle butts, dragged women downstairs by the hair, snatched away infants, shot feeble or sick people in their beds.

Out in the street, the people had to form by fours in a long, enormous column and march to the *Umschlag* and the boxcars, escorted by armed gendarmes who often struck and killed them on the way.

Calm was restored in the evenings, and then the survivors crept out of hiding. They began looking for relatives and friends, mourning their losses. Some who wished to share the fate of their relatives, or perhaps hoping to help them escape, voluntarily reported at the *Umschlag* . . .

We all—my mother, father, aunt Fela and her daughter Halina— sat out the first days of the "campaigns" at 23 Nalewki Street.

My elder brother was working in the hospital, which was still functioning for the time being. Hilek had been taken to the *Umschlag* to help remove dead bodies.

Storm Troopers and police broke into our yard like a herd of wild beasts: *"Alle Juden heraus!"* (All Jews outside!)

We bolted our door. We could hear the clatter of soldiers' boots on the stairs, the crash of doors being smashed in to neighbors' apartments, lamentations, outcries and appeals for mercy. Sweating, holding our breath, our hearts thumping like hammers, we waited for them to approach our door, to start banging . . . We expected this to happen at any moment, and trembled with terror.

The house on Nalewki Street was enormous, with three wings and three big yards. They kept dragging people out; I had the impression it would never end. Though we lived so high up, they banged several times at our door during the subsequent "campaigns"; fortunately, however, they came towards evening, and were only Jewish police, whom it was not difficult to bribe. So the first deportations passed us by, though our position grew worse every day.

Hilek used to come home in the evenings from the *Umschlag,* completely shattered and barely conscious after the things he had been forced to watch at the *Umschlag* during the day. He simply would not let himself be spoken to: "Don't ask me!" he exclaimed in desperation to my mother. He covered his face with both hands and groaned softly: "God, what are they doing? God, what will become of us?"

Hilek was nineteen. He was an involuntary, daily witness of the killings that went on around the boxcars at the *Umschlag.* He saw them ill-treating and killing his colleagues, our friends. The suffering of my big, strong brother depressed me. The look on his face revealed much more to me than all the talk of the grown-ups at home, though I listened to them with great interest and attention . . .

A terror emanated from Hilek, and it penetrated me through and through.

Of the family, only my mother behaved courageously, without giving way to panic. She alone could control herself, comfort the rest of us and devise new ways of saving our lives.

Hitherto my cousin Halina and I had been preoccupied with ways to beg my mother for an extra crust of bread or spoonful of jam, distributed as though it were medicine, or how to take advantage of her inattention, to sneak them. But now, suddenly, we realized from Hilek's few words and despair that there was something far more terrible than the hunger that tortured us. A great, incessant fear and dread of the "campaigns" became stronger than hunger—and made us forget it.

"Mama, what will they do to us?" I kept asking, and my mother tried to smile serenely, untroubled.

"Don't be afraid," she would say. "If they catch us, we'll go to work in the fields. They won't do anything bad to people who can work and are willing to. We are all young and strong, we can work well, and the Nazis need workers, especially now, after their defeats on the Russian front . . ."

Then she would add, gravely: "Remember, you must always, everywhere, say you are nearly eighteen."

This struck me as rather comical, strange and interesting. The role of a "grown-up young lady" impressed me. But I did not understand why my mother kissed me so often, looking into my face so searchingly and penetratingly. But, even so, I liked it. Before, my mother had been strict, constantly worried about something or other, and could not devote much time to me. Now she longed to avert the doom the Nazis had in store for me, and kept wondering whether I would pass in their eyes as a grown girl, even though I was not yet fourteen . . . By Nazi law, Jewish children, the old and the sick people were sentenced to death . . . My mother, like all mothers in the world, wanted to protect her children—she longed with all her heart for me to live, survive the Nazis and the war.

And she was searching desperately for a way . . .

After a time we, with my aunt and Halina, left the apartment on Nalewki Street and arrived early one morning at a small factory on Stawka Street, where my father worked.

The factory made army boots. It belonged to Toebbens, a German, although before the war it had been the property of a relative of my mother, who now acted as manager there.

My father obtained work in the Toebbens factory thanks to the influence of this relative at the start of the deportation "campaigns," when the Nazis had announced that only Jews working for the Reich would be allowed to stay in the ghetto.

German-owned factories seemed a paradise—life was assured to "productive" Jews and their families. But although we were equipped with an *Ausweis* (I.D. pass) that protected us from roundups and deportation, we soon realized it was safer to go into hiding with an *Ausweis*. Since these factories were not disturbed during the first period of roundups, we decided to take refuge there, particularly so since the Jews managing the factory gave us permission.

So we hurried at dawn along the streets from Nalewki Street to Stawka Street with indescribable feelings of terror. The ghetto was empty, as though dead. I took the slightest sound to be the echo of the footsteps of Nazis lurking everywhere to destroy us. The sight of the streets and sidewalks, stained in many places with blood shed during the "campaign" of the day before, added to the terror. It was eloquent, terrible evidence!

However, we reached our destination without anything dreadful happening. Nervous strain and palpitations—these were after all a low price for the journey. Terror, now regarded as a normal thing and as commonplace as could be, simply did not count any more . . . All that mattered was to survive, not to let ourselves be herded into the boxcars, not to perish—the rest was nothing, of no importance.

We breathed deeply with relief when we reached the factory where the survivors of my mother's family were. We felt more self-confident amidst the noise of machinery and the banging of the factory hammers, surrounded by relatives. The rapid and powerful rhythm of the factory, unconcerned by Nazis or "campaigns," aroused in us a new faith in life. Besides, we no longer had to worry about our grandparents or my mother's youngest sister, who was also here with her husband and two little children. After all, every moment during this period was so fraught with terror and frightening surprises, every step in the direction of a relative's home so risky!

We lay quiet for the next few days and nights in a corner of the factory, in the least conspicuous corner of all, without washing or undressing or even taking off our shoes. We had to be prepared for any eventuality. But we lived for the fleeting moment, trying not to think what the next hour might bring. Under the circumstances, we had to admire the way in which little children behaved, so patiently and sensibly, like grown-up people, as they suffered with us in the factory.

There were no children in the real meaning of the word in the

ghetto, and especially during the criminal deportation campaigns; they were all adults, they all feared for their lives
and struggled ferociously to prolong their lives, if only for
an extra hour. Even the youngest among us understood and
felt this.

The only food at the Toebbens factory was a little barley soup
which my mother cooked once a day, during breaks in between
"campaigns," in an empty apartment in a neighboring house from
which the owners had already been deported. I never left my
mother's side from the moment the deportations started. It was
only with her, and not anyone else in the family, that I felt safe—
in her presence I feared nothing. As she cooked, my eyes were
glued to the pot; I could hardly wait for the moment when I
finally received a few spoonfuls of the hot liquid, for my mother
always fed me before serving the soup to the rest of the family
. . . At the same time I would listen intently for anything suspi-
cious happening in the street and yard.

I do not know where my mother found the courage and willpower to cook in that alien, dead house, in someone else's
kitchen which reminded us of the misfortunes that had befallen
its previous tenants.

This sickly little woman, who suffered from frequent attacks
of gallstones, possessed an iron will and determination. She had
absolute control of herself, and knew precisely what to do in any
situation, without ever losing her serenity of spirit. Glancing
around all the time, so as to avoid Germans, she carried the pot to
the factory and there, spoonful by spoonful, justly and equally,
she served portions of food to each member of our family. Each
was as hungry as the rest! Of course, no one even dreamed of
satisfying his hunger, yet how we relished the soup and its delicious smell! This meatless, unflavored soup had a marvelous
taste. Except that it disappeared so rapidly . . . Then our bellies
would remind us yet again of their presence . . . The despair
emanating from the gaze of all these people, whom I so loved,
depressed me more than any hunger. Only the news that a "campaign" was in progress not far away, in our district, wrenched me

away from thoughts of food, from the torment of hopeless wandering in search of rescue from Nazis prowling through the ghetto.

However, the immunity of "productive" Jews in factories and workshops did not last. The terrifying news spread that the deportation campaigns were increasing in scope, that numerous units of bandits had been brought to Warsaw from various areas of Europe occupied by the Germans, that workers in factories were also being taken away and that people with even the best *Ausweis*, for which they paid large sums, were being herded to the *Umschlag*.

When the manager of the Toebbens factory learned this, he threw out everyone who was not working. He replied to our appeals and entreaties with bluster, pushing us by force down the stairs and into the street. He yelled that our presence threatened the life and safety of the people employed in the factory. That we threatened the very existence of the factory itself!

My mother's uncle also refused to stand up for us. When his colleague and partner threw out the "illegal tenants," he kept silent, as though he did not know us at all . . .

Opposite the outside stairway leading to the factory stood the ghetto frontier guard; the German gendarmes often used to fire in the direction of these stairs, and at the high porch in front of the factory door. More than one person had lost his life here through no fault of his own. When we were struggling with the manager at the factory door, all of us, and especially my mother, who was struggling with the greatest fury, were exposed to mortal danger . . .

But the manager, who knew this perfectly well, remained adamant. He would not let us back into the factory.

So there we were on the open stairs, facing rifle barrels, close to an area where a "campaign" was raging. At any moment it might seize us, or one of the gendarmes might fire at us.

In the twinkling of an eye, my mother realized she could not propitiate the manager. Dragging us after her, she ran down the stairs and made for the nearest gateway. Still agitated and indignant at the stony hearts of the factory managers, we ran upstairs into an attic. Here dozens of people were lying in deathly silence, scarcely breathing.

The heat and stench of the crowded, sweating bodies brought on nausea and faintness. The place stank of foulness, sweat, urine and excrement, for people relieved themselves where they lay, fearing to move while the "campaign" was in progress, lest they be heard from outside.

It is hard to describe what happened when the oppressive silence was broken by the crying of an infant; the cry was noisy, impudent, as though deriding our humility in the face of the Nazis and of Death. The crying of a child who did not know how and did not even want to control its rebellion, its protest against suffering, homelessness, wretchedness, injustice. The fugitives lost their self-control. Their nerves, taut from the constant tension, gave way. A crying child might be silenced by being stifled. And its mother had no right to defend her child or even mourn aloud.

Several dozen people must not die on account of one infant— this was the strict law prevailing in the hiding places of the ghetto.

I lay nestling close to my mother, famished and drenched in sweat. Thirst tormented me. Every now and then I dozed off from exhaustion. I knew that every sound that reached us from the street, every slightest rustle, could decide my life or death. When the noise of a "campaign" drew near, I silently prayed that the Nazis would not find us, that they would not come for us. When a "campaign" ended or moved away, I hugged my mother and relatives joyously. Every hour snatched from the Nazis was a great boon bestowed on me.

Day by day the ghetto grew emptier. Giving Death the slip, we hid in various attics, in different dark holes which, earlier, no one would have thought could possibly serve anyone as a hiding place. Our whole lives now depended on flight and finding ever-new hiding places. Neither our grandparents, nor my uncle, aunt and their two children were with us now. After a few days they had fallen into the clutches of the hunters. We mourned our relatives, many friends and acquaintances. We kept out of the light, avoided open spaces, apartments—our allies were inaccessible recesses, darkness, smelly attics, deep and damp cellars.

But even here the executioners broke in . . . systematic and accurate, assisted by traitors recruited from people of the *Judenrat* and the Jewish police . . . Finally they caught us too.

It happened towards evening, after a day-long "campaign."

We had left the attic, as usual in the evenings, to breathe a little fresh air in the streets, talk to other people and find out who had been taken to the *Umschlag* that day, what the morrow promised, where to buy a little bread or some potatoes which Jews working outside the ghetto boundaries would sell at very high prices. We were walking along together: my father, who had just returned from work in the factory, my mother and Hilek, who had also just come home from his forced labor at the *Umschlag*. I was feeling stupefied as a result of the stuffy attic, the heat and hunger.

Dusk was slowly falling. After a long period of lying motionless among the crowd in an overheated attic, the summer breeze was cool and pleasant. My mother had carelessly pulled on my little woolen jacket—after all, we were only going out for a moment, we had no intention of going anyplace. Besides, we had nowhere to go, no one to visit . . . It would have been hard now to find any of our friends or acquaintances who had not yet been caught, or even to guess where they might be.

Suddenly, unexpectedly, several rickshaws drove into the street—these bicycle-driven carts had been a widely used means of locomotion from the moment the ghetto was established. The rickshaws contained Nazis, Ukrainians and Lithuanians—

"specialists" in hunting down Jews. We were appalled. The
roundup included our street and a few neighboring streets. Never
before had such ambushes occurred so late in the day. Under the
circumstances flight to the attic was impossible. The armed
Nazis jumped out of the rickshaws and scattered, to cut off all
streets except those leading to the *Umschlag.*

We were caught.

With a gesture, they ordered us into the center of the street.
We were the first foursome in a column that grew and swelled
minute by minute.

My father, mother, Hilek and I stood obediently, without pro-
testing either by word or movement, so as not to infuriate the
Nazis or risk a beating or death. For we hoped we would somehow get out of the *Umschlag* because of my father's *Ausweis*
from the Toebbens factory, or of Hilek's string-pulling with one
of the Jewish police officers he knew at the *Umschlag* . . . Hilek
had a pass and was registered as a cleaner and disinfector working there. My mother's fate and that of myself caused the greatest
uneasiness, but we thought that if the Nazis saw fit, they would
free the family of a "productive" Jew, i.e., a Jew still of use to
them. But this was by no means sure. They rarely set free the
trapped wives and children of Jews who had passes and work
papers. If the worst came to the worst—my mother soothed me
on the way to the *Umschlagplatz*—we would go to work in the
fields. Nothing bad would befall us in the countryside.

I listened attentively, trying to read in her face whether she
really thought this, or whether she was afraid of something she
wanted to hide from me. I was extremely upset by this unexpected turn of events in the course of the last few minutes, and
the sudden reversal in our fortunes. I missed the dark hiding
place in the attic, but was not downcast; I did not panic. Clearly,
my mother possessed a miraculous gift for sharing her own calmness with the rest of us. She radiated serenity of spirit and
strength of character.

They brought us to the *Umschlag.* To that hundred-times accursed *Umschlag,* drenched in blood and tears, filled with the

whistling of railroad locomotives, the trains that bore away hundreds of thousands of Jews to the ultimate destination of their lives. The great square, near a building which had been a school before the war, was thronged with a desperate and highly agitated crowd. For the most part, they were workers from factories and workshops in the Aryan district—owners of an *Ausweis,* who until very recently had still possessed "the right to live." When they were coming home from work today, as usual escorted by Storm Troopers to the homes from which their nearest and dearest had been dragged after seizing all their possessions, they had been ambushed.

A high wall and living barrier of policemen, with not so many Nazis, armed to the teeth, now separated us from the ghetto and its hiding places. My elder brother was still there, with my aunt and her daughter, as they had decided not to go down into the street with us.

We waited in suspense for what would happen next, looking around in search of some way out. My father held us close, kissing my mother, brother and me. He held us tightly by the hand, not letting us move even a step away, especially my mother, who fidgeted incessantly, trying to tear us away from the crowd and somehow sneak into the school building, where there was a first-aid post and a Jewish police post. She wanted to hide us there, to prevent us from being herded into the boxcars.

My father was so upset and terrified that he was incapable even of thinking of escape; all he could do was to show his pass to the Hitlerites; he believed up to the last moment that we would all be saved by it. He was afraid. He thought that to disobey the Storm Troopers could only hasten our doom.

My mother was different. That was why I always clung to her, profoundly convinced that she would find us a way out of the worst situation . . . In my father's presence I had completely different feelings.

And now, in the *Umschlagplatz,* the same thing happened.

Freight cars had never before been drawn up at this time of day. So we supposed we would have to wait all night at the *Um-schlag,* until a train arrived in the morning. This gave us some opportunity of escape, of returning to the ghetto and the attic.

Then we saw the Nazis placing a machine gun in the center of the square, aimed at the enormous packed crowd of people, who responded with a murmur of terror. But, although everyone realized what was going on, no one dared cry out or burst into noisy tears. Silence prevailed, uneasy, heavy with tension. We embraced each other: my mother, my father, Hilek and I; we looked at one another in the way that people look for the last time . . . to take with us the picture of beloved faces, before moving into total darkness. Everything else, everything we had lived by and fought for up to now, ceased to matter.

My father was half-conscious, my mother—as always—serene. She even smiled at me.

"Don't be afraid," she whispered in my ear, "everyone must die sometime, we only die once . . . And we shall die together, so don't be afraid, it won't be so terrible . . ."

No, I was not afraid. I simply did not believe it.

I did not comprehend what death meant. I could not imagine there would ever be a time when we would not be in the world, or stop living. I could not comprehend that.

I waited for what would happen next with hope and belief in life and . . . with curiosity. I was seized by a strange, almost joyous mood; this moment seemed to me unusually elevated and very important, though not because it was going to precede death . . .

Suddenly, the whistle of a railroad train was heard.

The freight cars drew up. The machine gun was no longer

necessary. Evidently their plans had changed. We were not to be shot on the spot; a train from Treblinka had come for us.

The Jewish police began hitting people with their sticks and herding them furiously into the boxcars.

My mother seized me by the hand and began retreating in the other direction. She dragged Hilek, my father and me with her, spurning the police and indifferent to the blows of their sticks. If only we could get as far away as possible from the boxcars! She intended to hide for the time being in some corner of the *Umschlagplatz,* then sneak back into the ghetto. My father and brother preferred going to the train with the rest; they were afraid to escape, and thought that the Germans at the boxcars would check my father's pass, then let us go officially. "If they don't," Hilek said, pleading with my mother to listen, "then we will at least go together in this train. We shall share the fate of all the Jews here. I don't want to see them shoot you," he cried in desperation, breaking from her grasp. He urged her with tears in his eyes that when the train left, the bandits would search every nook and cranny in the *Umschlagplatz,* which they already knew by heart. Hilek had himself brought murdered bodies out of them . . .

But he pleaded in vain. My mother had made up her mind; we had to fight to the last, not let ourselves be herded into the boxcars. "We will get out," she said decisively, "we will get out."

And she stubbornly pushed her way through the crowd, energetically dragging us towards the school. She clutched my brother and me by the hand, and my father pushed willy-nilly after us. During these terrible minutes, a hurricane of blows fell on his already bent shoulders. Jewish police surrounded him and tried to herd him to the train. My father attempted to defend himself, to appeal. He shielded himself with his arms from the blows, tried to evade them, but was helpless against their brute force; he crouched down still further, but finally moved obediently to the boxcars. He certainly expected they would check his papers there and let him go, despite the policemen who would not even listen . . .

But no one was checking papers at the boxcars. Papers did not interest anyone, just as no one was interested in the fact that these wretched people were all being sent to execution.

I saw my father for the last time as he walked, bent and helpless under the police blows, to the boxcars . . . He was 47 years old.

But my mother managed to wrench us away from the driven crowd. First we hid in a toilet in the police post on the *Umschlagplatz*. Then we fled from the police, continually changing places as we slipped out of the grasp of some into the clutches of others . . . until the train left.

Finally all was silent, the darkness thickened.

The square emptied. Abandoned objects became visible: prams, pillows, clothing, single shoes . . . We were alone in that great, empty, terrible graveyard.

At any moment Nazi gendarmes might appear and shoot us like dogs.

Hilek and I could not endure the deathly silence, the sudden isolation and the uncertainty. We reproached our mother for keeping us away from the boxcars. After all, we knew there were no hiding places here which the Nazis did not know. And to make matters worse we were standing in the middle of the square, an excellent target for Nazi bullets . . . Hilek was sobbing with terror. He could have saved himself, as an *Umschlag* worker. At worst he would be ordered to remove our dead bodies. But my brother did not want to go on living, if we died.

It was already too late to induce my mother to change her mind; the train had gone. The next would not arrive until morning. Would we live to see that morning? Everything suggested that the worst would happen, just as Hilek feared.

Even now, my mother did not betray fear or hesitation by so much as a single word. She did not regret that we had escaped deportation. She was pleased we had avoided the police, and not been herded into the boxcars. She looked around intently, letting our reproaches go in one ear and out the other. She was wise and courageous. She soothed my brother and me, explaining mildly and kindly that the boxcars meant death (this was the first time she used the word "death"), so why not try to escape? We still had time to encounter death; we should not regret not having gone in that train! We must fight, not give way to fear, we must do all we could, not to be taken in the next trainload.

She spoke serenely, just as though we were sitting in the tranquillity of our own home. Then she straightened the jacket around her shoulders and, taking me firmly by the hand, set off towards the school building. She intended to come to terms with the policemen and hide somewhere in the building. She thought one of them would take us out of the *Umschlag* during the night, in return for promised money or jewelry. We did not have a single penny on us at the time.

Rejected and spurned by the Jewish policemen guarding the entry to the school, my mother appealed in vain to their consciences, she begged for a measure of pity. They would not admit us to the first-aid post. They would not even listen to the protestations of Hilek, whom many knew from his work in the *Umschlag* . . .

Yet they might have hidden us, and taken us back to the ghetto early in the morning, before the "campaign" began again, before the arrival of the train for new loads of people. They could do it, and did it every day, though only for large sums of money. They even had a set fee for taking people out of the *Umschlag* after bribing the Nazi gendarmes—10,000 zloty "per head" (as they expressed it). But my mother, with a child's jacket thrown over her shoulders, did not look like a person with enough money at her disposal for a bribe. Hilek's presence made them display a certain amount of tolerance, but they did not like it. This was why they refused to help us, brutally driving my mother away like an importunate dog.

Finally we managed to bribe one of them.

He agreed, in exchange for Hilek's watch, to let my mother and me into the building. We were to hide in a drain in the inner yard. During this transaction, a small but characteristic incident occurred, demonstrating the abjectness of the police. As Hilek handed over his watch, another policeman nearby noticed and interrupted at once: "What's this, you are taking a bribe from an acquaintance, an *Umschlag* worker, for rescuing his mother and sister! Aren't you ashamed?" The other thought this over for a moment, then reluctantly gave Hilek his watch back.

We were on the way to our hiding place when the "benefactor" who had appealed to the conscience of his fellow worker caught up with us and . . . demanded the watch for himself.

My mother and I suffered several hours in a narrow drainpipe, fainting and stiffening in a most uncomfortable position. We were shut off from the world by a tightly closed iron grating. Literally, we were in danger of stifling. And Hilek was trembling with fear all the time, lest the Hitlerites find us and shoot us. He had cleared away dead bodies from this very drain more than once.

Fortunately, it turned out later that there had not been enough freight cars for all the people trapped, and a number of them had waited until morning in the police post at the *Umschlag,* and Hilek, on learning this, removed the iron grating he had carefully installed earlier. If there were still people about, then we too could come out and join them without fear that the Germans would shoot us. They only shot individual persons who succeeded in some miraculous way in detaching themselves from a transport.

I scarcely closed my eyes through all that interminable night. Then my mother began again hurrying from one policeman to another, bargaining with them, imploring them to get us away from the *Umschlag* before the train arrived from Treblinka!

Finally, by promising a bribe (a ring, two kilos of rice and Hilek's suit) she managed to persuade a policeman. I could not believe our good fortune: the policeman attached us to a small group whom they assembled at the *Umschlag* gate. We were to go back to the ghetto!

And yet we would never have been able to raise the amount of money it "usually cost" for both of us to get out (20,000 zloty).

I owed this good fortune to my courageous and wise mother. How proud I was of her for not giving way to panic, and not taking any notice of Hilek's and my reproaches and hysteria. For showing such firmness and willpower, so much perseverance in dealing with the policemen!

We went back to the attic in Stawki Street. We found my aunt, Halina and Marek again. There was no end to the embraces during our joyful reunion; it was as though we had not seen each other for years, as if we had returned from the other world.

Perhaps we really had? At least from a hallway leading to the other world . . . There was no news of my father.

On the same evening when the Nazis had herded us to the *Umschlagplatz,* my uncle—manager of the Toebbens factory—was also accidentally seized. He was the man who had so brutally driven the women and children out at the height of a "campaign." My uncle had "ironclad" identity papers ensuring himself and his family safety, but he would have perished like my father had not Hilek saved him from the boxcars at almost the last moment and hidden him not far from us, in the police building. (My uncle's case was much easier than ours, as he had the wherewithal to pay the policemen off.)

When we left the drain and my mother was trying to get out of the *Umschlag,* my uncle, who was moved by Hilek's help and our common fate, promised he would give or lend us part of the money required to ransom us.

Soon, however, we noticed he had . . . vanished, without troubling himself in the least about us. He bribed a policeman who took him back to the ghetto.

All the same, they took my uncle, his wife and their three children to Treblinka soon after this incident. And his *Ausweis,*

money, factory job, and large stores of food, purchased for
enormous sums from smugglers and people working in the
Aryan district—all went for nothing. His egoism and indifference to the sufferings of others did not even assure him
people's remembrance.

So we went back from the *Umschlag* to our stinking attic,
bereaved and uncertain of the morrow. My mother began clinging still closer to her sister, the only person left of her numerous
family.

Terror, hunger and flight, the search for hiding places and
stubborn struggle for each moment of life once again became the
content of our days.

One evening, the German workshop owners Toebbens and
Schultz instructed all their workers to move with their families to
empty houses specially allotted to them. Toebbens's workers
were to move to Leszno Street, those of Schultz to Nowolipie
Street. In this manner they separated their workers from the other
Jews, and a kind of labor camp was created on these two
streets—those who lived there had a solemnly guaranteed immunity from roundups for the *Umschlag*.

Although my father was no longer with us, we took advantage
of the fact that he had at one time worked for Toebbens, and my
mother, Hilek, my aunt and Halina and I moved to 64 Leszno
Street along with the families of workers in that factory.

Marek was still working in the hospital on Leszno Street, not
far from us.

We made the journey from Stawki Street to Leszno Street one
evening; the deserted streets, so full of traffic and noise only a
few weeks earlier, now created an eerie impression. It seemed
that even the bricks of the houses, the sidewalks and streets were
soaked in the atmosphere of Hitlerite crimes!

We kept close to the walls. They might kill us here at any
moment, without troubling even to glance at our passes, or before
we could open our mouths to explain and refer to the orders of
Schultz and Toebbens . . . We were afraid to look around lest we
catch sight of Death in the shape of a green Nazi uniform. Worn

out by constant sojourn in an airless attic, we staggered along like people recovering from a serious illness.

But our "move" succeeded this time, too.

We occupied an apartment of several rooms at 64 Leszno Street. There were only a few other families besides us. We could choose among the empty apartments, whose owners the Nazis had already taken off to execution, though the question of an apartment was of no interest to anyone now. None of us believed in the assurances of the German industrialists, and we were less concerned with comfortable living conditions than with a good (i.e., dark) cellar or attic . . .

The apartment we occupied by chance and without forethought contained many fine things, beautiful furniture, many kinds of toys and splendidly bound books, which would have been an unattainable dream for me before the war. Now they were wasted, no use to anyone, lying in corners. I glanced through some of them, but they brought me no happiness. All the books and toys reminded me of the children to whom these treasures once belonged. Now they were no longer in Warsaw. I felt that they were no longer in this world, though no one had yet told me definitely what really happened to the people taken away in the trains. They disappeared. But was it so certain that they would never, never come back? Suppose they did? I put the toys down carefully, imagining the children coming home, and how I would tell them I had looked after their books and toys during their absence. They would invite me to stay, and we would play together. Then again I was overwhelmed with terror at the idea of what might have happened to those children. The first evening in our new home I could not restrain my indignation; I began to cry and pestered my mother with questions: why are things so terrible in the world, so awful, when would it all end, how much longer would we suffer? But my mother—could she possibly explain, alter, improve anything? Holding me close, she smiled and tried yet again to persuade me, serenely, that everything had a beginning and an end, that it could not be otherwise. "But shall we live to see the end?" I cried, somewhat comforted despite myself by the logic of her reasoning.

"We must fight for that," she said gravely, "fight with all our might and not be downhearted."

The last words were a gentle allusion to my lack of endurance.

I adored my mother. I admired her serenity, her self-control, her wisdom and the way she could fight so courageously for our lives, overcoming fear and withstanding panic throughout those hard, cruel times. I loved her for her unbounded self-sacrifice, for the great love she had for us, her family and everyone she encountered, for the smile that never left her face, even when confronted by death, as on that occasion in the *Umschlag* when the Nazis aimed their machine guns at us, and again later, in many other, equally terrible situations.

During those hard and dangerous times, she developed the habit of talking to us in this way: "I want very much to live and see the defeat of our executioners, which is why I am doing my utmost and will continue to do everything in my power for us to survive, for us to escape their clutches! If we do not succeed, that will be too bad. A person only dies once, and though I would regret losing my life, I do not fear death."

I knew that every word of hers was absolutely true. I longed to be like her. It was not easy. I was scared. I was scared of everything: the Nazis, the everlasting "campaigns," the continuous shooting that accompanied them. But what I dreaded most of all was losing my mother; I shuddered at the mere thought. I could not imagine life without her.

Since my father had been taken away, the bonds between my mother and me became still stronger. We were never apart for even a moment, we shared every glance, every feeling and foreboding, every smallest remark.

My mother now spoke to me as though I were a grown-up person, a friend. During this period I learned to understand her far better than in the good, old days. I read and divined in her eyes the slightest fear, her slightest care or wish in a gesture. She did not have to explain anything to me, nor to say anything; I knew what she wanted, what she was feeling, what she intended to do, or how she viewed anything.

And I tried to obey her in every way, to help her in every way I possibly could.

When my mother was pleased I was full of joy and indescribable pride. My mother's glance, pleased or grateful when I behaved properly without being told, made me happy. Before the war I had often misbehaved and deserved a scolding, and would sulk when my mother reproached me—unjustly, as I used to think. Even in the ghetto, before the deportation campaigns started, I was not a good little girl. But suddenly this all changed, I began seeing everything differently, and my mother became for me the supreme, most perfect of models to imitate, which was a great joy in itself.

Hilek used the last cash we had at this period to bribe the Jewish manager of a workshop, and after a great deal of effort (for the amount of money we had was much less than the amount asked) he obtained work in a group of laborers in the Ursus factory near Warsaw.

From that day on, when he left the ghetto in the morning, he always said goodbye to us as though he were leaving on a long journey. We never knew whether or not we would meet again that evening.

When he came home in the evenings, we would run downstairs to embrace him. For his part, he would loudly give vent to his joy at finding us at home and still alive. Sometimes he brought us a little food from the Aryan side of the wall; he obtained it in exchange for clothing smuggled out of the ghetto, which was a very risky undertaking. On the threshold of our apartment he would often ask uneasily whether anyone had been taken away. When the reply was negative, we would embrace and kiss again, and tell each other what had happened during the day; how the "campaign" had gone, how we had succeeded in hiding, eluded the hunters and emerged alive. Hilek described the cruelty of the Nazi overseers towards the factory workers, the everlasting searches during work, when leaving or entering the ghetto. Then Hilek would unload the contents of his rucksack. Hungry and impatient we waited for my mother to give out the treasures. We ate in the dark, without lights, so as not to attract the attention of patrols prowling the streets at night, and not run the risk of an unexpected "visit."

My brother often spoke of the Poles who worked in the Ursus factory and brought bread and other food to Jews, although they thereby risked death according to Hans Frank's regulation of October 15, 1941. These acts proved there were good people on the other side of the wall who sympathized with us in our misery and were ready to help us, despite the terrible danger and without even knowing us. So we listened to Hilek with emotion and increasing courage in our hearts.

Hilek never touched food at home. He tried to eat as much as he could at work so that the food he smuggled into the ghetto with such difficulty was left for us.

After a while, my mother found work in Schultz's tailor shop on Nowolipie Street. She was excellent at sewing, and on this account obtained the job without bribing the manager, merely making use of the good offices of acquaintances. Hungry and in perpetual terror, she worked twelve hours a day sewing uniforms for soldiers of the *Wehrmacht*, receiving a little soup and *Lebensrecht*—the right to live.

At first she took me with her. I hid behind her sewing machine or under her chair. The window of the room overlooked the yard of 64 Leszno Street. My mother watched everything that went on in the vicinity of our house: she saw whether Nazis came in, and could see what my aunt and Halina were doing in the apartment.

I nestled close to my mother's legs, squatting, always dreading someone might notice me, shout and send me away. I had no right to be there, because in the first place I did not work in the shop, and secondly I was a child, without any right to live.

Not until evening was I spared. At home I could straighten my stiff legs, talk, eat and drink without being afraid. In the shop my mother gave me her ration of thin soup but I was hungry again as soon as I had drunk it.

Daytime was Hell. Nor did we have undisturbed nights.

The Russians began bombing military targets in Warsaw and its vicinity in the summer of 1942. We had to run downstairs to the hallway, already exhausted after a hard day, after hiding from roundups, but revived in spirit by the bombings all the same.

One night, during an air raid, a bomb hit the Law Court opposite where Germans were stationed. Our house shook, and the explosion took off the roof; no one was killed.

But we had lost our hiding place in the attic, and were faced yet again with the question—where should we hide?

The following day promised to be hard: a long line of freight cars was drawn up at the *Umschlagplatz* . . .

My mother decided I should avoid this especially thorough "campaign" (as we expected it to be) in the hospital where Marek was working. My aunt and Halina would hide in our apartment, among rolls of bedding. Hilek went to work as usual, and my mother left for the shop. Early the next morning I went to the hospital with my elder brother. The weather was hot and stifling. Though it was still early, the heat was trying. A great deal of movement and indescribable uneasiness prevailed in the street. People were running aimlessly to and fro, agitated, depressed, feverish; some were going to factories, others to hiding places or brief meetings with relatives or friends. If only they could make it in time before the blockades of the street began, and the start of the "campaign" . . .

I looked around with curiosity and some pride, to be walking along the street so early without my mother, independently, alongside my brother. I wondered what the hospital was like, about Marek's work there and how this exceptionally frightening day would pass.

Marek put me in an empty little room while he went to the patients with whom the hospital was crammed. Every now and then he dropped by to see me for a few minutes and bring me some of his own frugal rations to eat. When he did so, he smiled and broke the silence, put on a brave face and assured me there was no danger here, and that the section of Leszno Street where the rest of the family were was not included in the "campaign." My brother's genuine concern truly relieved, though only briefly, my gloomy thoughts. But the stay in the hospital lasted for ages. My pride at being independent burst like a soap bubble; its place was taken by fear and remorse that I had let myself be persuaded to leave my mother's side, that perhaps I would never see her again.

Hospital employees were wandering about the entire building, conferring with one another continuously, telling one another fresh news of what the Nazis intended to do to the patients and staff. Hunting down Jews took on gigantic dimensions that day. The number of unfortunate people trapped grew by the hour, but there were so many boxcars that they were still unfilled. It was said that the entire hospital was to be liquidated, that Storm Troopers would shoot the chronically ill on the spot, that patients who could walk, and the staff, were to be taken to the *Umschlag*. People looked uneasily out the windows, fearfully awaiting the further course of events.

None of this escaped my attention. I listened in to every word the grown-ups said, seized every sound outside the door, read the gaze of people hurrying by. I understood perfectly well what was happening, and the fact that I knew nobody here, that I was in an entirely alien place, made me feel still worse. I prayed for evening, so I could at last go back to my mother. I vowed inwardly never again to let myself be persuaded to part from my mother, not even if doing so meant a sojourn in the safest possible hiding place! I yearned for my mother, as though I had not seen her in years, instead of only a few hours earlier. I was afraid that either she or I would be taken to the boxcars separately, and we would never see one another again.

However, the campaign did not extend to the hospital that day, nor did any of the terrible things predicted come to pass.

In the evening I walked back to Leszno Street with Marek, along the same streets we had come by in the morning.

Many of the people who had been rushing about here in the morning, seeking refuge and help, were no longer alive. Several tens of thousands had been loaded into the boxcars at the *Umschlagplatz* in the course of the day.

Marek assured me there had been no blockade at our house in Leszno Street, yet I approached with beating heart. I dreaded opening the door of the apartment, and finding no one there . . .

Fortunately my fears proved groundless. My mother saw us through a window, immediately opened the door, and I was in her arms on the threshold. Marek watched, touched and smiling, waiting for my mother to embrace him. At this very moment we heard an unearthly noise and uproar in the street. Alarmed, we rushed to the window. Crowds of Jewish police, armed with sticks and bludgeons, were invading Leszno Street. Like a herd of wild, famished animals provoked by the smell of blood, howling and yelling, they ran into the gateways of the houses.

A "campaign"! For the first time it was being carried out by policemen, without Storm Troopers, and for the first time at such a late hour.

We could not believe our eyes, until another tenant told us that each of the policemen had been ordered to supply four Jews to the *Umschlag*. If he failed, he himself would have to go to the boxcars.

We fled to the attic, which had no roof, but was shrouded in helpful darkness. We lay on the ground side by side. We could hear the police yelling, smashing down doors, sounds of struggling, coarse oaths, scuffling on the staircase. The police traded the people they captured with one another; a man who succeeded in catching more victims sold his "surplus" to a less resourceful colleague. The price was 10,000 zloty a head. As much as it cost to get away from the *Umschlag* . . . And after delivering their live "goods," the police came back to loot the abandoned apartments, as they always did every evening after a "campaign."

They did not find us this time, though they looked into the attic several times.

The next day I did not want to go to the hospital with Marek. My mother could not take me with her to the tailor's shop; the manager strictly forbade her, declaring he would throw out both her and me. And my mother had to work. At the time we thought, like everyone in the ghetto, that if at least one member of a family was working in a factory or outside the ghetto, then that fact provided some chance of survival. We also believed the "campaigns" would finally end. This was why people were now doing their utmost to get into factories or outside jobs; they were not discouraged by the fact that now and then people were dragged away from these jobs too, and taken to the *Umschlag*. Sometimes entire factories fell victim, together with the managers and tradesmen who, after all, were necessary to the Germans and worked for them "productively." But mostly the Nazis did not invade factories daily, as they did apartments.

When my mother and brothers left for work, I stayed behind with my aunt and Halina. A woman with two small children occupied the next room. We hoped that things would be calmer after the previous day's campaign, and that this time they would not blockade our street. It was too light in the attic, they would easily find us there, and the house had no cellars . . . Now and then we observed the street through the window. There was no sign of a storm.

Suddenly we caught sight of Nazis approaching along Leszno Street. "A campaign in our street!" my aunt cried in despair, seizing Halina and me by the hand. We ran up to the attic. Our legs were trembling, our hearts beating with terror.

The Hitlerites blocked the whole of Leszno Street and adjacent side streets. I could imagine my mother's horror as she sat by her window, sewing uniforms for murderers and executioners, watching.

The day was very bright, at the height of summer. The attic, without a roof, was drowned in sunlight, while hordes of Nazi hunters drew closer . . .

Yet we wanted to live!

My aunt hurriedly pushed Halina and me, and the neighbor's two little children, into a closet in one of the undamaged walls of the attic. She put Halina and me on the lower shelf, the two little ones on the top shelf. Then she locked the closet and barricaded it with some broken planks. She and the neighbor went back to the apartment and hid between rolls of bedding, as had been planned in advance.

We children lay with bated breath. The Hitlerites were running up and down the stairs, smashing in doors, shouting, laughing, firing shots . . . Now and then one would break into our attic, pass our hiding place and go on searching. At one moment two stopped right by us. They were talking. The slightest movement, even drawing in or out our breath a little louder than usual, and we were lost.

I tried not to breathe at all. The children above us—one was four, the other six—urinated, no doubt from terror. The urine ran down on my head and face . . . But I hardly felt it. I was shivering with terror lest one of the children involuntarily betray our hiding place. If they burst into tears, for instance, or coughed . . . I sweated with agitation and at the stuffiness prevailing in the crowded dark closet. The two Nazis went away, but the campaign continued. We sat out five hours in the closet.

When dusk came, people did not start creeping out of their lairs and hiding places. They were waiting for the police to finish looting apartments emptied by the campaign. We knew by this time that the campaign had passed us by, and we waited calmly enough, although we very much wanted to get out.

But neither my aunt nor the neighbor appeared, and time passed: people were coming home from work. The worst possible forebodings overwhelmed us; perhaps they had been seized? Perhaps my mother too had been dragged out of the tailor shop, perhaps nobody would come to let us out? And what would we do then?

At long last my mother opened the closet; she seized us in her arms, kissing and embracing us fervently. It turned out that my aunt and the neighbor had been herded to the *Umschlag*. Halina was now orphaned, and when the father of the two little children came home from work in the evening, he took them with him to the *Umschlag*, to join his wife. Hilek and Marek tried in vain to rescue my aunt through Jewish policemen.

My mother had watched helplessly all day through the window of her workroom, and had undergone tortures. When she came home from the tailor's shop and discovered they had taken her beloved sister, she almost gave way to despair, and aged rapidly; for the first time in my life I saw my mother cry.

The Hitlerites stopped the "campaigns" in the fall of 1942. Toebbens and Schultz, the two biggest German industrialists who employed Jews in the ghetto, had previously made huge reductions in the number of their workers, and by doing so, sentenced them to death. Those whom Schultz deigned to continue employing were given a green pass; henceforward only people with green passes had the right to be in the ghetto. Savage struggles to obtain these passes now began—to obtain the right to live.

As one of the best tailors, my mother obtained a green pass from the factory manager without influence or bribery; she brought it home joyfully.

After the reductions and the introduction of passes, the Germans announced there would be a "selection" among all Jews remaining in the ghetto, then the chosen Jews, i.e., the "necessary" ones, would be able to go home and to work; complete calm would then prevail in the ghetto, on the condition, of course, that its inhabitants properly carried out all regulations and orders . . .

For the time being, they ordered us all to assemble in Mila Street, where the announced "final" selection would take place. We went there with everyone else. At the exit from Mila Street was standing a group of armed Germans led by the Storm Trooper Hantke, notorious for his cruelty. He would walk through the ghetto during hours permitted to Jews with his rifle aimed at people, and shoot anyone he met in the evening after a campaign.

A huge column of many thousands of men, women and children moved in fours towards this armed group. The Storm Troopers directed people with the movement of a horsewhip—some to the right, to remain in the ghetto and work in factories; others went to the left—they were to go to Treblinka. The fate of old or sick people, and of children, was decided in advance. Some pinched their pale, sunken cheeks or painted them, straightened their clothing crumpled from attics and cellars, did everything they could to hide from the selection commission any traces of the persecution they had experienced, sleepless nights, continual moving from one hiding place to another, days of hunger and exhaustion. To get through the selection safe and then go back to slave labor for Schultz or Toebbens! Especially since the Germans had promised they would not hold any more campaigns, and the deportations would end. But everyone knew they would only leave a very small number of working Jews in the ghetto.

The tragedies which the great and notorious selection on Mila Street brought with it—the first selection of its kind, during which 100,000 Warsaw Jews were sent to Treblinka—cannot be numbered. What words can be used to depict the agony of mothers whose children were taken away from them here, the sufferings of divided families, human helplessness and the invincible desire to live?

I was in the column with my mother and Halina. My mother had lost her green pass. We had spent the entire night looking for it, but in vain.

We moved along in the crowd of helpless people, waiting for the verdict of the SS commission. Not all the crowd could get into Mila Street, so they filled several neighboring streets too. The Nazis surrounded the side streets, forming what was known as an "encirclement."

Only a few people were destined to get through. So people

devised the most dramatic and various stratagems, the most desperate ideas. They put little children to sleep with powders or injections, then hid them in suitcases or rucksacks, so as somehow to smuggle them past the watchful eyes of the commission. Infants were even abandoned on occasion . . . Many people prayed fervently for delivery, some asked others what to do, where to escape to, how they should comb their hair, make up their faces or dress, so as to look their best and pass through the selection successfully.

As usual, my mother encouraged Halina and me: after all, we were young, pretty, in good health. She braided up my long thick plaits in a crown so I looked much more serious and no one would think I was only 13. She kept straightening my crumpled dress, looked at me attentively, and asked neighbors in the crowd how old they took me for. She wanted me to look at least 17. She thought that only my age would decide my fate. She was most afraid for me. For she had deluded herself into thinking that the manager of the tailor's shop would get her out of the "encirclement," even without her pass, as she was one of his best and most necessary workers. Halina, on the other hand, was pretty, well-built and looked like a grown girl; in those days such girls generally succeeded in passing through this eye of a needle, past the sorting commission that was composed of executioners.

That day Marek was working in the first-aid post in the *Umschlag,* along with some others of the hospital staff, while Hilek was still employed in the Ursus factory on the Aryan side. The life of each one of us was hanging by almost a hair's breadth, but it seemed to my mother that I was in the greatest danger. She made an extraordinary effort to avert it, and at the same time not show that she was in fear and trembling of the result of the selection. If they took me, she would go with me to the *Umschlagplatz* without a moment's hesitation.

She told me this, but I in turn tried to persuade her that she ought not to come with me if they did not let me through, if they directed me to the left. She gazed into my eyes and asked with a smile, though seriously: "Do you really think I could possibly leave you?" I knew very well she could not. But I did not reply, for I was deeply moved and there was a lump in my throat.

We slowly moved forward in the direction of the exit, where the SS were standing. Hours passed. Amidst the uncertainty that prevailed, delusions started to circulate: surely some miracle would occur, the end of the selection, the deportations and all the other tortures would unexpectedly arrive . . . Various items of news ran through the crowd, each more terrible than the one before, of new tragedies, victims and crimes the Nazis were cynically and cold-bloodedly perpetrating during the selection in the streets and around the boxcars, before the ultimate showdown they were preparing for us in Treblinka.

We were not far from the SS commission when we suddenly caught sight of Mr. Melcer. He was a good friend of ours. This chance meeting with him abruptly altered my mother's decision. Mr. Melcer asked point-blank whether we all had green passes or an *Ausweis*. When he learned we had neither, he exclaimed: "In that case, where are you going, with children as well?! It is certain death."

My mother shivered as though suddenly waking from a dream that had obscured her mind. Without a word she looked at Mr. Melcer, then at us; I guessed from her expression that she was struggling with some inner reluctance, that she was pondering something deeply. Obviously she had all at once grasped the peril of our situation. Mr. Melcer's brusque words showed her just how very naive it was of her to nurse the dangerous illusion that the selection would work out to our advantage . . .

A moment later my mother regained her former vitality. She stopped pinching our cheeks and her own so they would look rosy, stopped asking people whether our appearance gave us the chance of getting out of the "encirclement." She began looking round for a hiding place, determined to escape the selection, the SS and death!

We had just stopped near 26 Mila Street, where workers of the Ursus factory were temporarily quartered. It happened, most unexpectedly, that Hilek was among them, because neither that day, nor for the next few days of the selection, did they take anyone to work. My mother instantly decided we would sit out the selection inside the house. A special guard from the factory was watching it. Hilek opposed the plan, fearing they might kill us. My brother always chose the simple way; he avoided any kind of stratagem and believed we should act accordingly to rules and regulations. Halina and I also opposed my mother's latest plan; we were angry at Mr. Melcer. We no longer had either the desire or the strength to drag ourselves around attics and cellars, in the dirt, stench and uncertainty. We believed (though I myself have no idea on what basis) that we would somehow squeeze through the selection fortunately, and would then at last be able to live peacefully and legally again, without the everlasting listening and terror.

But my mother would not give in. Unable to persuade us by logic, she resorted to a trick: she told us she would go into the house merely to cook us something to eat, and later, after we had eaten and rested a little, we would come back into the street . . . and be in time for the selection. So many people were standing in line ahead of us, there was no need to hurry! On this condition Hilek obtained permission from the sentry to go into the Ursus quarters.

So we went into 26 Mila Street. We stayed there two whole weeks. This refuge saved from death not only us, but also a handful of other people without an *Ausweis,* who, like us, were seeking safety. My mother at once struck up an acquaintance with them, learned of the existence of a well-hidden attic, and obtained their permission to use this hiding place. None of us could oppose her. When Halina and I smelled hot food and when the quiet of this house, with its safe hiding place, enveloped us, we stopped trying to persuade my mother to go back into the street, from which, in any case, increasingly bad news was coming.

We sat out the selection in a stuffy, smelly attic. The Ursus workmen were transferred after a few days to a factory on the Aryan side. Their living conditions were dreadful, nor could they make contact with their families in the ghetto. So we knew nothing of Hilek. Nor did we know what was happening to Marek.

Some tens of thousands of Jews remained in the Warsaw ghetto. They returned to the small factories and homes on Nowolipie and Leszno Streets, now converted into veritable labor camps. The rest of the Jews, around 100,000 people, including all the workers of my mother's tailor's shop along with the manager and his family, also the majority of those who had green passes ensuring them their lives—were loaded into the boxcars and deported . . .

For we learned that when the SS had selected a predetermined contingent of people for work, the remainder were herded into the boxcars without any selection, without inquiring whether they had passes, or were capable of work. Quite simply, they were not necessary. The streets covered in the "encirclement" were blocked for two weeks to enable a purge to be carried out. Every nook was carefully searched, using listening machines, dogs and informers recruited from the Jews. Sometimes the Hitlerites adopted strange tricks: in the evening after a "campaign" Jewish songs and traditional melodies were heard, to lure people from their hiding places.

They did not find us.

We lay for days at a time on the attic floor along with the score of people who had come there before us and had hidden the entrance.

The attic was situated high up, and was entered from a small empty room in the garret by an opening in the wall, now blocked by an old shabby cupboard with a mirror. Apart from this broken and empty cupboard and a pile of down from some torn pillows, it contained nothing else, and probably the fluttering down discouraged the Nazis. In any case, it never occurred to any of them during the blockade to move the cupboard.

Every few hours my mother gave us each two dumplings, soured by the heat, and a little tea or lump of sugar, just enough

to prevent us from fainting with hunger. She cooked the dumplings and made the tea in an empty apartment belonging to a factory
worker, in the same house, a few floors below. It was terrifying to
go down from the attic into that apartment. We crept as quietly as
mice . . . Any shadow, any sound filled us with terror.

By day we were haunted by the noise outside: footsteps,
shouts, firing. At night when silence and the saving darkness
came, we dreaded ghosts, phantoms, specters.

In such an atmosphere, in fear of our shadows and our own
breathing, my mother cooked dumplings and tea on a gas-ring.
German patrols kept roaming the streets . . . Halina and I would
lie down on a bed and doze. Then, before it got light, my mother
woke us after watching all night. She revived us with a scrap of
fresh dumpling and a few spoonfuls of hot tea. My mother took
the pan of food and a thermos of tea, and led us back up the dark
stairs to the garret full of down, and the attic. We wasted no time
on dressing, washing or other "toilet" operations. Ever since the
start of the deportations, when we left Muranowska Street, we
had been wearing our best clothes, with several changes of underwear, a few dresses, jerseys and topcoat—in case they sent us
somewhere to work. For we still believed to a certain extent that
perhaps they would not kill us, that perhaps they would let us
live, and then these things would assuredly come in handy . . .
So, though condemned to terrible suffering during heat waves,
we never undressed.

The same things happened in succession every day and every
evening. Everything as it had been earlier, as during the past
months of blockades and campaigns. Except that now the Jews
who had passed successfully through the selection were no
longer subject to the "campaigns," though to our great despair we
were unable to join them; a human wall of Storm Troopers cut us
off from them. The murderers never left their posts; anyone who
appeared in streets closed by the blockade died at their hands.
None of us knew how long the blockade would last. We were
afraid we would all starve to death before it ended. There was no
hope of our acquiring new stocks of food.

Meanwhile, the attic stank more and more of excrement, urine and sweat. Children were drugged with powders, sometimes stifled in sheer despair and terror. One woman gave birth; her baby soon died from lack of nourishment. During the birth pangs the woman did not utter a single cry: every sound, every murmur, even the slightest, caused antipathy and hostility among our companions of misfortune.

In the street, the shouting of the Nazis, the firing, the shrieks of people being dragged from various hiding places and refuges persisted. People were forced into lines in the street and herded to the *Umschlag,* to the boxcars.

One evening Marek turned up most unexpectedly in the apartment downstairs. He had come to Mila Street in a cart to take dead bodies away to the cemetery. He had expected to find Hilek in the house and to find out from him what had become of us.

Marek had been watching from the window of the first-aid point in the police building as the Nazis herded people from the "encirclement" to the boxcars on the *Umschlag.* He recognized workers from my mother's tailor's shop, and realized that the entire personnel had been sent to the *Umschlag.* He was certain that at any moment he would see my mother, Halina and me being herded into the boxcars. He lived through purgatory. He could not know that my mother had lost her green pass, that on the way we would meet Mr. Melcer who turned us back, nor that we would hide in the Ursus block . . . How amazed and happy he was! He covered us with kisses, wept aloud for joy.

I saw a grown man crying for the first time in my life . . . My elder brother crying! This was even more shocking than my mother crying. I felt confused by all these impressions and emotions. I just did not have the strength; I could hardly stand upright, exhausted with hunger and with lying motionless in the attic with its poisoned, stifling air. Only my mother tried to control her unhappiness and her joy. She smiled wanly, stroked our cheeks, encouraged us, inspired us.

Then we went back again to the attic, but we were in lighter spirits after meeting Marek. Marek promised he would soon be back; but he did not keep his word. In those days, no one could promise anything for certain. Nothing was certain, except death . . .

Marek did not want to stay with us, though my mother begged him to. Later, she fretted at the thought that she had not been able to persuade him. She began to fear he was dead, that she had lost him forever. But it would have been hard to keep Marek there. He could never have sat enclosed in a hiding place. So he left us. Neither my mother nor I could understand at that time that life in inactivity would have killed him.

We no longer believed that the blockades and campaigns would ever cease. Everyone around declared that the encircled streets would be cut off entirely from the rest of the ghetto; in the end, should the SS fail to hunt us down and herd us to the box-cars, we would die of hunger in this well-hidden attic.

Yet fate proved kinder.

After fifteen days the blockade was lifted. The sentries were removed from Mila Street, and we could contact inhabitants of other streets in the ghetto as well as the Schultz and Toebbens blocks. At first we believed the disappearance of the sentries to be merely temporary, or a trick designed to lure us from our hiding places. So we fiercely and angrily attacked those who brought the news and advised us to leave the attic. However, the news was genuine.

Worn-out and dirty, we went back to Leszno Street. Our apartment was so wrecked, we scarcely recognized it. Fresh signs of looting were everywhere, while on the floor, amidst a lot of rubbish, lay my mother's green pass—as if nothing had happened—to the disappearance of which we owed our lives . . .

The campaigns really had stopped, as announced before the selection, though only for a time. For a few months relative calm prevailed in the ghetto; single roundups to the boxcars and hooligan excesses still occurred by the SS. However, we could breathe again after the nightmare of the selection and "encirclement" in Mila Street.

Hilek reappeared on the first evening of our return to Leszno Street. He was still working in the factory on the Aryan side. We knew nothing about Marek . . .

The ghetto had diminished considerably in population: "In the 20 months from November 1940 to July 1942, about 100,000 persons died of starvation, epidemics, exhaustion, inhuman forced labor and of executions within the Warsaw ghetto. But in the less than two months from July 22 to mid-September 1942, the German occupants and their collaborators deported more than 300,000 inhabitants of the Warsaw ghetto to Treblinka or liquidated them on the spot."[*] The few spared from the vast "campaigns," roundups and selections worked day and night in two shifts in factories and workshops. Toebbens's workers were allowed to live only on Leszno Street, those of Schultz on Nowolipie Street, the remainder on Mila and Nalewki Streets. Each street was encircled by sentries—Storm Troopers and Jewish police, or fatigue units known as the *Werkschutz*. The laborers always went to work and returned in groups, escorted by Jewish police or the *Werkschutz*. A pass was required to cross from one block to another. No one, apart from the police, was allowed on the street during the day. That meant death by shooting. (Walking in the streets at night had been forbidden from the beginning of the occupation.) Only in the morning or evening, when workers were being escorted to and from work, could we stay outdoors for an hour. This was the time when people purchased a frugal share of the products with which the German industrialists paid their slaves.

The streets between Mila, Nowolipie and Leszno, which had previously formed part of the ghetto, were called "wild streets" after the last deportation; neither Poles nor Jews were allowed to live there. Most of the earlier inhabitants of these streets had been exterminated.

---

[*]B. Mark, *Uprising in the Warsaw Ghetto,* Warsaw, 1963.—Ed.

Winter came, accompanied by severe frosts.

Every day Hilek brought back food from the Ursus factory, bartered for clothing, bedsheets and ticking; he smuggled these things out of the ghetto. Soon after the blockade in Mila Street, he found his girlfriend, Hela, whom he had met before in the ghetto. Hela was 20, a pretty girl from Bydgoszcz. She had passed the selection, and was now working in a furrier's factory. She lived with a girl cousin at 30 Nowolipie Street. The Nazis had taken away her middle-aged parents to Treblinka, after the Mila Street selection. Depressed by this loss, Hela was now all the happier to find Hilek again, for she dearly loved him. Both decided to stay together, and a few days later we all moved into her apartment on Nowolipie Street. Moving, which in those days had nothing to do with moving furniture, took place in a much simpler way. In the evening, when the laborers were coming back from the factories, a person went with a basket of provisions into an apartment house where there was an attic with an opening in the wall, and passed through the attics to the staircase of the chosen house. This was the way we moved to Hela's.

My mother was no longer working. Her tailor's shop had been disbanded, and she did not even try to get into another. She, sick with gallstones, could not work at all, and had difficulty in even getting around the house. I often found her in bed, groaning with pain. Halina and I took her place in everything, and she merely gave us instructions from her bed. My mother placed most of the domestic duties on me; she did not want Halina to think that she was being made use of by the family because she was an orphan. My mother behaved in the same way to Hilek's fiancée. She tried to spare her every inch of the way.

Later on, when we started hoarding food—like all the Jews, expecting that the deportation campaigns would start again and that we would have to hide for a long time in a bunker—my mother often gave goodies from her store against a "rainy day" to Halina and Hela. She herself, my brother and I used saccharine in our tea, while my cousin and Hilek's fiancée had jam on their bread, and sugar or dry cookies intended for a sojourn in the bunker. I

devoured these goodies with my eyes, but never dared ask for
any. I was jealous and resentful. But whenever my mother noticed my greedy look, full of indignation, she tactfully drew me
aside and explained kindly: "I cannot love them the way I love
you—so I must reward them with something else because they
have no family."

Hilek married Hela.

I will never forget their quiet wedding during those days of
mourning and death, though I was not very happy about it—I
don't know why—I did not like Hilek's wife very much. I admired her graceful figure and pretty voice. She liked singing and
knew many songs. She was neat, and very gifted at any kind of
work with her hands. But something about her made me shy. Not
that she ever paid much attention to me in those days. On the
other hand, she loved my mother and Halina very dearly. Unusually cordial family relations prevailed between them. My mother
was wise and tactful; she knew how to get along with other people,
and to understand them, especially when times were hard.

Not long afterwards Marek reappeared.

One evening he appeared in the entry on Nowolipie Street,
wearing a ragged Chassidic coat, and begged the *Werkschutz*
sentries to let him through the Schultz workers' block; he expected my mother to be living and working there. When we
learned of this from acquaintances, my mother and friends of
Hilek and his wife immediately began making spirited efforts to
get Marek across the border at the Nowolipie exit, which was
guarded by Jewish police and *Werkschutz*.

Marek's tale was brief; immediately after leaving us, he had
been seized for work floating wood down the Vistula. He labored
very hard there. He bartered his clothes for food, and went
around in an old gabardine he found somewhere. When the raft-
ing was over, the Nazis loaded all the workers into trucks and

drove them to the *Umschlag*. Marek jumped out of the moving vehicle, hid by the roadside, then slipped back into the ghetto to find us.

After a few days during which we enjoyed Marek's presence, Hilek arranged a job for him in his factory; from that time on they worked together all the time, and together they smuggled out clothing left in apartments, deserted after the recent campaigns. During these few winter months of 1943, we finally had enough to eat, and I even got so plump that my mother did not like it. Fortunately for me, however, I now looked a good deal older than I was.

My mother continued to hoard crackers and sugar from the supplies which Hilek and Marek brought in every day from their factory. The thick books lying around the attic were now being consumed in the tin stove that served us both for cooking and warming the room. At first we used chopped-up pieces of old furniture, then—like our neighbors—wood from the banisters and bottom steps of the staircase; when this source was exhausted, it was the books' turn. There was no other way.

We lived through the last winter in Warsaw as if we were in a jail or labor camp, but at least we were together, and felt incomparably better than in hiding places in an attic during a "campaign." When my brothers came back from the Ursus factory in the evenings, we would sit around the little, red-hot stove and tell one another of the events we had lived through, seen or heard of. We would recall relatives deported from the *Umschlag* into the unknown. Deep down, we fostered the hope that they were still alive, and would at some time return to us . . .

Meanwhile the atmosphere in the ghetto was changing. As the extermination of most Warsaw Jews proceeded, the authority and influence of the *Judenrat* decreased. We saw nothing but enemies and traitors in them. Their blind fear, their passive willing-

ness to carry out the Nazis' orders disappeared. They were re-
placed by hatred, by the wish to rebel and be revenged. The
crowded area of the ghetto was now inhabited by people with
nothing to lose, each one of them mourning his nearest and dearest, and the enormous burden of suffering he himself had lived
through. No one could cheat or scare them any more.

Now the only people who were listened to were the leaders of
the secret resistance movement; they were trusted, their orders
awaited. They were our pride, they inspired our admiration. People
equipped themselves with arms, iron bars, even poison—anything
to prevent being herded to the boxcars. Weapons which—under
the rule of the *Judenrat*—people had not even dared look at too
closely, were now prized, joyfully tossed into the air. They became longed-for and priceless treasures. All the factory workers,
all the young men tried to acquire one.

They built deep, underground and well-equipped bunkers, they
set up various well-hidden hiding places, intended to facilitate
retaliation and resistance. They began issuing and carrying out
death sentences on sadistic Gestapo officers, on Jews who turned
informer, and on police.

Members of this resistance movement killed Hantke, the
Storm Trooper, and many others who had prowled the ghetto
sowing death. From places of concealment they shot many traitors among the Jewish people who collaborated with the Germans in destroying their fellowmen, including the commandant
of the Jewish police, a bloodthirsty dog whose death was greeted
with profound satisfaction by the entire ghetto. This was Joseph
Szerynski (Szenkman), commandant of the Sentry guards, the
official name for the Jewish police in the ghetto, who assisted the
Germans in deporting Jews. However, at this time he was only
wounded by Israel Kanal, an underground fighter.

From now on, the Nazis dared not go alone into Jewish refuges or hiding places during the subsequent "campaigns": they
went in groups, and pushed Jewish police in front of them, to
protect themselves against rifle-fire. The blood on their accursed
green uniforms—this was the only requital we had for the oceans

of misery, tears and blood innocently shed. The sight of ordinary, human terror in the eyes of our executioners, the proof that their wicked power was neither everlasting nor invincible—this gave us courage and raised our spirits.

Campaigns no longer swooped on the ghetto unexpectedly. The resistance movement obtained information about them and warned people in advance, so we had time to take shelter in bunkers. By night special sentries watched in the yards and woke people living in the houses when danger approached. And when danger had passed, we received a signal that we could return to our apartments.

How many such cold, uneasy nights I remember! Warned by unknown people, my mother dragged us from our warm beds almost by force. I used to sleep heavily. I could not open my eyes, could not understand what they wanted, why they were pulling the quilt off when it was so frosty outdoors! But there was no trifling with my mother in those days . . . I had to get up obediently and dress like lightning. My mother seized a basket of food and then, cautiously—lighting our way with a candle so as not to slip on the icy stairs or fall over the chopped-out bottom steps—we all went out into the great dark yard; we made for a hallway from which steps led into the cellars, where there was a concealed recess, our hiding place.

Like us, our neighbors crept in there, a crowd of silent, uneasy shadows.

It was crowded and stuffy in the recess. The glow of a candle did not disperse the darkness, but sufficed so people did not collide and could recognize each other. We sat there, agitated, half-conscious, sleepy. I put my head on my mother's lap and dozed off, or daydreamed of all sorts of good things. I pictured to myself the world after the war, meeting my father, my playmates from Muranowska Street, my relatives and friends who had surely only been sent away somewhere, very, very far away. This is how I sometimes took refuge from our horrible reality. This is how I endured the anguish and discomfort, and killed the time that dragged into infinity.

Hilek's friend, David Kaplan, visited us that winter. He had made friends with my brother before the war, at school and in the ghetto. Both boys belonged to the *Hashomer Hatzair* Jewish scouting organization. He met us again by chance. He no longer had any family. He too had been taken to Treblinka, but escaped and made his way into the ghetto again. He told us horrifying things; the hell people endured in the packed boxcars, the crimes being committed in Treblinka, which he had seen with his own eyes. Paralyzed with terror we listened to him, reluctant to believe.

But now for the first time we began to understand what really lurked behind the words "deportation," "campaign," *"Umschlag,"* and "boxcars." Here was someone we trusted, who had himself been in that almost legendary Treblinka, and had come back to tell us and to confirm all the tragic apprehensions, tales and rumors.

Very few victims succeeded in escaping from Treblinka; it was very rare that we met a refugee from the camp in the ghetto. This was why David's reports were little less than thunderbolts. So now we knew we could look forward to Treblinka with nothing but dread.

David's luck had held; he hid in a wagon among rolls of clothing that had belonged to the dead and murdered, which were being shipped to Germany from Treblinka, and he came back to Warsaw in the same railroad train; he slipped across into the ghetto, though he had no support there, at the risk of being caught and deported again . . . I could not sleep a wink at night, and neither my mother's persuasions, nor her assurances that Kaplan was exaggerating or at least partly making it up, could soothe me. It was hard for me to come to terms with the thought that this terrible fate had come upon my father and those I loved or liked, or merely knew . . . The same fate threatened us too, at every moment. Now I was afraid of the dark, of human voices and footsteps, even of my own shadow. The distant whistle of a locomotive went through my heart like a sharp knife, leaving me breathless. I kept examining corners, recesses and walls in our apartment, wondering desperately where to creep when the entry of hunters surprised us. I knew that my nearest and dearest had also examined the corners of our apartment with the same idea in mind—my mother, my brothers, all the grown-ups in the house. I longed with all my heart to become invisible, and wondered all the time how it could be done.

Then came April 1943.

The Nazi industrialists, Toebbens and Schultz, moved their factories and most employees to Poniatow and Trawniki near Lublin, where labor camps were established. Rumors circulated around the ghetto that the Nazis were planning the final liquidation of the Warsaw ghetto, which in their language meant *Warschau judenrein* (Warsaw purified of Jews). At the same time we passed from mouth to mouth the joyous news of the German armies' great defeats on the Eastern front; optimists predicted early liberation. Even little children in the ghetto knew of the Stalingrad defeat; people supposed that the Nazis, having enough troubles of their own, would leave us in peace or not have the time to execute their criminal plans. People comforted themselves with these ideas, though the building of bunkers and shelters persisted.

When people began repeating more and more insistently that the predicted liquidation of the Warsaw ghetto would assuredly occur in the spring, my mother obtained places in a bunker near 3 Mila Street, for us all, paying in dollars—we sold part of the food brought in from the Aryan side by my brothers. The bunker had been constructed underneath a cellar, and was provided with various kinds of equipment—a pump, electricity, ventilators, bunks, and wall closets for food supplies. All these fittings showed that this was no temporary hiding place for one or two "campaigns."

The shelter was under the ruins of a house bombed in September 1939; we entered through the cellar, then by a tunnel. It could accommodate a couple of hundred people. There were also stocks of weapons, as in all the bunkers at the time.

The unhappy though relatively calm winter had passed. Easter 1943 was at hand. Hela left her job in the workshop and we moved to Mila Street to be closer to the hiding place. My mother would not even consider leaving voluntarily for Trawniki, though many of our friends decided to go, in the belief they would be safer there than in the ghetto that was already doomed to destruction.

"To surrender into their clutches like that, without resistance," said my mother, "to go to their camp where we have no chance of hiding, to give up our fight for life? No, I will never agree to that. Unless they take me by force! But I will never go of my own accord . . ."

So we did not go to Trawniki or Poniatow. Just before Easter we crossed into the "small ghetto" (as they called Mila, Nalewki and part of Muranowska Streets) to an empty apartment—of which there were plenty here—to the first floor, so as to reach the bunker the more quickly in the event of a blockade. We regretfully took leave of our friends and neighbors, with whom we had spent the winter in Nowolipie Street. Bitter experience had taught us that a farewell in the ghetto was usually final; a change of living quarters or hiding-place often meant a change in destiny. Shared misfortune and misery brought people together, they became closer and dearer to one another.

The only way to cross from Nowolipie Street to Leszno Street was in a group of people with a special pass, escorted by Jewish police. On the day of our move to Mila Street we had to join a group led by police, notorious for their extraordinary intolerance and strict observance of the Nazi authorities' most minor regulations—this meant we were not able to take with us the supplies of food prepared for a long stay in our hiding place. For the time being we left them behind in the Nowolipie Street apartment. Marek was to go back later and bring them to Mila Street. As ill-luck had it, Marek was stranded in Nowolipie Street when the insurrection broke out in the ghetto and the bloody, systematic extermination of the Jews began—his route to us was cut off. So our family was separated again in this epoch-making moment on the first night of Easter.

We spent that night in the bunker celebrating the Passover Seder. Late at night, some unknown men of the night watch

knocked at our door and told us briefly that many Hitlerite units
were surrounding the ghetto from all sides; we were instructed to
take refuge in the shelter immediately. Guided through a laby-
rinth of many secret passages (in which it was hard to find one's
way, and we ourselves could not have found the way a second
time), we at last reached the bunker. I believed the "campaigns"
would cease within a few hours and we would soon be back in
our apartment.

Some two hundred people were lying here, packed together on
narrow bunks. It was hard to find any room: my mother and I
were together, Hela and Hilek separately, with Halina a little
closer to us. It was stuffy and crowded. The place smelled damp
and musty, like all cellars, and the air was foul, it was dark and
the atmosphere was one of agitation. From the very beginning,
more people came than had been bargained for. More and more
followed during the succeeding days, from other threatened hiding places or burning houses. The bunker grew increasingly
crowded and stuffy. Anyone who went to the water tap or toilet
collided with others or stumbled over their neighbors in the darkness. There was no end to the disputes and squabbling, fights
over nothing, insults, name-calling. Exhausted by the want of
fresh air and the most elementary facilities, tortured by incessant
fear and uncertainty, people began losing their self-control. The
bunker became a real hell.

Week followed week, and we lay in this cellar unable to tell
day from night. We were tortured by hunger—after all, our supplies had been left behind in Nowolipie Street. We had brought
with us only some sugar cubes and a few pounds of jam in a can.
My mother gave each of us a lump of sugar, or one or two
spoonfuls of jam and a little water to drink a few times daily—in
this way we prevented ourselves from starving to death for three
weeks. Even though other people's cupboards in the bunker were
full of crackers and all sorts of baked goods and conserves, nobody offered to help us. No one knew how long their supplies
would have to last, so their owners economized, even for themselves and their families. We were strangers here. Yet there were

also people in the bunker who had plenty of food of their own, but who nevertheless left the bunker at night to loot provisions from other hiding places, whose occupants had been taken away for execution by the Nazis. These people never had enough, and in their greed they ignored the risk of such nightly excursions. Sometimes these excursions ended tragically for the looters, and brought disaster upon the hiding places by leading the Nazis, or informers and spies in their tracks.

Sometimes I collapsed from hunger. Then my mother gave me an extra ration of jam or sugar, though this did not help much. I left the bunk only to go to the toilet. I dragged myself there with difficulty, my head reeled, I could not keep on my feet. Most of the time I dozed from exhaustion, the heat and stench.

But sometimes I talked to my mother about our position, our chances of survival, what might have happened to Marek and to friends in other shelters in other streets, and we discussed the behavior of our companions in the bunker. Serenity of spirit and hope never deserted my mother. She tried to convince us and everyone around that there was still no need to lose our faith in life. She kept rousing me from my dozing and half-fainting state. Then I would gaze with ever-increasing envy at people in the neighboring bunks, who always had something to eat. Eating! I recalled with grief and bitterness how my mother had hoarded food supplies in Nowolipie Street, fearing we would run short at a critical moment . . . But all those wonderful things had been wasted! I never mentioned this. I did not want to hurt my mother's feelings. I knew that as things were she was worrying about everything, and that thoughts of Marek were torturing her.

We talked little and rarely to the other members of the family— Hilek, Hela and Halina. We were at some distance from them, and frequent trips inside the bunker were impossible on account of the crowd and our weakness. We knew they too were suffering, the same as we.

Above us, on the surface, fighting was in progress. Units equipped with the latest type of machine guns were moving in on a handful of exhausted, ragged and almost unarmed Jewish insurrectionists, who preferred an honorable death on the field of battle to gas chambers . . . Heavy artillery, tanks, bombs, shells, accurate listening devices, bloodhounds—all were used. The Storm Troopers systematically burned down street after street, house after house. They murdered those they caught or found in hiding places—insurrectionists or not, all Jews, women, old people, children. They were afraid to enter bunkers, so they threw smoke bombs in, or flooded them with water. The Hitlerite bandits even blew up the ruins of burned-out houses, so no one could hide in the ruins. In this way thousands of people in the ghetto perished, burned alive, suffocated or drowned in underground shelters flooded with water; those who tried to escape death by flight were shot down by Nazi bullets. Only a few succeeded in getting through the barrier of fire, and to reach other as yet undamaged shelters, providing the people in them agreed . . .

Towards the end of the third week, our bunker was packed to the limit. We lay on the bunks in total darkness, as the external electricity cable and our supply of batteries had long since been burned out. Candles would not light on account of the lack of oxygen in the air. We breathed heavily and noisily, sweating, wheezing like old, broken-down engines. Every few minutes someone collapsed. The strongest, those who were still able to move, soaked sheets and towels in water, waved or hung them around their bunks for coolness. The situation was growing worse hourly, the more so because acrid smoke and the heat of the houses on fire overhead was penetrating into the interior; refugees from other shelters continued to join us.

Even the squabbling stopped; nobody had the strength. People
were dying like flies. Yet, in the midst of this suffering, there
grew up a solidarity, a mutual understanding and sympathy. It
was no longer necessary to shout for quiet, lest the SS track us
down, nor ask too long for neighborly help. People helped one
another, even shared the last drops of medicine, without caring
whether someone was a relative or a stranger, a friend or unknown, poor or rich. The differences between us disappeared. In
the end, our mutual and tragic fate had united us into one great
family. Although life in the bunker was purgatory, no one
thought of voluntarily leaving it and throwing himself on the
mercy of our murderers.

In the end, however, they discovered us too.

They began smashing their way in, pulling down the barriers
that shielded the bunker entrance. There were many barriers, and
it took several hours to remove them. One of the captured looters
had betrayed us, and described the location of the shelter to the SS.

Aware that we were lost, but determined not to let our enemies
in, we listened in silence as one barrier after another fell. In the
end they succeeded, and began hammering at the cellar door
itself, shouting, threatening, promising a reward if we opened it.
At first, when the sounds of hammering were indistinct, far-off,
we thought that perhaps we were imagining things on account of
our highly strung nerves and fear. But when the Germans' furious shouting reached us, we realized that our last moment was at
hand, that there was no escape.

I was so stupefied with hunger and the bad air which penetrated through a leaky ventilator that at first I did not realize the
catastrophe. I lay sweating, almost undressed, in a strange half-
sleep from which my mother tried by force to revive me. "Wake
up!" she kept saying, shaking me insistently. "You must not
sleep, you must get dressed and be ready to leave! Can't you hear

them knocking? Wake up, I say, wake up!" For a moment I opened my eyes, then sank back into sleep again, as though drugged. My mother's words did not sink in. Not until the sound of a terrible explosion did I regain my senses. The Storm Troopers had thrown a grenade at the trap that closed the ventilator opening in the ceiling, on the outside. (This trap remained closed throughout, even though we were almost suffocating for the lack of an air current; we were afraid the Nazis would notice it, and also that smoke from the conflagrations would penetrate to the interior.) Fortunately, the exploding grenade did not injure anyone. Finally air and daylight, which we had not seen since that Passover evening three weeks earlier when we went down underground, began flowing in from the ceiling. But then at once the Nazis let down a long ladder through the opening; one after another, our executioners in their green uniforms began climbing in.

Inside the bunker they tried to treat us "mildly," thus ensuring their own safety. They urged us "politely" to climb out by the ladder; after all, nothing bad threatened us, at the most they would send us to another locality where we would work. But we had to carry out their instructions to the letter and leave the bunker as rapidly as possible. They even helped the weakest people to climb the ladder. Despite what we knew about them and what we had hitherto undergone at their hands, these "benevolent instructions" acted soothingly on people. Some underwent the delusion that perhaps, after all, there had been changes in the Hitlerites' plans, perhaps they would let the remainder of the Jews they caught live . . .

But on the surface we realized our naivete yet again.

They took us to Muranowski Square. It was full of soldiers. All around were ruins and smoldering buildings. Amidst a crowd of Storm Troopers who dragged us out of the bunker stood the traitor who had informed on us, and thus saved his own life, impudent, his arms folded. We recognized him instantly. He had come upon us by following the tracks of nocturnal looters from our bunker and had begged to be let in. Who would have thought he would repay us in this way for the kindness shown him? But it was too late now to wonder at the vileness of this informer . . .

They added us to a crowd of people dragged from other bunkers. Machine guns surrounded us. Armored cars and tanks were moving along the streets—it was just like the front line.

We were all ordered to take off our upper layer of clothing in the middle of the street, then go to the wall and turn our backs, with hands up. The Storm Troopers demanded jewelry and money, threatening to shoot. They stormed upon and searched the people, and those who resisted, also old and little children, were shot on the spot. Anyone who spoke, burst into tears or made any rash gesture, was shot into the blood-stained gutter. All this went on under the windows of our original home in the ghetto, where we had lived through the first two years of the occupation, never dreaming at that time that such monstrous things could happen in our town, in our street, in front of our house . . . The dark, fume-infested bunker now seemed to me to have been a cozy, quiet refuge. Even the sky, for which I had so yearned while in the bunker, was cloudy and threatening that day, as if to fit in with the general background. But on the other side of the wall, in a house on the Aryan side, someone was— perhaps by accident—playing a piano . . . This is how our last hours in the Warsaw ghetto were passed. For many thousands, these were the last hours of their lives.

Dusk was falling as they herded us to the *Umschlag.*

We left behind—most of us forever—everything we had formerly loved in this our native city; the homes in which we had been born, grown up, lived with our own people, gone to school, learned to be human beings, the houses whose cellars and attics had for so long been witnesses of our humiliation, terror, sufferings and longing for freedom.

The train was not due to arrive until the next morning. For the night, the Nazis packed us into the former school on the

Umschlag—I knew this building from the first roundups in the ghetto—several dozen people to a room (the rooms were not large). We sat on the floor, crouching in an indescribable crush, literally one on top of another. Time and again Nazis burst into the room, called us foul names, hit people, trampling on the heads of prostrate people, demanding gold, jewelry and money. And when a dead silence was the only reply (after all, most people now had nothing left but their ragged clothing), they picked out individuals at random, tortured them into insensibility, or shot them dead with a pistol in full view of everyone else.

Then I envied rats and mice . . . they were not so helpless as we, that night on the monstrous *Umschlag,* as we awaited the train to the extermination camp of torture. Rats and mice had holes, where they could hide from enemies and danger. But we were not allowed to leave the room, even to go to the toilet. I also began to envy people who had died earlier; they left the worst behind them, they were free.

I remember a Storm Trooper pushing his way into the room with some empty bottles in his hand. He stamped loudly on the floor with the iron-tipped heels of his shining top boots. He was armed, as they all were, and like his colleagues he demanded money and jewelry. Nobody answered. People only shrank further back, pressing to the floor and walls. Then the Storm Trooper announced he was going to throw the bottles at us; anyone hit must rise, and if the individual did not hand over money, he would bitterly regret it. He raised one hand, aimed a bottle.

My mother covered her face with her hands, and crouched over to protect me. I closed my eyes, clenched my fists; I was too terrified to move or even turn my head, lest I drew the Storm Trooper's eyes on myself. I waited in terrible tension for what would happen. Whom would the bottle hit?

There was complete silence in the room. It was as though nobody in the crowd was breathing. Then came the sound of smashing glass, someone's uncertain steps and the blows of a horsewhip, regular as the ticking of a clock.

I kept my eyes shut, not wanting to know who the victim was

this time. I did not want to hear, and put my fingers in my ears. I nestled close to my mother as she crouched over me. Then I felt her body trembling with spasmodic sobbing. At first I did not understand why my mother, always so self-controlled, had suddenly broken down. I opened my ears; a dead silence reigned in the room. Only the horsewhip went on striking, though the man under torture did not even groan or beg for mercy. Then I opened my eyes and looked up to see why my mother was sobbing so bitterly, though without a sound. And I saw Hilek.

The bottle had hit him. He had no money or anything that might have saved him. The Storm Trooper was beating him sadistically and cold-bloodedly. He kept striking Hilek about the head. He smashed Hilek's spectacles and blooded his face. Hilek stood there as though he did not feel the blows at all. He did not utter the slightest groan. And he endured this to the end of the bestial torture, when the Storm Trooper finally got tired or bored, for I doubt whether Hilek's calmness and his endurance impressed the bandit. However, he spared my brother's life. Hilek crawled over to us on all fours, with his face bloodied, blind without his spectacles, his head splitting. When the Storm Trooper went out, Hilek still did not utter a word, merely crouched on the floor beside my mother and Hela, wiping off the blood that poured from his wounds with a handkerchief.

Before dawn, two Storm Troopers again pushed their way into the room. One was Hilek's tormentor. He looked round the prostrate people, caught sight of Hilek and again called him into the center of the room. We froze in horror. We were certain that this time he would kill Hilek . . . But the bandit merely wanted to boast of his "prowess" to a comrade. Perhaps both were surprised that a Jew had not uttered a groan under torture.

In the earlier period, when the Hitlerites ran rampant in the ghetto and ill-treated us, Hilek had been beaten by them more than once. This had happened when he left the ghetto to work on the Aryan side, or when he came back to the ghetto, for the Nazis searched people at the gate. After all, Hilek was engaged in smuggling, and bringing back food he received from Poles at the factory. So he often got horsewhipped or rifle-butted on the head. And even then he submitted to these terrible beatings in silence, never cried out, never groaned, never begged for mercy. His colleagues, other factory workers, sometimes joked that he had a head made of iron . . . Hilek really was exceptionally resistant to physical pain.

Now, the worst was that he had lost his spectacles. He could scarcely see without them.

Cattle cars arrived for us in the mornings, the kind in which the Nazis usually deported Jews from the *Umschlagplatz*. They rushed into the school building like a herd of wild, enraged beasts, beating people with whips, rifle butts, firing into the crowd of people who were insane with terror. This was the Nazis' usual way of driving people into the boxcars. In the panic and confusion some screamed, wept aloud, calling on God for help, others prayed fervently, yet others cried out as they sought lost children. Everyone pushed and crowded the rooms, corridors and stairs; everyone wanted to get out of the building as fast as possible, to get away from the bullets and whips of the SS. The route to the boxcars was strewn with corpses. We had to trample on the bodies of the dead or dying. Finally we reached the box-cars, trying not to lose one another in this enormous, seething crowd. We held hands tightly, trying at the same time to avoid Storm Troopers who might be provoked into firing by some involuntary, unlucky gesture. We considered it extremely fortunate that all our family got into the same boxcar!

The boxcar was crammed to overflowing. We could only stand. The Storm Troopers had difficulty in closing the door. I thought they would take some of the people to another boxcar, but I soon realized they had better methods; they began hitting those standing nearest with their rifle butts, and firing—everyone shrank back instantly inside the door. Then the SS shoved a few more people in, and when there was no room for even a pin, they slammed the door and sealed the boxcar. People raised an outcry, trampling on each other and swearing.

Finally we had come face to face with that from which we had been trying to escape for so many long months, from that which our relatives and friends, and hundreds of thousands of unknown Jews had experienced. Our turn had come . . . The train moved off amidst incessant shrieks, cries and rifle shots. We were leaving Warsaw. We were leaving Warsaw! Our infernal ride to the death camp had started. People were quarreling and fighting over every inch of space. The wheels rattled along the tracks, the train rocked—it cared nothing for our sufferings . . . The strongest, and especially the tallest people blockaded access to the small window; we had no light or air. The heat and stuffiness intensified our thirst. A few bottles of water, which courageous Poles managed to throw to us on the way, were snatched from hand to hand, seized by force. The Poles hastily drew this water from ditches or streams near which the train stopped. Mostly, however, those by the window or those who had enough strength to snatch it from others were those who got it. The water was muddy, sometimes smelly and dirty, but who cared for that? It was priceless!

The train proceeded very slowly, sometimes stopping, sometimes reversing—all in order to increase and prolong our sufferings, so that as many as possible would die of suffocation inside the boxcars.

The journey lasted all day, until late at night.

People collapsed, trampled on each other, raged, prayed. When anyone collapsed with exhaustion, they were crushed to death.

At that time no one wondered where they were taking us, nor what they were going to do with us. What significance did that have, with death threatening us here at every moment?

They placed a layer of dead bodies and half-dead people on the boxcar floor; underneath were the weakest, then the stronger—the number of victims kept increasing. The noise of rifle shots outside reminded us time after time that we were not alone here, that Nazi death was lurking not only inside the box-cars, but outside too, all around. They fired at the daredevils who jumped in despair from the windows of the moving train.

My mother wanted to try escaping through the little window too. Hilek and Hela refused; they did not believe such a risky step would succeed, and besides, they longed to be together until the last moment.

I struggled for a long time with the mass of people pressing upon me and with my own weakness, to prevent myself from falling to the ground. I gazed, stupefied, at the little basket my mother was carrying—a bottle of rapeseed oil. Why had she brought that oil instead of water? I had a bottle full of liquid before my eyes, but a liquid that was undrinkable. I stared at it in despair. I wanted a drink! A drink! A drink!

At first, I deluded myself into believing that my mother, or Hilek, or Hela would push their way to the window and get water. Soon I realized my mother was too frail, and Hilek could not be counted on after his recent beating by the Storm Trooper. Hela could not be considered.

A lump of sugar my mother put into my mouth seemed dry and hot. It cracked between my teeth like sand, and I really had the impression I was eating hot, dry sand . . . I concentrated on the rattle of the wheels, so as to tear myself away, if only for a little, from reality. I asked my mother whether by any chance they were taking us to the place Hilek's friend Kaplan had told us of. My mother assured me we were on the way to a labor camp, and none of us was in any danger. This was just what I wanted to hear, but David Kaplan stood continually before my eyes, talking about the murder of Jews in Treblinka . . . I did not want to believe in death; I preferred any lie a hundred times, as long as it gave me the hope of surviving . . . Then everything grew confused; the noise of the train, the shrieks in the boxcar, my mother's words, the sinister thoughts and my fear of Treblinka. My head reeled and I plunged into an abyss.

I collapsed on a pile of alive, half-dead and dead bodies, shaken by the movement of the train. I no longer felt any pain from my bruised legs, no heat, no thirst, no fear. My clothes ceased burdening me. The faint voice of my mother, who was lying somewhere beside me, barely reached my ears. She was certainly trying to bring me back to consciousness, but I could no longer catch the meaning of her words . . . It was completely dark inside the boxcar, or perhaps my eyes were closed. Collapsing people kept giving way around me. They collapsed across my legs, my stomach, I could not move, could not free myself from their weight. By a strange chance, only my head was outside. I do not know how long I lay thus. Suddenly I felt something pressing upon my face, my lips, my nose—I was suffocating! And then the invincible will to live awoke in me, the will to extricate myself from the inert bodies pressing down on me.

I began struggling with this enormous weight. With a kind of insane, purely animal strength, I struggled until I finally gained the surface, leaving my laced boots and clothing underneath the nightmare-like heap. I stood up on my own two feet, barefoot and almost naked, but erect and breathing freely. I threw off the rest of my clothes, clambered over the heap of rags and bodies, and reached the window. The open window! Outside it was already night. I stood alone by the little window. No one pushed me away—almost everyone was lying helpless or unconscious.

I leaned out of the window and began greedily breathing in the fresh, cool, reviving air. But right by my face, almost touching my chin, a rifle projected. A Storm Trooper sitting on the boxcar steps had dozed off, probably with boredom. Perhaps the regular rhythms of the train had rocked him off to sleep. He did not notice me stealing air that was not intended for me.

We reached Lublin late at night.

The train stopped. The SS opened up the boxcars and began brutally herding out all those who were still alive and could move. Yet again the cries, the calling and the shrieking began. People were searching for each other, pulling on the clothes they had discarded on account of the heat. I found that all my nearest and dearest had survived. I grabbed the first garment that came to hand in the darkness from the pile of rags over which we scrambled. It was a man's topcoat; I pulled it over my naked body, jumped down to the ground goodness knows how, for the boxcar door was very high up. I could have broken my arms or legs. The encircling SS drove us on with blows and shouting.

It was drizzling; on leaving the train we stumbled through thick mud. The sharp chill of night penetrated to the marrow of our bones, especially after the stuffiness inside the boxcar. I was barefoot, my feet hurt as I trudged along in the crowd being herded to the Lublin *Umschlag*. Had it not been for the darkness of night, the SS would have shot me on the way, as they shot all sick or frail people.

Once more they packed us into some building, on a muddy and dirty floor. We were perishing from thirst. Not until early morning did Hilek manage to reach a water tap, drink his fill, and bring some back to us in half a broken bottle. We shared it like some precious medicine. Later, when we had quenched our thirst, it turned out that there was a gold watch in the topcoat I found in the boxcar. My mother exchanged it for bread from a Polish policeman. Thus we were able to appease our hunger for the first time since going into the Mila Street bunker.

Getting the water and the bread, and the fact that we were not in Treblinka (we thought it was only in Treblinka that they killed people) encouraged us. We thought it a lucky sign.

The building stank of excrement, foul air and mold. Dead bodies, their skulls shot in, fragments of clothing, shoes lay scattered in the corridors and yard. An atmosphere of apathy and depression prevailed. People relieved themselves where they lay—nobody paid attention any longer, or was disturbed by anything. People stared ahead, unseeing, no longer understanding. Hours dragged by like centuries.

By chance we met some former neighbors from Nowolipie Street at the *Umschlag*. We barely recognized them, so greatly had they changed during the train journey. Neither we nor they could force ourselves to talk. We were no longer ourselves, and now everything that had formerly existed, before we were herded into the boxcars, belonged to an alien world. We were all haunted by the questions: what were they going to do with us? Would they really kill us? Was this really the end? No turning back? But no one uttered these questions aloud.

Our neighbors from Nowolipie Street had a son my age, named Sewek. We had been inseparable friends in the ghetto, after the Mila Street selection, during the few winter months' respite from "campaigns." Our families even stayed together in hiding places. Sewek and I always had a great deal to talk about. He was a very intelligent and well-read boy. He wrote poetry about our life in the ghetto, the persecution and longed-for freedom. Grown-ups said they were very good poems, and they impressed me as unusually fine.

But now, at the Lublin *Umschlag,* even Sewek's poetry lost all its meaning . . . I only exchanged a few words with my friend on the subject of what the Nazis would do to us children, if they took the grown-ups to a labor camp. How unreal, how stupid our earlier speculations and guesses as to our unknown futures seemed! Always optimistic, Sewek assured me even now that children would work as messengers in the camp, that the Nazis only took away infants, and we were almost grown-up already. But he spoke in a feeble, low voice, as if he were about to collapse. He was terribly exhausted by the journey from Warsaw to Lublin, by hunger and lack of sleep. He looked still smaller and younger on this account.

Meanwhile, terrifying rumors began circulating in the *Umschlag* that a "selection" was due to take place the next day. The Nazis would separate men and women, and send them to different labor camps; the old, the sick and children would be exe-

cuted. I told my mother, as I had done before the Mila Street
selection, that if the Nazis did not send me to a camp for adults
capable of work, I did not want her to come with me. However,
my mother smiled in her own way, and looking affectionately at
me, vowed she would never consider a separation. And there was
so much determination and serenity in her face that I was
ashamed of my plea. Besides, I knew that I too could never part
from my mother, should anything threaten her. I could not even
imagine a situation in which we might separate. Hilek was also
hopeful, and said I looked older and prettier than ever, and that I
would certainly get through the selection successfully. There was
a little truth in my brother's compliment; the sufferings I had
endured, the sleepless nights, had added years to my appearance.
The crown of thick plaits which my mother carefully piled up on
my head, and my plumpness—all suggested I would be sent to
the Majdanek camp with the grown-ups and those fit for work.

In the morning, the Nazis ordered us to get up off the floor. In
a long column we marched under strong armed guard to
Majdanek. We trudged through the mud stumbling and falling.
We passed crowds of men in strange, striped prison uniforms,
with odd striped berets on their shaven heads. They were carrying rocks or pushing wheelbarrows full of earth, and the mud
greatly hindered their labor. I wondered whether my mother and I
could do such work? I also saw women working, in striped
prison clothing. These people did not say a word to us as we
passed, though we tried to question them and find out what
awaited us here. Storm Troopers were watching them all the
time, and would beat them savagely for the slightest thing. The
SS were assisted in this by prisoners armed with clubs, wearing
armbands that said *"kapo."*

Before we left the Lublin *Umschlag,* my mother took the shoes
off the feet of a dead woman, and told me to put them on. They
had high heels; at first I could not even walk a step, as my feet
were cut and sore. Then I plucked up all my energy and concentrated on mastering the pain. I leaned heavily on Hilek's arm. I
would have lost my balance without his help. Finally Hilek took

one of my shoes and broke off the heel. A lot of nails remained in the sole. He was about to do the same to the other shoe, but we were too late; we had reached the spot where the Nazis, shouting and hitting people, were separating the men from the women . . .

We kept retreating, to postpone the moment of separation from Hilek. Other families were doing the same. Sons, fathers, brothers and husbands hastily said goodbye to their womenfolk. People embraced and kissed. The SS brutally pushed them, fired at those retreating, beating people blindly. We must have been harder than iron, for our hearts did not break with the pain!

Hilek kissed me, my mother, Halina. He held the sobbing, desperate Hela in his arms. We had never expected to be separated so abruptly. When saying goodbye to me, Hilek gave me strict instructions not to lean on my mother, for she was frail, and could not bear such a burden; it might kill her.

A few more loving, powerful embraces, and the whip of a Storm Trooper reached us . . . They took Hilek from us. Forever.

A gusty, cold, cruel wind was blowing.

We were standing in a crowd of women and children in the center of a great open space, shivering with cold and exhaustion. But this was nothing compared to the separation. The menfolk had been driven away somewhere, we did not know where—and now we had no idea where they were to take us, nor what they would do with us.

Noon approached. The SS went on separating groups of men from the crowd and herding them into barracks huts standing nearby. What was inside those huts? No one came back from them, so we could not tell.

My mother covered me with her coat, and cuddled me lovingly. The wind drove sand into our eyes, it was so powerful that we could barely stand after the many hours of waiting in the square, the sleepless nights, the nightmare we endured in the boxcar. I thought—come what may—if only this suffering would end! I just don't care any more what they do to us.

My mother stroked my head, comforted and soothed me. "Just a little more patience," she said, "and soon they will take us to the bathhouse, we'll wash and change our clothes, then we'll go into the camp, to the huts you can see beyond the barbed wire. We will rest there, then they will surely assign us to work in the fields . . ."

"You don't think they will kill us?" I asked.

"Of course not," she replied, "after all, we saw women prisoners in prison dress on the way here, and now you can see them in the distance, behind the camp wires."

"Will there be beds in the huts, and blankets, and food?" I asked.

Persuaded by my mother's words, I began daydreaming about a bath, and the hut where I would rest, eat my fill, and get warm. The slowness with which the line was moving agitated me. How much more time would it take before we got to the bathhouse, into which the SS kept leading more and more groups of women?

How could I have foreseen that these hours in the empty space in front of the bathhouse were the last I was to spend with my mother? That these were the last hours of her life? And I wanted to hasten on the moment of entering the bathhouse and the camp! Yet how could I have known?

Finally our turn arrived. The Storm Troopers added Hela, Halina, me and Eda Wilner (Hela's cousin, thanks to whom we had obtained places in the Mila Street bunker) to a group. Remembering Hilek's admonition not to lean on my mother, I took the arm of my cousin, a tall, plump girl, who offered me it (she did not survive Majdanek, but was one of the first of our group to die in the camp). My mother walked behind us, with Hela, and I did not even look around to see what was happening to them, being absorbed in setting down my feet, for each step caused me incredible pain. To this day I do not know when and how I found myself inside a large hut, piled to the ceiling with heaps of clothes and shoes. The Nazis ordered us to strip naked and throw everything except our shoes on this pile. At this point, Hela exchanged her light shoes for a pair of high top boots which she slipped furtively out of the pile. She winked at me to do the same, but I was afraid and too exhausted; I no longer needed anything, I did not even have the strength to think of my wretched shoes . . .

Driven on by hundreds of naked women, I eventually reached a shower: "A bath!" I thought joyfully. So this was the bathhouse, which meant we would soon be in a warm hut. My mother was right; they were not going to kill us, we would live and work! How good that was!

I wanted to throw myself into my mother's arms for joy, to tell her of my love and complete faith in everything she said. I looked around, seeking her in the crowd of women under the showers. But she was not there. I began looking for her more and more frantically, I could see Hela, her cousin, and Halina, but my mother was not there. Where is my mother? My head reeled, there was a lump in my throat, I could not get the question out. "Where is my mother?" I finally managed to whisper, turning to my sister-in-law.

Hela looked at me, I saw her unhappy face, then she looked away and although she spoke quietly, I distinctly heard her say: "She is not here."

I felt as though my hands and feet had suddenly been cut off. Yet I still did not understand the meaning of her four words. I had not seen them take my mother away, nor how it happened, nor why. Besides, all our friends from the *Umschlag* were here. My mother was young, with her pink cheeks she looked much healthier and prettier—or so it seemed to me—than many other women. Yet they had taken her! Why? I could not come to terms in any way with the thought that she was really not here, that I would never see her again. I kept looking at the door; she should be coming in at any minute, to embrace and comfort me. But my mother did not come in. I moved in a circle like an automaton, repeating mechanically: "My mother is not here!" Everything else stopped existing for me. I was incapable of anything, even tears. When they handed out clothing that had to be put on quickly, without drying ourselves, Hela energetically took care of me, seeing I was half-conscious.

"From now on I am your mother, do you understand that?" she said firmly.

But I said nothing. I could not bring myself to express my gratitude. Although when I later recalled this moment, I was always aware of gratitude. But at that time, in the bath-house, I was still with my mother, cuddled up to her in the empty space in front of the bathhouse, protected by her coat, in the cold wind; all I had to do was put out my hand and touch her. Then someone nudged me, and the vision fled.

They gave me a floor-length black ball gown, with lace. Hela put the dress on me and tied string around my waist to pull the skirt up. I was to start prison life in Majdanek in this ball dress. Everyone was handed these weird party clothes, as if to jeer at us.

The Storm Troopers assembled us in groups of five, outside in the yard, counted us, and took us into the camp. Those who failed the selection (mostly from the Warsaw transport) were taken to the crematorium. I did not realize this until much later. My mother was among those sentenced. But Hela and acquaintances from the bunker kept telling me she had been taken to another camp, to easier work harvesting potatoes, and that I ought to be glad . . . Perhaps they really believed this, for at that time none of us knew there were gas chambers and crematoria in Majdanek.

I consoled myself to a certain minimal degree as I listened to my companions; I refused to admit the fact that they had driven my mother and all those other women to death! My longing for my mother did not lessen on this account in the least. More and more I wanted to have her close to me, and I realized with ever-increasing clarity that this was already impossible.

The camp—especially the watchtowers bristling with machine guns and the electrified barbed wire—horrified me. I was used to cellars, attics and other hiding places in the ghetto, and feared open spaces, coming face to face with our executioners. The shock that followed the unexpected loss of my mother, my frantic terror at the sight of the watchtowers, the machine guns, the green uniforms of the SS, and finally the impossibility of escaping everything I had learned to run away from in the years in the ghetto—drove me almost to the point of insanity. I did not even recognize my own face; I had a ferocious look, and my eyes grew huge, bulging. Sometimes Hela turned away when I looked at her, and would implore me: "Don't look at me like that, you frighten me! Don't look at me like that!" But for a long time this was the only way I could look at other people.

The reality of Majdanek weighed me down even more than that pile of bodies under which I almost stifled in the railroad car. The "labor" camp proved entirely different from the picture my mother had drawn for me. It was not a question of work, cozy huts and rest after work—it was nothing but ceaseless fear, penal servitude, and a bottomless pit of hell. How can anyone find words to describe it?

Had it not been for Hela, her boundless devotion and constant care, I would have perished after a few days. Hela had vowed inwardly to my mother that she would take her place, and she kept her vow. She was a true mother to me, up to the end of her life.

I was thirteen. The years of persecution in the ghetto, the loss of my father and my brother, and—most painful of all—the loss of my mother, had impaired my nervous system, and at a time when I should have forced myself to be as resistant as possible, I broke down completely.

Fortunately, however, I was physically robust and plump enough not to be taken for a child, and the many "selections," during which weak, pale and thin women were sent to the gas chambers, passed me by.

We had to fight for everything in Majdanek: for a scrap of floor space in the hut on which to stretch out at night, for a rusty bowl without which we could not obtain the miserable ration of nettle-soup with which they fed us, or yellow stinking water to drink. But I was not capable of fighting. Fear and horror overcame me at the sight of women prisoners struggling over a scrap of free space on the floor, or hitting one another over the head at the soup kettles, snatching bowls—hostile, aggressive women, wanting to live at any price. Stunned, aghast, famished, terrified, I watched them from a distance.

Meanwhile Hela fought with redoubled strength—for herself and for me. She shared every bite she acquired with me. As for energy, Halina did not yield to Hela. She learned how to make her own way in the camp from the very start. We stayed together, though Halina did not like this very much; she had to share with me and help me, to bid for a place for me on the floor, or for a blanket, which I could not even take care of, so that time and again someone would take it from me by force or trickery. This infuriated Halina. She tried to make Hela rebel against me, saying I was only pretending to be weak, and that I wanted to make use of them.

Halina was fifteen at this time, plump and well-built. Even at home in Warsaw, she liked avoiding her duties, and was always concerned for herself, her own comforts. She had been spoiled, especially by her father, who adored her. Of course, Hela did not give way to her hints; on the contrary she showed me more affection and attachment every day. She gave me all the love she felt for my brother, and did everything in her power to make easier my life in the camp. For a long time I could not rouse myself from my state of listlessness. Had it not been for Hela's efforts, I would not have roused myself from my apathy and despair. But there was no room in Majdanek for the feeble or depressed.

Only here did I recognize the true nature of my sister-in-law, and only here did I come to love her. Later, I was ready to make any sacrifice for her. Out of regard for her, and thanks to her help, I too finally joined the fight for life in the camp of death.

Hela was almost twenty-one. She was a graceful, slender and blonde girl, energetic, serious, taciturn and collected in her ways. She had struck me as inaccessible, even alien. Her gravity, her calmness made me shy; I used to accuse her of being overly self-assured. But she had reason to be proud: in addition to being honorable and noble, intelligent, wise and resourceful, she was also very talented, could sew and crochet beautifully, could sing, and was greatly liked by our family—people reckoned with her views. She accepted admiration as natural. Her family was quite wealthy, and she had two elder brothers, but was not spoiled. Before the war she graduated from a sewing school. I was slightly acquainted with Mr. and Mrs. Herzberg, Hela's parents. I used to see them in the ghetto before the first deportation campaign; they were sweet and well-bred people. Hela's brothers fled to Russia at the start of the occupation, when Hela and her parents came to Warsaw from Bydgoszcz.

Roll call was being held when we entered the area of Majdanek. That evening it lasted a very long time, longer than usual, apparently as a punishment. *Kapos,* Storm Troopers, and German women overseers counted us many times, and watched that no one changed her position.

This was the first time I had ever seen women in uniform, armed like Storm Troopers with revolvers and horsewhips. Hitherto I had thought that only men were in the SS, since it was hard to imagine women capable of beating, torturing and killing people.

Hela surreptitiously borrowed a pair of scissors that was passing from hand to hand during the roll call; swiftly and nimbly she cut off both my plaits and rubbed them into the ground with one foot. Scissors, a comb and a little mirror were rare treasures in the camp, and this was why Hela took advantage of the opportunity, and spared me the trouble of looking after my long hair. I accepted the cutting of my hair with the utmost indifference.

There were about a thousand women in our barracks. They slept on the ground. At night they trampled on each other when they went to the lavatory, or for water.

The camp soup and contaminated water gave most women diarrhea, so that troublesome nightly trips to the lavatories let no one sleep. Often the sick women did not get there in time . . . The lavatories in Majdanek were out in the open, near the barbed wire that divided the women's camp from the men's. We had to stand with our buttocks naked, while men were walking about not far away, and the guards in the watchtowers often fired at this "target" out of boredom, or to amuse themselves.

I shivered with terror, shame and cold whenever I had to relieve myself, and tried to use the latrine as rarely as possible. But soon I too contracted diarrhea, I too had mishaps on the way to the lavatory. We had no clothes to change into, often it was not possible even to wash, and the women I involuntarily soiled did not spare their blows, curses and insults. Helpless and miserable, I used to wonder at such moments what my mother would have said to it all. Perhaps it was better for her not to be there, not to have to endure such terrible humiliation.

Every day at dawn, *kapos* rushed into the huts and, beating us around the heads and shoulders with planks from their wooden beds or with whips, cursing and abusing us, they woke us and herded us out to the morning roll call. Sore from lying on the floor, shivering with cold, we sometimes stood for hours in the huge space between the barracks. Those in the front rank were the most visible, and were in danger of the Storm Troopers' and *kapos'* sticks. It was somewhat safer in the middle ranks and . . . warmer too. This was why we all tried to acquire a place in the central ranks, we fought for it as though it were literally a place in paradise . . . We nestled to one another, forgetting recent quarrels and fights, only trying to get warm, though when a *kapo* or overseer approached we drew away quickly to arm's length, and the rain, wind and early morning cold struck us with renewed force. Mostly we were in summer dresses with short sleeves— that was how they dressed us. In the afternoons we suffered from the heat, having no place to shelter from the sun. Our arms, legs and faces became covered with blisters. There was nothing with which to tend infected wounds. The worst was that the SS would take people away to the gas chambers during a selection for having such a thing the matter with them.

Female Storm Troopers in thick uniforms and raincoats with

huge hoods, and wearing tall boots, roamed around the square, counting us continually and wreaking their bad tempers on women prisoners, arousing the fear and terror of us all.

After several hours, when it was light, a terrifying whistle indicated the end of the morning roll call. The *kapos* began herding the women away, forcing them into labor gangs before marching them out to work. Running about the entire camp, blowing whistles, they hurled themselves on us, pushing and pulling, beating us. On these occasions the seriously ill, the wounded or feeble were killed off. I could not walk; my injured feet, a festering wound on my heel, and those accursed shoes, one with a high heel, the other full of nails—how in the world could I survive a 12-hour working day? Even grown-up, healthy, strong prisoners collapsed, pushing heavy wheelbarrows loaded with earth or stones.

I hobbled along, biting my lips with pain, in panicked flight from the *kapos* as they ran about the square. I hid behind the huts; when they caught me, I showed them my injured feet and begged them to let me go—sometimes they actually did, after hitting me with their whips.

In any case, I dodged work all the time, only pleading with God that they hit me with a whip rather than a plank. The dry, hard blow of a plank hurt a great deal more.

On the day after our being brought to this camp, the commandant entered the hut to which we were assigned; he ordered everyone to sit on the floor, took up his position in the center with a revolver in one hand, and began a "speech of welcome." From this speech it proved that henceforward each of us was to be only a number—we had immediately to sew scraps of canvas bearing numbers to our clothes, on our chests; the camp regulations meant severe punishment for the slightest transgression, from shooting and hanging to twenty-five strokes of the whip on our bare buttocks. He spoke of this in such a casual manner, and as calmly as if he were talking of the most ordinary, everyday matters.

He made a much more terrifying impression on me than the usual enraged Storm Trooper. The face of that Nazi and his speech haunted me for a long, long time afterwards. Even today I have not really freed myself from the terror I felt at the sight of him.

The next "selection" in Majdanek came upon me as suddenly as that first selection in front of the bathhouse, when my mother was taken away. But my shoes unexpectedly helped me.

During dinner, which they allowed us as an exception to eat in the barracks and not outdoors as usual, a woman overseer appeared in the doorway. *Kapos* then rushed in, and began laying about them to right and left with their whips, striking bowls out of prisoners' hands, herding us all towards the door, where the overseer carried out a "selection."

I had been sitting on the floor beside Hela (we always stayed together), and was finishing some soup that Hela had procured for me. I was drinking the thin liquid straight from the bowl, as—like most new arrivals—we had no spoons.

At first we did not realize what was going on. We failed to notice the overseer in the doorway . . . Not until women began throwing down their bowls of soup and rushing into the depths of the hut, or jumping out of the windows, did terror seize us. There was already a great rush at the windows . . . and in any case, with my injured feet, I could not have jumped . . . Yet we both realized we must get out of the hut, if only to avoid being beaten.

Hela pressed the tin bowl to her chest and began pushing her way towards the door. I followed. I always followed her blindly. After a few minutes of dreadful struggling, Hela found herself outside the hut. But I, completely indifferent to what was happening all around, limping, finally reached the door, only to hear a loud, harsh "Halt!" I looked around and came face to face with a female Storm Trooper, who barred my way with a whip. I did not understand why they were detaining me in this manner, when they were driving everyone to the door. Obsessed by the single thought of joining Hela as soon as possible, I forgot my injured feet and did not know that a "selection" was taking place, or that the overseer was paying special attention to our feet. So I was more startled than frightened, thinking there must be some mistake, and I looked at the female Storm Trooper impatiently, even angrily. This gave her pause. She looked at me again—at that time my face was still full and fresh—she hesitated, then turned her gaze to my feet: she had seen me limping. Then she caught sight of my shoes—one with a heel, the other without. She raised her whip—I could pass. Hela had been watching the incident from outside, half petrified with terror. For, outside the hut, there were trucks containing the women whom the overseer had "selected" for the gas chamber. Fortunately I did not realize this until after the event. Had the overseer seen fear in the eyes of a limping prisoner, she would not even have thought of glancing at her shoes.

The frequent "selections," though they entirely paralyzed our senses, were not the only tragedies in the camp. We were tormented day after day by the roll calls, starvation, slave labor, beatings and vermin. Lice devoured us at night.

Death in all shapes and forms decimated the camp, striking down even the strongest, fittest and most resistant women. We all grew thin, emaciated and feeble. Overseers guarding us at work would sometimes throw meat to their dogs, then give us the leftover bones to gnaw.

Faced by neverending suffering, I had to arouse myself from the state of apathy and despair that followed my mother's death. I learned to push when standing in line for wretched portions of food, to dodge adroitly during *Arbeitsappell,* to flee and hide from the *kapos* (one of them called me an "old camp-follower"), to control my trembling and terror so as to walk erect and assuredly during a selection. My youthfulness was no longer a danger—dirty, sunburned and lean, I looked like a worn-out woman . . . Hela proved weaker than I; I dreaded the thought that I might lose her too . . . The sight of her gray, earth-colored face and her famished, profoundly unhappy eyes now oppressed me more than all the horrors of the camp. She felt cold all the time. I used to cover her with part of my own clothing, tried to warm her with the heat of my own body. Gradually we changed roles.

The longer we stayed in the camp, the more we gained in experience, our instincts sharpened, our vigilance developed and our reactions quickened. We acquired a greater capacity for adapting ourselves to conditions. We learned that staying inside the camp during the daytime was not always safe, on account of the ever-increasing number of selections. Better drag rocks all day, or dig under the blazing sun, than to shudder every time a whistle blew in the camp.

As our stay in Majdanek lengthened, we learned to distinguish between the easier and harder labor gangs, which to avoid, who were the "better" overseers and *kapos,* and who were the worse, those to keep away from. Prisoners trying to get into the better labor gangs were generally not particular what methods they used, so fights broke out, there were incidents of informing and toadyism.

When we worked in the fields near Polish villages, it was sometimes possible to bribe an overseer or *kapo* so as to allow peasants to toss us food—bread, sugar, sausage, hard-boiled eggs . . . Sometimes the peasants would give us this food out of pity, disinterestedly, or sometimes in exchange for money or jewelry which some women had smuggled into the camp. If a "bad" overseer caught sight of one of these transactions, it would end with the gallows for the prisoner and severe punishment for the Pole. Poles also paid with their lives for being helpful to Jewish people. Hela had smuggled a little money into the camp, and sometimes we spent it to buy bacon, bread or sugar lumps. She did not tell me about this money at first, fearing I might blurt it out to someone who might inform on us, and such things were punished with the utmost severity. The food we bought was divided into three shares, one for Halina, one for me, and the third for Hela herself. I admired her resourcefulness and courage. I gained still more trust in her, and respect for her. It was not everyone who would so gladly share with others, especially food.

When Hela had spent all the money (there was not much), she sold her top boots, which she had pulled out from the pile in the hut before the bath, to a *kapo*. She got several hundred zloty and an old pair of men's pants. Other *kapos* had already tried to snatch the boots off Hela's legs, but she fought back.

One day as we were weeding beets in the vegetable garden, Hela recognized Hilek among some men working not far off.

"Hilek!" she suddenly shrieked with inexpressible joy.

"Hilek!" I cried too, forgetting we were not allowed to speak to other prisoners.

Hilek turned, smiled and waved. This did not escape the notice of a *kapo,* who rushed at Hilek with his stick. We crouched over the beets, gritting our teeth so as not to cry out for pain and despair. Hela moved closer to me; her eyes blazed with anger.

We never saw Hilek again; when the Nazis began sending transports of men and women away from Majdanek to other camps, he sent us a card by someone else, informing us which transport he was leaving on, and asking us to try and join the same transport of women. That card was the last greeting from my brother. He has remained in my memory as I last saw him in Majdanek: tall, lean, in striped prison uniform, with a round, striped cap on his shaven head—crouching beneath the blows of an infuriated *kapo*.

Hela never knew that he died, as she herself suffered the fate before he. This I was told by one of his friends, shortly before the end of the war.

Sometimes we worked in fields only a stone's throw from a village hut—armed SS sentries cut us off from freedom. Then I used to look with envy and longing at the children playing freely in the peasants' gardens, at the hens pecking the dust, the people bustling about . . . I just could not comprehend that there still existed another world, in which people were allowed to move around open spaces not cordoned off with barbed wire, and in which children played! But at the same time the faith quickened in me that we too would at some future time be people. The existence of life outside the camp, the sight of the bright sky and green fields alleviated the tragedy of the camp. More than ever before, I believed every rumor of the defeats of the Reich at the front, of the approach of Soviet troops and the liberation that was at hand. Here, in the open fields, closer to people's houses, it was easier to hope. I thought it only necessary to muster all our strength in order to survive . . . But where was I to get this strength? It was ebbing away, and our sufferings grew daily.

In Majdanek, light work was considered to be weeding the grass between two rows of electrified barbed wire separating our camp from that of the men. It was a narrow strip of space which could accommodate a slender person. Squatting one behind the other, we moved cautiously forward; a careless movement meant death, and every now and then someone was killed by touching the electrified wire. Neither the overseers nor the *kapos* dared come between these wires, so no one urged us on, or struck or

rushed us. We could sit and rest, picking at the weeds and grass . . .
I preferred this work to any other. Here I had the peace I longed for.

More transports from various parts of Poland kept arriving in
Majdanek. We, the old and experienced inhabitants of the inferno, taught the newcomers the laws and regulations, and ways
to avoid punishment and death. The terror and stupefaction of the
new arrivals, their simple questions, their complete ignorance,
sometimes appeared almost absurd to me. Yet I myself had behaved
in the same way at first. My past was, as it were, no longer mine, it
did not in any way concern the present reality. The camp had made
me a being totally different from the person I had been before.

One day they brought in women from two localities in Southern Poland from which my father had come, and where his family lived. The arrival of people from this area aroused earlier
feelings in me . . . It was worth making inquiries, in case anyone
knew my father's relatives. So it was that I found my cousin
Rachel, who was twenty. We gazed at one another like strangers,
asking one another about the fate of various members of the
family. Rachel was surprised when I introduced her to Hela; she
did not know of Hilek's marriage. After all, we had had no contact since the outbreak of war . . . My appearance shocked Rachel, while her childish questions and fear of things we already
regarded as unimportant mere trifles shocked me.

Shortly before the war, Rachel's mother visited us in Warsaw,
then took me back with her to their home in Southern Poland for
the vacation. Their house was solid and welcoming. I was then
eight or nine, and missed my mother dreadfully. Rachel, who
liked children, looked after me and did all she could to render my
stay of two months a pleasant one. Her parents and younger
brother showed me great affection. My grandparents, whom I had
not known at all, could not make too much of their "grand-
daughter from Warsaw."

Now I gazed at Rachel, involuntarily recalling the past happy days and . . . I had nothing to say to my suddenly rediscovered relative. The past was forever buried, the present was terrible, the future threatening—what had we to talk about?

Rachel was a well-built, tall, plump and robust girl. Looking as she did, she had every chance of successfully passing selection and getting better work, which in turn meant better opportunities of surviving. I told her this frankly and openly, but she was hurt. She wanted affection and comforting from me, not brutal words bluntly expressing the naked truth. Alas, I could not bring myself to feel affection for anyone except Hela. To the end of our stay in Majdanek, I remained entirely alien to Rachel, though she tried to become intimate with us both.

The talk with my cousin only added to my sufferings. Rachel's father and 15-year-old brother had been shot in Pinsk by the Nazis, in a sawmill to which both had been recruited to work. There also the Nazis shot my father's two younger brothers, both still unmarried. Rachel's mother died in the freight car on the way to Majdanek. When the people, unable to endure the crowd and the stench, started shouting and banging on the walls of the car, the Storm Troopers answered by a salvo of shots through the window. My aunt was hit, and died in her daughter's arms a few hours later, before they reached Lublin.

How was it possible to cope in Majdanek with the burden of memories, cruelty and pain? There was one remedy: Majdanek itself. Majdanek gave no one time for memories, sorrow or despair. The threat of death and torture meant that every minute spent in the camp dulled the mind while it sharpened the animal instinct, and killed all other human impulses.

After a two-month stay in Majdanek, the SS began selecting the healthiest and best-looking prisoners, whom they deported in groups of several hundred to unknown camps.

In general, the women believed they would have easier work and better conditions there. In fact, the first transport, consisting of the prettiest, youngest and best-built women, went to a labor camp near Czestochowa, where things were better than in Majdanek or other camps, and most of them managed to survive until they were liberated by the Red Army. Rachel was sent in this "best" transport.

"If only Hela looked like Rachel, she would have had the same opportunity," I thought involuntarily, as I said goodbye to my cousin.

During the next "recruitment" for departure, the Nazis picked out Halina and me, but I slipped away at the last moment, to remain with my sister-in-law, who had been overlooked. I would not leave Hela for anything, just as long as I could be with her, everywhere, to the last!

A few days later they assigned us to a third transport. The uneasiness that prevailed in Majdanek after the departure of the previous transports was still more intensified by the news that the Hitlerites were about to liquidate the camp, and that those remaining in the place would be exterminated. This was precisely what happened, soon afterwards. So Hela and I were fortunate in getting out of threatened Majdanek. The moment when we passed out of the women's camp, holding hands tightly, has remained deeply impressed in my mind. It was a moment of great joy and great hope. I had no suspicion of how much suffering awaited us in the not so distant future. But those who remained in Majdanek genuinely envied us. Their own forebodings, unfortunately, came to pass . . .

They took us to an empty hut in the men's camp, where very many wearisome formalities took place: copying down our camp numbers, our surnames, our first names, place and date of birth; they kept counting us over and over again. This went on for hours. We sat crowded together on the floor. Now and then SS officers came into the hut, and we froze with terror at the sight of them, trying to guess their plans from their expression.

Men prisoners brought in soup; it was possible to exchange a few words with them. Many women received greetings from relatives, or passed on greetings, while some fortunate ones even met their dear ones, a husband, son, brother or friend. The men tossed pieces of bread to us. An unusually feverish, lively mood prevailed in the hut until evening.

Neither Hela nor I met anyone we knew in the men's camp. No one knew Hilek. But my sister-in-law struck up a chance acquaintance with one of the prisoners, who was much interested in us, asked about our experiences, and later brought us some bread.

When it was dark outside, the Storm Troopers locked the hut and switched off the light. I nestled up to Hela, and we both fell asleep on the floor, dreaming of a better camp, easier work, tolerable living conditions . . .

In the middle of the night, the SS noisily threw open the hut door, arousing us with their shouts and beatings; they began herding us out, making sure that no one hid or escaped. A fearful confusion ensued.

Sleepy, frightened to death, we crowded to the door, pushing and trampling on one another in the darkness and panic. The Storm Troopers ran around like mad dogs. They made us form fours, lit electric lamps, counted us, swearing.

"They are taking us to the crematorium!" The terrible news fell on us like a thunderbolt and spread like lightning through the ranks.

My heart beat rapidly. I could not believe it. Once again I could not believe that death was possible, as months earlier, on the Warsaw *Umschlag,* when the Nazis set up a machine gun in front of us . . . And I did not yield to the general despair.

The SS gave an order and we moved off . . . in the direction of the crematorium. Some women were weeping, others tearing their hair, praying, or bidding farewell to mothers or sisters.

They herded us into a hut, the interior of which resembled a bathhouse. Despite the darkness, we observed stacks of empty gas containers on the ground in front of the hut. There was a strange, sweetish odor in the air. There was no doubt now that they were taking us to execution. The women went out of their minds . . . They groaned, wailed, had convulsions.

They herded us into this bathhouse, and barred the door behind us. Now we had to carry out an order given previously: undress and hang our clothes up on hooks on the walls. Obediently we undressed in silence. We knew there was no way out. We hung our clothes up, then sat down on benches along the walls, waiting in extreme agitation . . . when and how would death come?

Time passed. Hour followed hour. But nothing happened, no one came. It was silent both inside and outside the bathhouse. Perhaps they had forgotten us? A faint hope slowly began emerging . . . Towards morning they came back; after the nightmare of waiting for death in the gas chamber, we went outside. They counted us again (as though anyone could have escaped from that locked building!), and took us back to the men's camp, to the same hut as the day before. There we learned from the prisoners that the supplies of gas had unexpectedly run out during the night . . . We had been spared on account of this accident.

We ate "dinner" in the same camp in an almost joyous mood. We were like people reborn! To emerge alive from the gas chamber— that bordered on the miraculous! After dinner they distributed bread (one loaf to four people), counted us again, then herded us to the boxcars.

We sighed with relief. For the time being we had no idea of the location of the camp to which they were taking us, nor what it was called. We did not find out until we arrived.

They ordered us to sit down on the floor of the freight cars in rows, our legs apart and round our companion in the row in front, so as to utilize all the space. This time they left the door of the boxcar open: two Storm Troopers took their places at it.

The Nazis ran around the train for some time, blowing whistles, shouting, looking into the boxcars now and again, checking, counting—finally the train moved off.

So my second journey into the unknown began. We believed that no matter where they were taking us, it could not be worse than Majdanek, for it was hard to picture anything worse than Majdanek. Especially after a night spent in the gas chamber . . .

"After all, had they wanted to kill us, they would not have let us out of the crematorium, or be taking us away from Majdanek . . ." we kept saying during the entire journey.

It was the height of summer. The train dragged along; the journey lasted two days and nights. Hunger, thirst. We were forbidden, on pain of death, to change positions.

Our limbs grew stiff, we could feel the pricking of thousands of pins all through our bodies. Our legs weighed like blocks of wood. I cannot describe the agony. When I stood for hours during roll calls in the camp and my legs gave way with exhaustion, or when I dragged heavy rocks about for twelve hours at a time under the blazing sun and whip of overseers or *kapos,* I longed to be able to sit down for a moment. I never dreamed that sitting could be such torture. Every nerve, every muscle cried out for a change of position.

All of a sudden, my neighbor moved slightly in her place. The Storm Trooper hurled a threat at her, but she ignored it and began begging him to let her stand up for a moment. Without waiting for his reply, she tried to rise, leaning on the shoulders of her teenage daughter who sat in front of her. The Storm Trooper aimed his rifle. Half-standing, she kept begging him for mercy. We held our breath. The Storm Trooper was an elderly man, he looked about sixty to me. Would he really shoot her? After all, the poor woman did not intend to escape, or even to stand, but merely to straighten herself a little.

The Storm Trooper fired. The bullet struck her in the temple. We watched in stupefaction as she slowly sank down on the shoulders of her daughter, as if she still could not believe that the old Storm Trooper would carry out his threat . . . Her face grew paler moment by moment, life was ebbing away from her incredibly fast. But the Storm Trooper, apparently pleased with himself, slung his rifle over his shoulder, as if nothing had happened.

A terrible silence filled the boxcar, broken only from time to time by the convulsive sobbing of the young girl supporting the fresh, still warm corpse of her mother on her slender shoulders . . .

This tragic scene made us forget our stiff legs, hunger and thirst. We had learned yet again that our lives were worthless as long as we were in the clutches of murderers. The Storm Trooper's inhuman act strengthened our belief that nothing good was awaiting us at the end of this nightmare journey. The harsh voice of the murderer tore us from our stupefaction: he ordered that the body be thrown out of the boxcar.

"You will not live long, either," he said to the young girl. "What are you blubbering for? Silence!"

She stopped. Tears were pouring down her cheeks. She was like her mother, a dark, pretty little thing, with great brown eyes and black hair. I was very sorry for the orphaned little girl. I also missed my mother, but at least I had Hela. Later, when I had lost Hela, I made friends with this sweet girl. Her name was Sabina. But I was doomed to witness not only the death of the mother, but of the daughter too.

The train stopped. They herded us out of the boxcars, and those who had died or been shot during the journey were thrown from the windows like sacks. Shoved brutally and beaten, we moved

in a column from the railroad station of Birkenau (Brzezinka). So
the problem of our destination was solved!

Nazis as well as *Judenrat* officials in the Warsaw ghetto had
terrified us with the name *Auschwitz* (Oswiecim). For a long time
we had shuddered at the very name. Now our column was passing through a wide gate with the sign *Arbeit macht frei F.K.L.*
[Frauen Konzentrations-Lager] (Work Will Make You Free:
Women's Concentration Camp).

There was an area much larger than that at Majdanek, surrounded by barbed wire, with many watchtowers not far from each
other, and machine guns emerging from them, long rows of gloomy
brick barracks, thick and stinking mud everywhere. Shaven heads
appeared in the windows, colorless faces that might have belonged
to men or women—we could not tell. In Majdanek the barracks had
been made of fresh planks, usually everything was made of wood.
But this camp seemed solid, expansive, precisely organized, built as
though meant to last forever, for centuries! Could any power change
things here, crumble it, or liberate us?

Auschwitz had been in existence a long time; even when we
were all living together in Muranowska Street, and I used to play
happily with my little friends on the stairs and in the yard—people
were being tortured in Auschwitz! We shall never get out, I
thought in terror.

Gorged, insolent *kapos* in dark-blue striped dresses and beautifully sewn aprons* herded us, swearing and beating us to a large
hut near a bathhouse, where we waited long hours as they
counted and recounted us, registered us, shaved our heads, tattooed numbers and marks on our wrists—the emblem of Auschwitz, proofs of identity . . .

I was collapsing with exhaustion. I was panic-stricken with
fear of another "selection," and separation from Hela.

The woman prisoner who tattooed me was unexpectedly kind.

---

*I later discovered that these aprons were all the fashion among the "aristoc-
racy of Auschwitz." They were worn by block overseers and *kapos* who had
the means to pay women prisoners to make them—mostly Greek Jewish
women, distinguished by special skill in sewing.

She saw I was a child, shivering with fear at the thought of this operation. Gently, she began asking me about my experiences. She spoke in Czech but I understood her very well, for the words sounded like Polish, except they were diminutives, caressing . . . I felt a little better.

But the worst of it was that during the registration, shaving of heads and the like I lost sight of Hela. At first she was assigned to another group. I went almost out of my mind with agitation lest they take her as they had taken my mother. Finally I rediscovered my sister-in-law at the bathhouse entrance, and threw myself into her arms. Hela had been given a summer dress, very short and ragged. The clothing and shoes in which we traveled from Majdanek were taken away from us before the bath. So I gave Hela my things and slipped back into the crowd of naked women. My heart was beating like a hammer. However, I was lucky about the *kapo* distributing clothing. The first time they had given me good, warm clothes, and the second time I did not fare too badly . . . I went up to another *kapo,* who was abusing prisoners with great relish, but she treated me fairly well, and did not even hit me.

Had they caught me during this stratagem, I would have been given 25 strokes on my bare bottom; that was one of the lightest punishments in Auschwitz.

During these hours of agony, as they transformed us into inhabitants of the camp, I wandered almost deliriously around the barracks looking for water. A drink, a drink, a drink! But there was nothing to drink. Until I caught sight of a bucket containing a dark liquid through the half-open door of a block overseer or *kapo*'s little room. I ran in, crouched over the bucket and began greedily and without thinking to lap up the fluid. It was dirty soapsuds. For long afterwards I could feel the loathsome taste in my mouth and throat, increasing my thirst. Towards evening, when they herded us under a warm shower, I opened my mouth wide, but the thin spray of water splashed in all directions . . . They did not even allow us to get properly wet. From the shower we had to run naked into a large, very cold and draughty hall.

Shivering, our teeth chattering as if with fever, we hastily pulled clothes over our naked bodies. They also painted a huge cross on our backs with red paint. Then they took us to Block 15 in groups of five, into quarantine.

It was already night when we entered the block. On either side of the dark and narrow passages rose three-tier plank beds; women prisoners lay closely packed together on them, covered with rough, dark blankets. A feeble bulb shone all night in the center of the hut. Room overseers ordered us to find places on the bunks. We wanted nothing better, but how could we, when there was not even room for a pin? The other prisoners pushed us away from the edges of the bunks, the overseers beat those standing below, and this would have gone on until morning, were it not for the block overseer who—awakened by the uproar—came out of her room and drenched us with a bucketful of swill and excrement.

Not until this "bath" was room found by some miracle, and we fell asleep for a few hours, packed sixteen to a bunk.

The barracks contained around 1500 women. The tiny windows were shut, the stench became unbearable.

Roll calls at Auschwitz lasted three or four hours, mornings and evenings—as in Majdanek. Hela, Halina (whom we met here) and I tried to stand together, to support each other and obtain a bread ration for three, as the bread in Auschwitz was distributed during evening roll call. Rations cut in half or quartered were not equal, so we took unsliced rations and when roll call was over, Hela cut the bread into fair shares with a borrowed knife.

During the two-week quarantine, we only worked inside the camp area, but since there was not enough work for everyone, the great majority were herded out daily to the *Wiese* or meadow. The *Wiese* was a large empty area surrounded by barbed wire. Nothing grew in this Auschwitz meadow. It consisted of dry sand or hard, cracked earth (or mud), and sharp stones. We sat here for days at a time, shivering in the morning chill and sweltering in the afternoon sun, always hungry and thirsty.

Kapos with thick sticks watched that no one could get into the washrooms and drink the yellowish water that was permeated with the smell of rust. We waited impatiently for the bread and soup made from leathery colerape or turnip, though neither the bread nor the quarter liter of muddy swill satisfied our hunger.

Food was the object of barter in Auschwitz. Bread was bartered for soup, clothing for bread, cigarettes and other things with prisoners whose work in the camp brought them into contact with new transports of people, also with Aryan prisoners who received packages from home, and with Polish workers (not prisoners) employed in the Auschwitz area. Mostly, however, things were smuggled in by women working in stores known as "Canada," where they sorted the clothes of people who had been dispatched to the gas chambers and who were being brought here all the time from towns in Poland and other occupied countries for execution.

Most block and room overseers sold soup and bread stolen from our meager rations. These women were always well fed and well dressed; they did not want for cigarettes or even vodka . . . They were German, Jewish, Slovak, Czech or Polish, prisoners like the rest of us, but marked by exceptional cruelty. They caused us greater terror than the German wardresses or SS because they were always around; in the barracks, at roll call, at places of work, in the washrooms, even in the lavatories. It was they who distributed the bread, taking one-third of each loaf for themselves, it was they who put the lid back on half-empty soup kettles and opened the next one, leaving the thicker soup at the bottom. And if one of the ill-used prisoners tried to complain, they would hit her on the head with the iron ladle and make her go without food entirely. It was they who herded us to selection, making sure no one gave them the slip, it was they who eagerly pointed out exhausted women to the SS, should the latter by chance overlook them. Hunger and "selections" were the two matters on which all thoughts and the entire attention of prisoners were focused. It was they who prohibited the use of toilets and washrooms, they who beat the feeble and the sick, and vied with one another in ideas how to make our lives utterly unbearable. They preyed especially on Jewish women, whom they could immediately identify by our numbers and the Star of David.

In Majdanek, I had heard from women that Jews were being gassed and cremated in Auschwitz; I did not believe them, and thought it was the stupid invention of anti-Semites and our enemies, rumors set in currency to frighten us. But now, a few dozen yards from our camp, behind barbed wire I could see a huge building with tiny barred windows and an enormous chimney. It was the crematorium. I saw that chimney smoking almost daily; of all the people brought here in the trains there remained only heaps of ashes; for many months I breathed air infested with the stench of burning corpses—and then I realized that nothing people had said could vie with reality.

There were people among us who had lost strength for the struggle for existence due to the beatings, mud, physical and spiritual anguish. They preferred an instantaneous death on the camp's electrified wires, or they reported sick, which amounted to suicide. Yet most of us wanted to survive at any price, and we clung to life with all our might.

After quarantine, Hela and I found ourselves in camp "b." Our new block overseer, a 20-year-old Jewish woman from Slovakia, had come to Auschwitz in one of the first transports, and had succeeded by this time in learning all the secrets of Hell and becoming a monster.

In camp "b" Hela and I first worked in the laundry; in other words we had a comparatively easy job by camp standards, since at least we worked indoors, not exposed to rain or the heat of the sun. In the laundry, too, we could wash ourselves and our clothes, and sometimes cook a little soup of potatoes bartered for bread, or warm up the camp soup, thinning it with water. At least there was no shortage of water here.

But the work was exhausting. For over twelve hours a day we scrubbed dirty, torn rags, listening all the time to the derision and curses of the *kapos* and German overseers.

One *kapo,* a German named Emma, was supposed to have been sent to the camp for being a prostitute. She was a good-looking woman, with pale blue eyes and dark hair; she smelled of vodka and cigarettes all the time. Her assistant Lotti was a tall blonde woman, also German and also sentenced for prostitution. Lotti had already been sent several times to the SK *Straf-kompanie.** Lotti was sentenced for having forbidden sexual relations with men working in the women's camp, and for drinking. She ill-treated us more often and more ferociously than the *kapo.* Watching her furtively, I thought her nothing but an animal.

But the *kapo* showed me a certain leniency—if it can be called that—from the first day. Once she even drew me to her, sat me on her lap, began asking me where I came from, how old I was, what my name was. Then she announced she would make me her *pipel* (like a little pet), and she suddenly kissed me. I caught the smell of alcohol, drew back in disgust, and got off her lap.

The custom prevailed in Auschwitz that *kapos* and block overseers kept favorites, a kind of pet servant . . . They chose as their favorites, young girls (of the few that reached the camp) who could sing, sew, embroider and so on. Their "foster-mothers" lavished affection on their little favorites, dressed them up, gave them all kinds of tasty things to eat—in a word, spared them none of the delights of Auschwitz. A "little pet" had to be on call

---

*A punishment unit to which prisoners who infringed camp regulations were sent, or on Gestapos' orders, for a specific period. The SK prisoners lived in a separate locked barracks and were employed in particularly hard labor.—Ed.

all the time, ready to flatter, fawn and inform on her companions, so as to remain as long as possible in the favor of their usually capricious and changeable patronesses. I preferred hard labor and hunger. During my two-year stay in the camp I was never a "little pet," though I would have suited the role very well, on account of my age.

Emma's "little pet" was a small, sly and shrewd Jewish woman, Henia from the laundry; later, she caused the dismissal of Hela and me from the laundry, and had her own protegées appointed in our place. Although Emma did not try to demonstrate her "affection" for me again, she remained quite kindly disposed toward me to the end. She never shouted at either of us, sometimes she assigned us to lighter work, or gave us a little extra soup from the kettle. I always thanked her, but never did I fawn. Kuk, the German SS overseer in the laundry, a plump young blonde woman, also treated me reasonably well. Sometimes I saw her watching Hela or me at work with a sort of curiosity, perhaps even with sorrow or pity. Once she brought me a piece of bread, on another occasion an apple . . . Apparently she had a little daughter at home. She never spoke to the women working there. Her behavior towards Hela and me was astonishing. She did not beat or bully us. I had the impression she pitied us.

Our colleagues in the laundry envied me the German overseer's "consideration," though I never sought it; they bullied not only me but Hela too, though they knew she was ill. Most harassment came from Henia, who intrigued and stirred up the other washerwomen against us . . . I watched this strange human malevolence and envy, from which there was no escape, with bitterness and fear!

Despite everything, I still looked quite well. I was starving, but did not show it, my cheeks were rosy, as before. But to my despair, Hela grew thin and more frail day by day. Her eyes, in her gray and contorted face, grew huge and protuberant, with a penetrating and immeasurably unhappy expression; her hands and feet were as brittle and slender as a child's . . . Her teeth began working loose in her gums, which bled. In my struggle for this ebbing life, I was armed only with my great love for Hela. Unfortunately, in the conditions that prevailed in Auschwitz, feelings could not save a human being from slow death by starvation. I often hid Hela in a corner of the laundry, covering her with linen so she might warm herself—she was always cold—and at least doze a little. I made sure her absence was not noticed, and was ready to warn her if a German overseer or *kapo* came in. Sometimes I gave her my bread or the extras which were doled out frugally: a thin slice of sausage, a scrap of cheese, a spoonful of jam; each time I had to induce her to take them, by saying I loathed the taste of camp food . . .

I still believed Hela would regain her health, though she knew that my little sacrifices, the only ones I could afford, were already in vain.

When Emma's "little pet" was promoted to Lotti's post as manageress of the laundry (Lotti had been sent to the SK again for punishment), the constantly drunk Emma finally yielded to vicious promptings and dismissed us from the laundry. We left with tears in our eyes and grief in our hearts; the blow had been delivered by a fellow prisoner who was Jewish too . . . The complacent looks of her friends pained me: they were enjoying our defeat.

An incident that concerned Hela was the direct cause of it. One hot, stifling August afternoon, we were tired and hungry, waiting impatiently for a rest and the bread distribution. Hela was hanging up linen on the clothesline outside; I stood inside the laundry, scrubbing linen with a big, hard brush. Recently Hela had been having a high temperature in the afternoons, and on this day she could scarcely walk. So I kept going out to see how she was. Just before work ended, I took another look. Hela was no longer there.

I began looking for her, asking the other women, but in vain. I wondered if she had run across to the toilet, or crept back into the block, but my uneasiness mounted, for Hela never went anywhere without me, or telling me where she was going. The time of roll call drew nearer, still no Hela. In my agitation I sought her everywhere, calling her name. Time passed, whistles resounded on all sides for the roll call.

The *kapo* counted us, inspected the ranks; one prisoner was absent! The other women scowled at me with hatred, aggressively. The *kapo* and overseer panicked—everyone knew what a roll call like this meant in Auschwitz. We went back to the block, and my last hope vanished: Hela was not there either.

We were standing in fives in front of the barracks, as always, as they counted us again, then sought Hela in various nooks and crannies, in the washrooms, the toilets, then they counted us yet again—one was still absent! She had vanished as though at the touch of a magician's wand.

Up came a Storm Trooper. The block overseer stiffened to attention, casting me a glance full of hatred and terror. She reported that one prisoner was absent in her block. The Storm Trooper counted us again, slowly and precisely, he inspected all the ranks (our heads were almost reeling from the counting!) and after a time the ominous news spread throughout the entire camp of thousands of women—Someone was absent in Block 27. This meant that instead of going to the toilet, resting after a day's hard work and finally eating a crust of bread, we had to stand in line until she was found.

I sensed looks of hatred, while the burden of my responsibility and my anxiety for Hela weighed me down.

At last they found her; she was lying unconscious in the grass not far from the place where linen was hung to dry. The *kapos* dragged her triumphantly over the ground as though she were an escaped convict, through the stones and mud, they kicked and belabored her, then—half-dead and bleeding—she was handed over to the block overseer for "correction."

After roll call, when the crowds of women dispersed to the barracks, or to the washrooms for water, or to the toilets, like a herd of animals cooped up too long, I pulled Hela onto the bunk, washed her wounds, scratches and bruises with a herb concoction we were given to drink, then I wrapped her in a blanket, and tried to comfort her.

So I told her we should certainly live to see the day of liberation soon, as everything was pointing to a rapid end to the war. My words, though very far from reality, clearly brought Hela relief. I could see this, even though she could not answer me.

It was the day after this incident that they dismissed us from the laundry.

Fortunately we did reasonably well at our next work, which was in an underwear workshop. The *kapo* was Anushneni, mother of our block overseer. We had easy work, "sitting down." The *kapo* did not beat us, nor did she insult us coarsely as the others did, though she treated us very sternly. We repaired camp linen, darned stockings (never knowing for whom they were intended, as we prisoners rarely received whole, good clothing), we sewed on buttons, and so on. At noon we went back to the block for our soup ration, and we did not have to stand outdoors in the hard frosts of winter for evening roll call. They counted us in the workshop, and we finished work after roll call. They had two shifts here: day and night. The night shift was especially exhausting, as it was not possible to rest or sleep in the block during the day. The room orderlies drove us to perform various tasks in the barracks, cleaning or carrying soup-kettles. Apart from this we were exposed to frequent and unexpected "selections," and—later—to visits from Dr. Mengele.* Dr. Mengele

---

Hauptsturmführer, an officer in the "Adolf Hitler" SS *Leitstandarte,* and garrison doctor in the Auschwitz camp in the 1943–1945 period. He was an anthropologist and was sought for criminal, pseudo-scientific experiments on prisoners and especially on twins. Mengele escaped prosecution after the war by living secretly in South America. He reportedly drowned in 1979; his remains were identified by means of forensic evidence in 1985.—Ed.

used to roam the huts, looking for women to serve as subjects for his scientific experiments. We used to run away from him by jumping out of the window, or hiding between huts and in toilets.

The night shift in the workshop dragged on interminably. It was always stuffy and hot there. Dozens of exhausted women, collapsing from hunger and weakness, sat at tables in the feeble light, crouched over sewing machines or their needles. Talking was forbidden. The night's darkness was illuminated by the burning crematoria, the silence was broken now and then by the whistle of locomotives or roar of trucks, in which the Nazis were bringing Jews, and in which they took away the dead for cremation (in the fall of 1943, the trains did not yet bring people to the crematorium in Birkenau itself, only to the railway ramp in Auschwitz).

When the *kapos* took us in groups to the lavatory at night, I eyed the hearse trucks, and although I knew what was going on here, I still could not believe it. Later, when the transports of Jews from various countries in Europe became incomparably larger, the Nazis improved their methods—gas chambers were built, and the railroad tracks extended to the crematorium itself.

Hela and I worked for a time on laying the track to the crematorium, mostly on Sundays or holidays, which is why we called this work "Auschwitz days off."

The day shift in the workshop was easier, and we awaited it like salvation. We could sleep at night, and at least we did not suffer from hunger, or have to listen to the noise of trucks, shrieks of despair, groans, sobbing and praying lamentations of those condemned to die.

If the German overseer was in a good mood, she would pick out singers from among us. Listening to the beautiful songs of many countries, we forgot our own tragedies for a moment . . . There were excellent singers in the workshop, with a very wide repertoire. Especially the Jewish women from Greece, who were frail and suffered greatly from our climate and the camp's wretchedness.

At the end of the summer of 1943, the itch began raging in the camp, causing us additional suffering. We were covered from head to foot by red scabs, which we scratched until the blood flowed, the sores filled with pus and itched mercilessly. As we slept eight or ten to a bunk in the hot August nights, drenched in sweat, sticking to one another, quarrels and fights broke out. In the mornings our sores, which had stuck to the straw mattresses, began festering again . . . It was hard to draw stockings on over the festering ulcers. When we had to tear our stockings off in the bathhouse, our legs were drenched in blood.

Lice added to these inhuman sufferings; they swarmed about our open sores, swollen and aggressive, satiated with our blood!

I became so upset by the itch that I lost my temper at the least occasion, quarreled over the slightest thing even with Hela and was bad-tempered and unfair. Hela had more patience and showed me unlimited forebearance. In the evenings she put my clothes in order which, when scratching myself furiously, I threw around. She sat by me for hours at a time, sometimes until late at night, fanning me with a piece of rag to bring coolness . . . She was good to me, not like a sister-in-law, but like a true mother.

Affectionately, she called me her "little chicken."

Ever since my hair began growing again, after it was cut off on our arrival at Auschwitz, Hela called me her "chicken."

As there was a small group of children in the concentration camp, ranging in age from one year to 14, some *kapos* and even block and hut orderlies showed a modicum of interest in them. The sight of live children was a novelty and rarity in the camp—and they attracted the attention of the Storm Troopers in the *Kommendatura* . . .

One fine day they assigned a special block to the children; the conditions there were supposed to be much improved: clean, four-person bunks, new straw mattresses, warm blankets, large rations of bread—and white bread at that—a piece of butter every day. Not to mention the promise that the children would not be forced to work. In other words—a small paradise inside the hell that was Auschwitz.

Consequently many young girls dreamed of this paradise, as did a handful of grown women who, with their heads shaven and their slender, small and terribly thin bodies, might indeed have passed as children. White bread, milk had a great power of attraction. So they adopted the most various of devices and tricks— anything, if only to get into the children's block, and those who succeeded aroused general envy.

As for me, I would not go to the block with the other children. I declared I was 17, and insisted stubbornly on this, for I did not want to leave Hela for anything!

The prisoners mocked me, but I let their jeers go in one ear and out the other. I kept going to the underwear workshop, suffering and starving. Yet I retained my good appearance and health. I myself still do not know to what I owed this physical resistance.

I was afraid that within a few weeks trucks would be driven up to the children's block, that they would be taken away—every single one of the inhabitants of the "marvelous" barracks— naked, confused, terrified, to the gas chambers.

The white bread and the milk would prove to be merely bait . . .

The fate of the Jewish children in Auschwitz confirmed my belief that in the fight with hunger and misery, a person must listen to the voice of instinct, and never forget his or her own dignity. I always stood aside when prisoners surrounded the soup kettles, trampling on one another, pushing, so as to obtain a couple of potato peelings, or the thicker liquid. This kind of behavior resulted in hilarity and jeering laughter from the Storm Troopers and those who toadied to them. Sometimes I told Hela that we, at least, gave them no cause for mirth. But Hela no longer had the strength to starve, or even to think straight . . . She often begged me to go to the room orderly handing out food, and ask her for another helping.

"You are a child, she will not refuse you. Try—after all, they will not kill you for it."

I suffered extreme anguish on such occasions. Hunger drew me to the soup kettle as though it were a magnet. And I felt I ought to do what Hela asked. I felt it, but could not bring myself to overcome my fierce resistance. Sometimes, though very rarely, the room orderly herself would call me over and pour out more soup for me. I put down the bowl, furious with myself for not being able to control the trembling of my hands, starving for food and a little human kindness, but at the same time proud that I had not demeaned myself to beg.

Such occasional incidents rendered me stubborn later on to my sister-in-law's pleas: "Halina, go and ask her, please try . . ." I dared not look her in the eyes then. I could hardly prevent myself from stopping up my ears. My feet were rooted to the ground, my lips sealed. The thought that the orderly might hit me, push me away, speak crossly or make a coarse joke—while I was standing in front of her with an empty bowl and outstretched hands—this thought tortured me even more than Hela's hunger and her beseeching expression.

I realized I was doing Hela an injustice, that I was behaving stupidly, childishly.

"Are we the only ones going hungry?" I wondered, trying to find some justification for myself. "Others are crazy with hunger too. What of it? They are not ashamed, they keep asking for more, and usually get a blow on the head from the ladle, instead of soup. And insults."

I obeyed Hela in everything. But in this one matter I could not bring myself to obey her.

Hela's condition worsened daily. She had become a living skeleton. No one would have recognized her as the young, graceful and charming girl with golden hair and merry blue eyes. Terrifyingly thin, her head shaved, protruding eyes and earth-colored face, she looked like an old woman or physically underdeveloped child. Some of our neighbors on the bunk advised me to abandon her, as she assuredly had TB and would soon die. I listened indignantly and angrily to these diagnoses, made with all the inhuman frankness of Auschwitz. I loved Hela and believed she would conquer even TB, recover, and live to see liberation with me . . . At the same time I watched as our neighbors in the bunk—who had the greatest chances of survival, being healthy and strong, though afraid of contracting TB—slowly broke down and became groups of what were called *Moslemesses* (women who had lost the will to live). The camp authorities and their prisoner assistants ill-treated the *Moslemesses* with outrageous cruelty. They beat them to death at every opportunity.

When a German doctor accompanied by SS officers and the *Lagerführer* picked out *Moslemesses* from a crowd of prisoners by a movement of one finger, the unfortunate women were taken directly to the gas chamber or to Block 25. This block was separated from the rest by a high wall. Its inhabitants, in total isolation, deprived of food or drink or the opportunity of using a toilet, sometimes waited entire weeks for death. They usually went towards this death without the slightest resistance. They certainly saw it as their only escape. When anyone spoke of Block 25 in my presence, I forgot my hunger and exhaustion at once.

Daily, during roll calls and often during sleepless nights, I would stare at the crematorium—a long, innocent-looking building, with a large, factory-like chimney, smoking incessantly day and night. I could not fathom how it was that crowds of people herded from trains and from the camp disappeared in that building forever! The extermination process was going on under our very eyes, beyond those wires, opposite, so close.

Later, when I was working in the *Aussenkommand* (outside the camp), we often passed people on the road to the gas chambers; they asked us where they were being taken, and they believed— as we had formerly believed in Majdanek—that they would be given a bath, then start work in the camp . . . Mostly they had no idea of what was going to happen until the last minute. A few hours later, their things were being sorted in "Canada" (a rich country; *"keine da,"* in German, no one there") before being loaded into special trains: the murderers' loot was sent to Germany. A bloody pillar of fire rose from the chimneys, scattering a bitter acrid smoke and the stench of burning bones.

It cost Hela even more effort to climb into the bunk and get down again. She could hardly stand for roll calls. She sat hunched up over her work at the table in the underwear work-shop. She was tortured by a cough, the itch, diarrhea, scurvy. During the night shift she often collapsed. I had to hide her illness from the block and room orderlies and, during work, from the *kapo*. I was afraid they would send her to the sick bay, to the "hospital." That was the equivalent of death.

The entire block had a very hard time during the *Blocksperre.**

We lay sweating and suffering on the packed, crowded and low bunks. Quarrels kept breaking out over even an inch or two of space.

Prisoners continually crowded around the hut door and in the little hallway in front of it, begging to be allowed to go to the toilet. But the block and room overseers set about these unhappy women with fists and clubs.

Neither beating, threats, insults nor soaking in swill had any effect. The crowd did not yield; on the contrary it increased as the *Blocksperre* continued.

Unable to withstand the pressure on the door, the authorities finally began allowing a dozen or so women through at a time, counting them carefully several times. Room orderlies then took them to the toilet.

In order to get out with a group of lucky women, we had to carry on a fierce, violent fight with other prisoners at the door.

Only comparatively healthy and fairly strong women could fight thus. What can be said of the sick, especially those with diarrhea? They could not even reach the distant lavatories. There was nothing with which to wash their legs, soiled with excrement. A change of soiled linen was out of the question. Water—musty, yellow, full of rust—was very hard to come by. There was not always enough to quench our thirst.

Many women with diarrhea relieved themselves in soup bowls or the pans for "coffee"; then they hid the utensils under the mattress to avoid the punishment threatening them for doing so:

*An order prohibiting prisoners from leaving their blocks and preventing them from observing "selections" inside the camp for the gas chamber. This also rendered impossible flight from one block to another.—Ed.

twenty-five strokes on the bare buttocks, or kneeling all night long on sharp gravel, holding up bricks. These punishments often ended in the death of the "guilty."

Diarrhea deprived Hela of what remained of her strength. When she tried to get down from the bunk to relieve herself, she was suddenly seized by a spasm of the bowels. I concealed her with a blanket and myself, so she might relieve herself unobserved into a pan . . . This required great caution, for if a neighbor in our bunk or nearby were to notice, she might report us to the room orderly . . .

Then, with beating heart, maneuvering and dodging about like a criminal, hiding the sinful pan that gave off a foul and powerful stench, I struggled to the exit, fought other prisoners, scratched and kicked in the unearthly crowd. I had to get to the toilet at any price . . . On the way there, in a close-packed group under the guard of numerous room orderlies, I shifted the pan from one hand to the other, manipulating it in all sorts of ways, guarding it like a treasure. Alas, it was never capacious enough, it filled so fast and was so often required!

I smuggled out the stinking pan innumerable times during the *Blocksperre*, undergoing panic and terror each time. Fortunately, however, they did not catch me committing this crime. Hela was already so frail and exhausted by illness that she wanted to go voluntarily to the sick bay. But I opposed any such thing categorically, assured her it would pass, though I was inwardly dying of despair . . .

That fall, heavy and persistent rain made Auschwitz life additionally hard. In mud up to our ankles, puddles, soaking and rotting clothes, cold, the Storm Troopers deliberately prolonged roll calls. On rainy days they seized any pretext to give us "exemplary punishment." We were forced to kneel down in the mud, or run holding rocks, because we marched unevenly, out of time with the band that accompanied labor gangs going to work; or because our shoes were not properly cleaned; or because we did not behave quietly enough during *Blockruhe,* and the like. There were any number of such pretexts. We froze in the cold and rain.

In the evenings, after hard days like these, they herded us into the bathhouse straight from roll call; but when we went back to the block, we discovered they had taken away our straw mattresses for disinfection, our few blankets had gone for delousing, and the bunks smeared with a stinking fluid, also for disinfection. We never felt the blessed results of these hygienic activities.

When we came back to the block from night shift one morning, drunk with exhaustion, and lay down on the hard mattresses after placing our dirty, wet boots under our heads to the accompaniment of the inhuman yelling of the room orderlies, suddenly terrifying whistling arose on all sides of the camp: "Get up for roll call! All Jewish women for roll call!"

The orderlies pulled blankets off sleeping women, belaboring them with their fists and cursing.

My teeth were chattering with cold, agitated, I pulled on my rags and finally both of us—Hela and I—went out to where the ranks were being assembled in front of the huts. We had no doubt what this special roll call for Jewish women meant, especially for those staying in the barracks during the working day. In terror and nervous strain, we looked at one another. Which of us would pass through the "selection" and go back to the block? I was seized by the monstrous and desperate certainty that this time they would take Hela away to the gas chambers. I had long since ceased believing in miracles. Feverishly, I began persuading my sister-in-law to run away; she could hide in the toilet, or some other nook . . . But Hela firmly opposed this, she remembered how they had beaten and ill-treated her when she collapsed while hanging out the washing . . . She would rather die than go through anything like that again.

We proceeded in fives to the large empty space in front of the bathhouse. Stripped naked, we all stood in line as the Nazis ordered, singly, one behind the other. Hundreds of women from numerous countries and towns; speaking various languages; tall and short, fat and thin, healthy with smooth skin, or sick, with scabs, wounds, bruises all over . . .

An uncanny SS tribunal took its place opposite; the little finger on Dr. Mengele's hand passed final sentence: to the left meant death, to the right—more life in the Auschwitz torture chambers . . . The line of naked bodies moved towards the bathhouse; Dr. Mengele, accompanied by *Unterscharführer* Taube, was sorting out his victims with deliberation. The women whose lives he spared went into the bathhouse, and after a brief shower returned to the block. Those he condemned to death by burning assembled, herded by *Lagerkapos,* on the left side of the square; their numbers were written down, so they could be crossed off the list of the living.

The day happened to be fine and beautiful. The sun shone in a clear, bright sky. To the satisfaction of the "Master Race" the selection was proceeding smoothly and correctly, as usual. The doctor's finger, on a hand covered by an elegant glove, moved slightly: right . . . left . . . left . . . right. Jewish people who threatened the "German new order and the purity of a superior race" must perish. Now or later, what was the difference? There was no problem. The Nazis had decided to murder them all, and were doing so accurately and systematically.

I walked immediately behind Hela, to keep her in my sight all the time. As we came closer to the judges and executioners, I moved nearer to my sister-in-law. The line moved on relentlessly. There was no way to stop it, to retreat, or to hide.

My heart was beating so hard that there was a darkness before my eyes. Mother, what was going to happen? A few steps more, one step . . .

We were standing face to face with the fresh, green uniforms, round green caps with stiff peaks, cold eyes calculating our usefulness, our physical condition.

I pressed close to Hela, wanting to protect her from their eyes with my own body. At this very moment, the gaze of Dr. Mengele fell on us. Cool, calculating, ironical. His finger moved without haste and divided me from Hela. To the right—to the left. My heart stopped beating. I embraced Hela. I no longer saw or feared anything, all I knew was that I had to be with Hela no matter what happened. Curiously enough, I suddenly felt young, healthy, strong. This feeling lasted only a few seconds, but already a tumult had broken out in the square. The progress of the selection had been interrupted, the iron discipline broken. Everyone was staring at us. The Storm Trooper Taube was dumbstruck, apparently with amazement. Meanwhile *kapos* were running up from all directions, trying to tear me away from Hela. I would not yield: I clenched my fists spasmodically, kicked, shrieked. Who knows how long they would have gone on scuffling with me, a naked little 13-year-old girl, clinging for dear life to a half-dead skeleton, had not Taube decided that since I did not want to part from a woman condemned to death, I should share her fate? So the *kapos* wrote my number down in the list of those "selected."

Meanwhile, the group of SS officers in the center of the square, shading their eyes from the sun with their hands, had been watching the entire incident. The scene apparently amused rather than angered them, since not one reacted or was indignant at my act of insubordination. Such things rarely occurred in the camp; people were used to blind obedience. My childish resistance had a sort of attraction for these sadists. At least, this is the way I explain it to myself today. Especially as something happened immediately afterwards that none of us could even have imagined. Hössler, the deputy camp commandant, beckoned to me with one finger.

I clutched my dress and ran over without thinking to the group of Storm Troopers. I looked up into Hössler's face.

All of them were tall, straddling and self-assured. Hössler seemed even more formidable and ruthless than the others. I grasped the meaning of his question at once. He wanted to know the identity of the woman for whom I was fighting so hard.

I began explaining in a rapid, unrestrained flood of Yiddish and German, as though I had been waiting a long time for the opportunity to give voice to everything that filled my heart.

"She is my mother, my sister, my family, I cannot live without her," I cried.

The officers listened in silence. Not one of them moved or altered his stiff attitude.

Then, in the tone of voice people use to scold a disobedient child, Hössler told me to be silent: "Otherwise," he said, "you will go in there with this *Schweigerin* of yours, do you understand me?" and he pointed to the crematorium smoking beyond the wires.

Did I understand him? I shut my mouth instantly, though involuntarily a single, brief, incredulous, hopeful word emerged: "Yes?"

The Storm Troopers burst into harsh laughter, imitating me with a kind of fiendish, cruel mirth: "Yes? Yes?" Hössler called the *Lagerkapo* and, in my presence, ordered her to cross our two numbers off the list. At this, I could not restrain my wild joy and—forgetful of everything—rushed towards Hössler to thank him . . .

A hard slap blinded and stunned me. I lost my balance and fell. The pain of the blow was nothing in comparison with my feeling of shame . . .

Beasts will always be beasts, even if they make a gesture that seems human. How could I, at such a moment, influenced by joy and gratitude, remember that? So I was punished; the brutal slap brought me back to reality. But this reality—Hela's and mine—had been miraculously spared! They had spared our lives. Our lives!

Now the *kapos* smiled indulgently, vying with each other to show us "kindnesses." A crowd of women surrounded us in the bathhouse, and later in the block. All that evening, people in the camp talked of nothing but my "adventure."

When our block overseer—a nasty, bad-tempered woman—

heard of it, she smiled with a touch of pride that anything of the kind had happened in her block. She wanted to know which little girl had saved her sister from "selection" (camp gossip made Hela into my sister; apparently this caused my deed to be more understandable), and had dared to try and embrace Hössler.

When the other prisoners produced this "heroine," she came over to look at me closely, and I saw amazement, contempt and disappointment on her face. I was nothing but a starved, unhappy child, looking like many of the victims here, who would any day join the crowd of *Moslemesses* . . . Yet, even though she could not understand how I had "won over" the Nazis, she stopped preying on Hela and me. After our victory in the fight with Dr. Mengele's sentence, Hela did not regain her belief in a better future. Only her love for me kept her going. Sometimes, indicating her arms and legs, which were thin as twigs, she would say, "As it is, I am no longer alive. I only live through you, Halina, with your breath." Then she added thoughtfully, in amazement, "I never dreamed you could bring yourself to anything like that, or that you would want to go with me to . . . the very end." I replied frankly that I had not expected it either, that if I had been asked before the "selection" whether I would go with anyone to the gas chamber, I would have to say "No." Otherwise, I would have been lying, for in reality I was terrified at the mere thought of death, of gassing, the crematoria. But when I was faced with the threat of losing Hela, I could not resist the promptings of my heart. I acted without thinking, instinctively.

Hela looked at me with great affection, and I felt an upsurge of warmth flowing through me. I kept telling her she would survive and live to see the day of liberation. But she persistently and sadly denied this; she knew she was mortally ill, that her days were numbered.

Soon afterwards they again took women from our block to the bathhouse and a "selection" . . . This time Hela obeyed me, and hid in our barracks. This was feasible when the selection did not cover the entire camp, or did not occur during a roll call.

Hössler recognized me instantly among the hundreds of pris-

oners assembled in the same area as before: "Ah, that's the girl
who made a scene recently," he exclaimed, as I passed by him in
the ranks. "And where is your sister-in-law?"

Scared to death, I replied that Hela had gone by earlier. Fortunately, Hössler was satisfied with this evasion. Had it occurred to
him to check whether I was telling the truth, there would have
been no help for either Hela or me.

In November 1943, the early frosts really began making themselves felt. An epidemic of spotted typhus broke out in the camp.
Thousands of sick women, half-conscious, their eyes burning
with fever, and with parched, cracked lips, were dying in their
bunks, during roll call, at work, in the sick bay, in the gas chambers.

The barracks became ever emptier. The number of women
prisoners shrank at an incredible rate. In our block, which had
housed 1300 prisoners before the outbreak of the epidemic, only
two or three hundred remained within a few weeks.

Hela's life was ebbing like the flame of a dying candle. I began
to realize that sooner or later I would have to give up the fight, and
agree to having her taken to the sick bay. I continued, more often
than before, taking her pan to the lavatory, or burying the places
where Hela relieved herself during roll call, hidden by me . . . Now
I was no longer as much afraid of the block overseer, or of our
companions. Somehow no one dared bully us.

One morning the whistle summoning us to roll call no longer
penetrated Hela's mind. She remained deaf to my appeals and
urging. She failed to understand what I wanted her to do. She lay
motionless, helpless, resigned to her fate. I had to leave her in the
bunk and go to the roll call alone—for the first time since we had
been in the camp. Strictly speaking, the block overseer dragged
me away from Hela immediately before the German overseer
came in. The room orderly put Hela on a stretcher and placed her

alongside other sick women, also on stretchers. After roll call, they would all be taken to the sick bay; this had been happening daily, for months. Except that now Hela was among these unfortunate women . . . She lay on the stretcher as though it were a coffin. Only her eyes, huge and wide-open, were still alive, staring at me, as though bidding me farewell, as if imploring my forgiveness, or pleading to be remembered. No, I cannot describe all the things Hela's dying eyes expressed. I cannot describe how terrible this 20-year-old girl looked.

Today, when I recall that scene, I cry. But at the time I was too stunned with misery to cry.

I was left alone, in an enormous crowd of women—suffering, indifferent and hardened to the suffering of others. Each had her own past, her own tragedies. I was of no use to any of them, my fate was of no concern to anyone—on the contrary, we hindered one another in the crowded barracks, in the lines for soup or bread. There was not even enough air for everyone. So the stronger defended herself from the weaker, pushed them away, killed them off.

They often threw me out of the lines for food, stole my blanket at night, or pushed me off my straw mattress to the bare boards or on the muddy boots along the wall. I was surrounded by hostility, but this hostility was no one's fault—it just could not be otherwise under such conditions. Hela—who though sick and weak had always stood up in my defense and would not let me suffer injustices—was no longer there.

I fought for myself as best I could. I did not cry or appeal to anyone for help. I grew vigilant and watchful, indifferent, like everyone else, to anything that did not threaten me directly. It was as though I had become a different person after parting from Hela!

I saw her once more before she died. The deputy block overseer, a Polish woman named Zosia, who had known us before the celebrated "selection," took me with her one morning to the sick bay, after roll call, as she was taking more victims there.

I barely recognized Hela in that hospital hut, among hundreds of semi-corpses.

"Halinka, is it you?" she whispered in a feeble voice, as though aroused from a deep sleep. She had not expected me here . . .

I could not speak. I placed some bread, hoarded for several days, ever since Zosia promised me this visit, beside her. Hela's eyes did not leave me, though she paid little attention to the bread. When I managed to control myself and was about to say something to her, they drove me away.

Great heaps of corpses rose between the barracks in the sick-bay square where I waited for Zosia; they reminded me of corded, dried-up and frozen blocks of wood. The corpses were naked and stiff. Shaven heads thrown back, their limbs mere thin little bones. Every few days, trucks drove up and prisoners from the *Sonderkommando* (crematorium and gas chamber labor gangs) threw the corpses in like stones, then tipped them as if so much rubbish, into the crematorium stoves. I had never seen so many corpses at the same time. And my sister-in-law, though still alive, differed but little from them. I went back to the barracks half-conscious with grief, terror, despair.

Some weeks later, when Zosia was counting us and passed me, I shyly asked whether she knew anything about Hela.

Zosia was in constant contact with the sick bay, so she always knew when anyone from our block died there, or was getting better, or had been taken to the gas chambers. She recorded these facts on the list of inhabitants of our block. However, she never spoke of Hela to me. Like almost all officials in the camp, she treated the prisoners with contempt and bad temper. This was why I hesitated a long time before daring to ask her. In addition, I was afraid of bad news.

Startled at first by my question, Zosia said nothing. I was sure she would instantly snap at me or curse, but she looked me straight in the eyes in silence. For a long time nobody had looked at me with such a human, everyday expression.

"She is dead," she replied briefly. But she did not go away, I could still see her face through a mist, through the darkness that suddenly surrounded me. I still had to learn what had happened to Hela: had they taken her in a "selection," or had they gassed her, or . . . Every detail was indescribably important to me. "She died a natural death," Zosia said with a grimace or strange smile, then I heard her a moment later shouting at a woman further down the line.

There were severe snows and frosts that winter. Our wretched clothing, torn stockings that stuck to injured legs; heavy wooden clogs, far too big, to which the snow clung, making it impossible for us to walk fast, though the Nazis ordered us to move on the double. The itch, hunger, lice, diarrhea, spotted typhus; this is how our situation looked in the 1943–1944 winter.

People in the blocks and labor gangs kept decreasing in number. On my bunk, where hitherto nine women had perched and badgered one another, six fell ill with the typhus. I got up in the morning drenched with their sweat. Soon only three of us were left—in good health for the time being; Sabina, daughter of the woman they had shot in the freight car on the way from Majdanek to Auschwitz, a 16-year-old girl (whose name I cannot even remember: she was from Bendzin in South Poland), and I. The rest had either gone to the sick bay and never came back, or had died in the hut or during a roll call.

We three were more or less the same age, and were linked by similar experiences. We had a language in common, we understood each other very well, and began helping one another. Sabina was the strongest and tallest. We shared everything, even additional rations of soup or a few potato peelings, which we as children occasionally got. Such "good fortune" would happen to one of us from time to time. During heavy frosts, we sometimes did not go to work, by permission of a "better" room orderly. We came back to our bunk after roll call, and cuddled up to each other under the blanket, warming ourselves from each other; we slept like this until the distribution of soup, forgetful of cold and hunger, though we were constantly in danger from overseers checking the barracks. When hunger and lice prevented us from sleeping, we would tell each other tales of past times as we huddled under the blanket, we remembered our families and lost homes. But this idyll soon ended. The typhus raging in the camp took Sabina. She suddenly fell ill, began wandering around the camp like a shadow, with a bag of uneaten bread. She had livid, parched lips and staring eyes, dilated with the fever. A week later they took her to the gas chambers during a "selection."

More than half the women working in the underwear workshop suffered from spotted typhus. But here it was easier to conceal and endure the disease. In the first place, we worked sitting down, and indoors. To be sure, it was a 14-hour working day (including evening roll call), with almost no food, but it was warm . . . From the start of the winter, a stove with a long pipe across the entire room was kept burning in the underwear workshop. The *kapo* was not bad; she often allowed us to warm up a little water or "chamomile" from the morning ration. We also dried out the sticky and sour bread on this stove.

The hot beverage brought great relief to the thirsty, both those who were sick and those who were well. It became a regular custom in the workshop—bearing witness to increased solidarity—that a jug of warm liquid or bread slops passed from hand to hand, among all those at the same worktable. Each woman took a sip, first the sick, then the healthy, by turn . . . If anyone managed to flavor the water with a pinch of salt acquired somewhere, a scrap of margarine, or clove of garlic, all her comrades without exception enjoyed it. This was a good custom, a humane custom, even though the conditions of our lives were becoming increasingly bestial.

My closest neighbor at the workshop bench was 20-year-old Basia, from Zaglebie, a tall and robust dark girl with fine skin and dark, sparkling eyes. Basia had been in Auschwitz a much shorter period than I had; Jewish women had been deported from Zaglebie later than we. She was therefore stronger and more resistant. I looked like a *Moslemess* beside her, though I still kept going well enough. I made friends with Basia, and became genuinely fond of her. I introduced her to my friend in the bunk, and finally Basia moved in with us; the three of us now slept together.

After a time our new friend Basia also caught the typhus, but it was a slight attack, and as we did all in our power to save her, she recovered.

My first friend, the girl from Bendzin, worked outdoors, not indoors as Basia and I did; the hard frosts and heavy labor, all day on her feet—none of these presaged she would survive the typhus . . . However, a stubborn, invincible will to live evidently came to her aid, for she too managed to defeat the illness. She only became paler, more frail and weak . . .

Somehow I did not catch the disease. Typhus passed me by for a long time . . . But sores all over my body tortured me, my bladder became infected, I had the itch, sometimes diarrhea. I was less afraid of "selections" at this time. Since the typhus epidemic had been raging, the Nazis simply looked at our tongues and took to the gas chambers only those with white "typhus" tongues.

I was more concerned at this time with getting rid of the harassing itch, dirt and lice than with obtaining additional rations of soup. Sometimes, when I stayed in the barracks after a night shift or thanks to the favor of a room orderly, I would creep into the washroom—its entrances were usually guarded by a special sentry or *kapo* with a heavy stick—in order to wash myself in icy water, to bathe my continually scratched bites and sores. Frozen with cold, I hastily pulled on my lice-infested rags—without drying myself—and would run back to warm myself on the bunk and "thaw out" under the blanket. These risky bathings soothed the itching for a few hours; unfortunately I had few opportunities to take advantage of them. In the evenings after roll call, or in the mornings before it, there was such a crowd in the washroom, with everlasting quarrels and brawls, that there was no question of reaching the taps.

I learned from one of my fellow prisoners that some Ukrainian women in Block 13 were bringing in from the labor gang a tar ointment, said to be very effective against the itch. Many women had already purchased some in exchange for bread.

I instantly hurried to Block 13 with my daily bread ration. The sacrifice was hard, but not in vain. The revolting, black and stinking tar ointment liberated me from the itch.

While in Block 13 I accidentally met Celina, a former school friend of my elder brother. She was glad to see me, and inquired about my experiences. That evening I learned from women working in the same labor gang as my cousin Halina that they had taken her not long ago to the gas chamber during a "selection." According to her comrades, Halina had been in excellent health and looking well. But during the selection, the block overseer (Ela, a Jewish woman from Czechoslovakia) had turned to the Storm Troopers and pointed at Halina: "Her too, maybe, *Herr Unterscharführer?*" The Storm Trooper did not refuse. I heard the news of Halina's death with horror, indignation and despair. She had left us long since, and stayed away from Hela and me; she believed that being in good health, and stronger than we were, she would do better for herself if she were independent, without having to share her food with us. She went to work in a hard labor gang, where a *Zulage* (extra pay) was distributed twice a week—extra bread and a piece of sausage. Then she had been transferred with the labor gang to Block 13. She visited us only once, after the famous "selection" when I tore Hela from the clutches of Dr. Mengele. News of this reached her block too, so she hurried over, full of surprise and admiration. But from that day on, I never saw her again.

As I was coming away, depressed, from Block 13, Celina stopped me, embraced me affectionately, and took me to her bunk. There I met her fellow prisoners and "fellow tenants," a Mrs. Prajsowa and her daughter Rozka, who was a year older than I. Both began asking me questions about my past life. I told them briefly of my experiences, and felt an enormous relief. Moved by their kindness and concern, I had the impression that the armor of indifference with which I had encompassed myself since Hela's death was breaking down and crumbling. Mrs. Prajsowa could not stand by and watch other people's tragedies calmly, especially when a child was suffering. She, her daughter and Celina listened to my tale with tears in their eyes. And when I left, Mrs. Prajsowa stroked my head and asked me to visit them whenever I could. "We will always find a way, we will help you," she said, pressing some onion and garlic into my hands.

I went back to the barracks as though on wings; it seemed to me my feet were not touching the ground, so light and good did I feel. That evening I regained my shaken faith in people, in their goodness. I went to see Celina and Mrs. Prajsowa almost every evening after roll call and often took Basia with me. Celina worked as a nurse in her block. Her duties were very limited— after all, the sick were not nursed in Auschwitz. She simply took them to the sick bay. Sometimes she applied minor remedies. However, she was on good terms with block and room orderlies, and took advantage of their "patronage." Most important, she obtained food without having to push her way to the soup kettle; she could barter soup and bread, or extra items (a piece of sausage, jam, margarine) for clothes and shoes, she slept on a clean, upper and uncrowded bunk, could wash and change her linen. Upper bunks were a privilege in the camp—they were lighter, more spacious, and so were usually occupied by room orderlies, or their assistants, persons who were patronized or "important."

Being on good terms with block and room orderlies gave us protection against "selections," prolonged standing outdoors in the rain, and the numerous punishments which the great majority of ordinary, run-of-the-mill prisoners endured. All this facilitated life a little, and increased a person's chances of survival.

Celina often gave me a piece of bread, or a little soup. She always welcomed me affectionately and warmly, and in those days I needed affection no less than I needed food. For my part, I always tried to sneak something from the underwear workshop that Celina might find useful. I brought her warm socks, underwear, thread, needles—almost unobtainable in the camp, very useful to Celina, her friends and the room orderlies.

Mrs. Prajsowa and Rozka worked in the block as assistants to the room orderly, and strictly speaking it was they who did the hardest work in the hut; when the other prisoners went to work in the mornings, they cleaned out the hut, scraped off the mud brought in by hundreds of women's clogs, chopped excrement frozen solid during the night from bunks and floor. Their hands swelled and turned livid from this daily labor. Both also worked for the block overseer, cleaning her room, washing her laundry, and taking into safekeeping such forbidden things as cigarettes, vodka and so on, in view of the frequent searches made by the SS.

Mrs. Prajsowa was sometimes deputized for the "night watch," or helped her during the night in the block. She carried her buckets to the lavatory, cooked (arranging things so that she could also cook something for the sick and unfortunate, whom she looked after all the time). Often she risked severe punishment by helping them. Rozka and I—in the later period they regarded me as a member of the family—often scolded her because she would forget about herself, and might also bring down disaster on us.

Mrs. Prajsowa and Rozka, like Celina, had certain privileges in the block. They did not always have to go to "selections," they received a little more food, better clothing, shoes; they usually invited one of the other prisoners to their bunk, where they slept by themselves. It was somewhat easier for them to manage than it was for me or many others. This was why I sought their protection and shelter.

The typhus epidemic intensified in January 1944. Death claimed thousands of victims. The crematorium chimneys breathed fire and smoke incessantly. They were not only burning corpses dead of typhus or starvation, but also hundreds of thousands of Jewish people, herded here from all over Nazi-occupied Europe.

On New Year's Day, colored decorative bulbs glowed on a Christmas tree, placed opposite the crematorium as if to mock it. On this day we received a holiday dinner: cabbage with minute scraps of sausage and in the evening—instead of a decoction of herbs to drink—cream of wheat in milk . . . The next day a selection took place. Anyone with a white tongue went irrevocably to the gas chamber.

The night following this selection, we were herded into the bathhouse, supposedly for delousing. We had to carry our mattresses and blankets there on our backs; our clothes were taken away for disinfection, then we waited hours, almost naked, in the frost and snow, until they were returned to us. On this occasion various garments disappeared, more rapidly and radically than the lice. Clothing, mattresses and blankets underwent destruction in the steam machine. But the lice went on multiplying as though nothing had happened, they devoured us mercilessly and spread infection.

I usually came back from these delousings almost naked, sometimes in nothing but a topcoat, with no stockings, in enormous rotten boots which infected the open sores on my feet. It was even worse when they stole my shoes—one of the hardest treasures to acquire in Auschwitz. A Polish winter, barefoot, was no joke. But here too Mrs. Prajsowa came to my help, nagging me for my sluggishness and inattention. How in the world could we let people steal our shoes? I accepted her scolding with humility that was all the greater when Mrs. Prajsowa would have given me her own daughter's shoes, rather than let me go barefoot.

My tongue did not betray me; it changed color, but not until after the "selection." I fell ill at a time when the epidemic was on the decline. Good luck was evidently on my side. One evening, after the latest New Year "selection," I contracted a high fever, with a raging headache. I suffered thus two weeks. I would sit at the table in the workshop, overcoming my sleepiness and weakness by an enormous effort of will, thinking only of not falling off the bench. I was overcome by an irresistible desire to lie down, somewhere, anywhere, to stretch out and close my eyes . . . "But not in the sick bay, not in the sick bay," I kept saying inwardly, stubbornly.

Basia never left my side; she and the girl from Bendzin looked after me during the evenings in the barracks. Had it not been for them, I would have been defeated in my fight against typhus. At this time I was cut off from Celina and Mrs. Prajsowa, as visiting other huts had been forbidden on account of the epidemic and incessant "selections." In any case, I would not have had the strength to visit them, as my legs gave way under me . . .

One evening, Stasia, the Polish room orderly, gave me a little water in which she had cooked herself some noodles. The hot, salty water had a splendid taste!

My inflamed bladder tortured me more than anything else during the typhus attack. Every few minutes in the night I had to scramble out of the bunk, find somewhere to relieve myself, for I could not reach the distant lavatories along the frozen, slippery path. Buckets for excrement, placed in the barracks in the evening, filled up like lightning; others were reserved for the room orderlies and their protegées. A person could get into very serious trouble for not observing the unwritten laws. I tried to elude the vigilance of the "night watch," and would relieve myself under the shadow of night somewhere nearby, behind the hut. Once the night watch, a Ukrainian woman named Shura, caught me in the act. I was beaten senseless, cast on the barracks floor; Basia and the other girl had to lift me and lay me on the straw mattress.

Slowly I began to recover, feeling increasingly hungry, much worse than before. I could not control it. By the next "selection," my tongue had regained its natural color. I was exhausted and still very feeble, but no longer sick. When the Storm Trooper shouted *Umdrehen!,* the order acted on me like an electric shock: this was a yardstick of whether a prisoner was in good health. I swiftly turned on my heel, without losing balance for a moment. The Storm Trooper looked at me with irony and disgust—my body was still black and blue from Shura's stick, sores and wounds. "How old are you?" he suddenly asked. Without a moment's hesitation I told him I was 17, and was myself surprised to hear my own voice; it was so self-assured, almost impudent. He let me go, but snarled something to the block overseer who stood alongside, writing down his "verdicts"; I only caught the end of a phrase ". . . mug of a woman of forty." Evidently he did not believe I was 17, for in fact my face was that of a woman of forty. The block overseer put a mark by my number and name on the list. When the Storm Trooper turned to the next prisoner in line, I glanced imploringly at the block overseer as I passed her; she turned to me and whispered: "All right, you have passed . . ."

Only then did my self-assurance and courage desert me.

This "selection" was carried on in a manner different from hitherto. All those who passed, and those who did not, were ordered to go back to the block and to work. There was no segregation this time, no dispatching to the right or left. Something was noted down by our numbers—that was all. For the next few days we wondered uneasily what this meant, but soon the "selection" was forgotten in the face of the daily tragedies of camp life.

Two weeks later, after a morning roll call, a strict *Blocksperre* was announced. No labor gangs went to work that day. As there was a fierce, hard frost, we gladly obeyed the order and went back to our bunks, to warm up and doze a little. But hardly had the three of us crept into our bunk when strange things began happening in the hut, which we did not notice at first. Two *Lagerkapos* appeared in the block, with lists, and began reading numbers off them—it was hard to make out which women were concerned, and why they were being called out. Those called assembled by the barracks door, undressed and handed over all their things. We did not pay particular attention to the fact that the number of women by the door was growing minute by minute. Perhaps they were going to take them to work of some kind? Basia was asleep. The other girl began recalling pre-war days, and I listened to her enchanted, quite forgetting camp reality. Suddenly, after the calling out of a number, complete silence fell on the hut. We too paused in our talking—but the girl from Bendzin went back to her tale immediately. Irritably, the *Lagerkapo* shouted the number a few more times. No one an-

swered. Finally the shouts reached our ears, and we both froze
with terror—it was the girl from Bendzin's number!

She jumped down lightly and quietly from the bunk. Not a
word of goodbye. She went, breaking off her tale of good times.
Tiny, naked, she went on foot with the others to the crematorium
that was burning on the other side of the wires. Under the blanket
I could still feel the warmth of her body, and her soft, emotional
voice still sounded in my ears.

Shortly afterwards fire burst from the crematorium chimney . . .
Such was the end of that strange "selection," after which we all
went back to the blocks. Our bunk became empty, terrible.

I also lost the friendship of Basia. Not by a "selection," nor
death, though I suffered it grievously.

By chance Basia met a man cousin who was working in the
Sonderkommando (labor gangs) at the crematorium. This cousin
began helping her by sending food or clothes through men who
worked in our camp as carpenters, electricians and the like.
Members of the crematorium labor gangs burned corpses at SS
orders, and they also supervised those condemned to the gas
chambers as they undressed and sent their things to a labor gang
where they were sorted and disinfected before being sent to Germany. So these men always had more than enough to eat, clothes,
even jewelry. Most of them helped relatives and friends in the
camp, or sometimes strangers too, if the opportunity arose. Basia
obtained various gift packages from her cousin. Some made a
considerable impression on her. She immediately stowed them
away in her bag, and looked after them watchfully. She began
avoiding people. She became increasingly taciturn, distant in
manner, secretive. She behaved begrudgingly and rudely to her
comrades in the underwear workshop. To me she spoke pee-
vishly, dismissing my questions or giving elusive answers. After
some time I realized she wanted to get rid of me, so as not to see
my hunger. I had my own pride; I would never force myself to
beg for her favors. The situation became so unbearable that I
myself decided to withdraw, without waiting for an outright
quarrel to occur between us. I sat at another bench in the work-

room. Basia now sought comrades among the "important" and influential women.

So I was once again solitary in my bunk and at work. I had lost all my former friends, and did not find others, nor did I try to. At least I would not have to mourn anyone. I was never reconciled with Basia; we did not even speak to one another after our friendship was broken off. In time, we were each transferred to other work in the camp, and to different barracks; I do not know what became of Basia in the end. I quite often visited Celina and Mrs. Prajsowa as before, finding encouragement from them in my loneliness. Living conditions were growing worse; my strength was ebbing. To make matters worse, the number of women in the underwear workshop was reduced towards the end of the winter, and many were sent to work outside, digging ditches and on construction sites. I found myself in this group.

Labor gang 103 was notorious in Auschwitz for its exceptional hard penal servitude, bad *kapos* and Storm Troopers, who often set their huge dogs on prisoners. At noon, after six hours of backbreaking labor, we obtained a half liter of turnip soup and, toward evening roll call, a ration of bread. This was all . . . The *kapos* and overseers drove us on; we pushed wheelbarrows loaded with rocks from one place to another, or carried rocks in hands stiff with cold. Here women collapsed like so many flies, more than one preferred death to this agony . . . Sometimes I tried to hide in the temporary lavatories, from which *kapos* drove us out with beatings, curses and shouts. I recalled the days spent in the underwear workshop, and envied those who had remained there with all my heart. Now I even stopped visiting Celina and Mrs. Prajsowa, I was so exhausted when work was over.

"This will surely be the end of me," I thought, resigned. But at the last moment, before breaking down entirely, I was fortunate again; the block orderly apparently took pity on me, and transferred me to the *Weberei* (weaving shop). This could indeed be regarded as a true miracle.

Meanwhile another "selection" took place . . . The Nazis held it on a Sunday (when we did not work), and as this had never

happened before, we were caught unprepared. The morning roll
call lasted longer than usual. We froze to our marrows. Impatiently we awaited the end. When the longed-for whistle was
heard, the camp square seethed as the women ran off in all directions to their huts. Suddenly an SS order halted us: "All Jewish
women stay where you are! Jewish women, come back! Do not
go back to your huts!"

Room orderlies and voluntary helpers among the non-Jewish
prisoners at once started watching lest any of us try to escape.
The judging commission of executioners arrived. Orderlies assembled us in rows in the *Lagerstrasse.** There was no way for
me to get through to the barracks area. That day I was feeling so
bad that I did not believe for a moment I would succeed in
passing through the "selection." I stood far away from the Storm
Troopers who were sorting out women, in the back rows, and as
we had to pass in single file in front of the executioners, I had to
freeze a long time before my turn came. Suddenly another order
came from the Nazis: "Strip naked, take off your shoes!" No, that
is impossible, I thought, but other women had already started
taking their clothes off. I undressed . . .

The SS were sorting us out calmly: to the left, to the right . . .
As always. What was unusual was that this was taking place not
in the bathhouse, as was done in winter, but outdoors in the
terrible cold.

We moved slowly forward. Livid, benumbed.

At one moment I found myself immediately opposite a side street
of the *Lagerstrasse;* here the way back to the blocks was guarded
by my room overseer, Stasia. This Polish woman sometimes called
me to her room when she was distributing soup; she would give me
a bowl of the thickest soup from the bottom of the kettle.

Stasia was strict, austere, but fair by camp standards. She
could not bear officiousness or toadying. She could not bear

---

*The camp's main thoroughfare, to which all side streets led: labor gangs and
camp authorities were allowed to move along the *Lagerstrasse*, but ordinary prisoners were forbidden to appear there, especially during working hours.—Ed.

those who pushed their way to the soup kettle, hitting and driving away others. Stasia was around 35, with blue eyes and dark hair, cropped like a man's. Once, at Yom Kippur, she ordered Aryans to replace Jewish women in all work in the barracks and fatigues. She managed to acquire candles somewhere, and in the evening we Jewish and Polish women gathered together in a solemn and impressive silence. Each of us prayed inwardly in her own fashion: for liberation from the hell of Auschwitz, for the end of the war, for peace in the world.

Now, in the *Lagerstrasse*, Stasia gave me an intent glance; my body was lean, ulcerous, almost blue with cold. She moved a trifle closer.

"How are you?" she asked in her rough way, as though reluctantly.

I expected no help from her—how could she help me now? But I felt a little better as I gave voice to all my fears in one breath. Stasia gazed indifferently round, as if not listening to me at all, and in the same indifferent way she eyed the women standing by me. Then she leaned towards me and, with a meaningful wink, she murmured: "Run, quick!" She turned her back on me, pretending to be interested in something in the rear ranks.

Like a bow from an arrow, as fast as my legs would carry me, I rushed down the alley between huts: several women standing near me also managed to escape.

When the "selection" was over, delousing took place; my shoes were stolen in the bathhouse. But this time I did not give up for lost; unobserved, I seized the first pair of shoes that came to hand, and ran for it. The only trouble was that the stolen shoes were enormous, my injured feet were lost in them, and they caused me terrible pain. When the opportunity arose, I exchanged them for a smaller size, and was proud I had learned to manage for myself.

The *Weberei* labor gang worked in a barracks that was a long way outside the camp. On our way there twice daily we passed a ramp and people being herded out of the boxcars. The road to the *Weberei* ran close to the crematorium and a small wood, where corpses were burned en masse, in heaps, in ditches, when the crematorium could not keep up with the great number of transports. The stench of burning bones was even stronger here than in the camp.

In the *Weberei* we worked at tables. We wove upholstery for tanks from scraps of various rags, clippings, bits of cloth. We worked fast, tensely, for the Nazis set very high work norms. We were punished terribly for not fulfilling the norm. To make matters worse, we did not receive enough raw material. Several times a day they threw a heap of rags on the hut floor; dozens of women snatched them from each other, to ensure achieving the norm and not being beaten . . . The Storm Troopers watched, grinning with satisfaction. I could not cope with it all, and was constantly in danger of a flogging . . . twenty-five strokes on my bare bottom . . . It was difficult for me to evade the evening checkup. Indeed, it would have been unthinkable for any long period, but fortunately I found a good and sincere friend here, who rescued me from my oppression.

Polusia was my nearest neighbor at the worktable. She came from Sosnowiec, was twelve years old, smaller than I, a tiny creature—it was strange they had let her into the camp at all . . . Dark, curly hair encircled her round, pink little face; Polusia had lost her upper teeth, which gave her a still more childish look. Cheerful, lively, nimble and unusually resourceful, she had learned very well how to "organize" rags; she weaved the braids so fast and skillfully that my eyes almost jumped out of my head as I watched her fingers fly. She outdid everyone else, and obtained a prize, an Auschwitz "reward"—an extra bread ration. She had been in the *Weberei* labor gang since her first day in the camp; she knew every nook and cranny in the place; sometimes a *kapo* would toss her material so she could earn a prize, and they gave her larger rations of soup. Polusia enjoyed the friendship of a certain young room overseer in Block 2, a Czech woman. I took a liking to Polusia and soon we were as inseparable as sisters. We moved to the same bunk, ate together, stood together during roll calls. We shared everything, as Hela and I had done earlier. Polusia taught me how to achieve the norm, and I finally lost my fear of checking and punishment.

Increasingly good news started reaching us from the front line in the spring of 1944. By summer, we realized the end of the war was at hand. A large area of Poland was liberated by troops from the East, and the victorious armies were approaching Auschwitz. Our hope and impatience grew.

But at the same time terrifying reports circulated around the camp of the murder of all Jews in the camps at Majdanek, Trawniki, Poniatow and Lublin—at the very moment, literally, when the Russians entered these areas. We feared a similar fate would be ours. Frequent air raid alarms and the panic of the Nazis at the mere sound of the alarm signal made us joyful; the sight of terror in the eyes of those savage, self-assured execution-ers used to give us intense satisfaction.

That same summer we heard from Polish women whom the Nazis brought to Auschwitz after the Warsaw insurrection that Warsaw was already liberated. My heart yearned for my native city, though nothing was left of it but ruins.

As we were coming back from work one day and were only a few steps from the gate, Soviet aircraft flew over and began circling low. The Hitlerites did not let us into the camp, and they themselves scuttled to a nearby shelter. For the first time since being brought to that hell, we were left outside the camp, with no escorts, no sentries! At liberty! . . . We craned our necks and, unable to conceal our great joy, we waved our hands and hand-kerchiefs to the pilots, enthusiastically shouting: "They are ours! Ours!" We could jump up and down, shout, laugh to our hearts' content—the Nazis were squatting deep in their underground shelters, scared to death . . . Suddenly bombs began falling; we threw ourselves to the ground, surrounded by a ring of explo-sions. A deafening roar, dust and smoke darkened everything around . . . A bomb had ploughed into the earth a few yards from the gate and the place where we were lying. Fortunately it did not explode . . . After the raid, the Nazis ordered it to be taken away, that great bomb "of ours."

Anticipating their own defeat, the Nazis began bringing enormous transports of people to Auschwitz at a hitherto unprecedented rate. That summer Auschwitz became a gigantic combine of destruction, pillage and genocide. Even the oldest inhabitants of the camp had never seen anything like it . . . The crematoriums proved too crowded, the days and nights too short, there was not enough gas or human hands to dig the ditches in which the additional corpses were burned.

"Selections" and roundups of the strongest, healthiest women started, to work in the gas chambers themselves where they had to assist undressing the children brought to be killed, to keep order and hurry on the grown-ups. Other women were selected for work in "Canada," where the belongings of murdered Jews were sorted. We translated the word "Canada" as *keine da* ("No one there!") or—more precisely, there is not a single Jew, all had been exterminated by the Nazis and their "New Order." Before the arrival of transports of Jewish people from Hungary, several hundred women as well as men worked in "Canada": they lived in a separate hut, and were mostly Jewish. They were not troubled by hunger, they did not require camp rations of bread and soup; they were in good shape, more resistant to the diseases decimating the camp. They rarely underwent "selections," and could at any moment buy themselves out of various dangers by winning over block overseers, *kapos* and even German women in high positions by some fine "present" or other. But the threatening shadow of death hung over them all the time. They knew that when the transports of Jewish people to the gas chambers ended, the SS would liquidate "Canada" and murder the witnesses of their crimes and pillage.

We unexpectedly learned that all the women working in the *Weberei* were to be transferred to Block 26, which was next to ours. The block overseer there was notorious for her cruelty, and the room overseers were just as bad. Crowding and confusion prevailed in the barracks to a greater degree than anywhere else. We dreaded that block as burned children dread fire, and I was particularly afraid, on account of my sick bladder and whooping cough that had been troubling me lately. But chance had it otherwise; instead of sending me to Block 26, I was unexpectedly sent to "Canada."

Polusia's friend, the Czech room overseer, promised to try and find her a place in "Canada" too. Weeks passed, they had even stopped taking more people into the labor gang, but Polusia was still working in the *Weberei,* though she kept making various efforts to obtain a transfer. One day, she copied out a list of numbers of all our youthful group and handed it to her room overseer, asking her to submit the list to the camp HQ. We had no chances as candidates for the work in "Canada," after all, they required a healthy appearance, physical strength and so on. No one believed anything would come of this, or that there would even be a reply. We laughed at Polusia's simplicity . . .

To our amazement, the letter reached HQ and . . . On the day when they were to take the women from the *Weberei* to Block 26 after evening roll call, a runner from HQ hurried in with urgent instructions for the block overseer, and after a short discussion, my number was called. Ready for the worst, I all at once learned I had been transferred to "Canada." What had happened? Someone at HQ must have crossed out all the numbers from the room overseer's list for a joke, leaving only one at random. Polusia was very resentful.

The runner took me to the bathhouse (for the first time I did not fear "selection" or the crematorium), then to the *Bekleidungskammer,* or clothing store, where I obtained thick, clean underwear, gray with white stripes, a quite new dress, also striped, an apron and a red kerchief (all the women in "Canada" wore red kerchiefs). After this I was handed over to the overseer of Block 12.

After a warm bath, dressed in fresh and clean clothes that were free of lice, I felt reborn. At first it was strange and depressing in the block. I knew nobody, nobody took any interest in me, they did not even pay me the slightest attention. But that evening I could eat as much soup as I wanted. Full kettles stood in the hallways, but no one except the room overseers and I even looked twice at them. I lay down to sleep alone, on a plank bed

that was clean and spacious! Also for the first time since being in
Auschwitz, I did not eat all my bread ration at once. I hid it, and
this without being afraid anyone would steal it from me in the
night. I wanted to take it to work with me, for I did not believe—
despite all assurances—that there was always enough to eat in
"Canada." The next morning I set out to work clutching the
bread. My new comrades in the ranks laughed at me mockingly:
"Taking bread to 'Canada'! Give it to someone here, silly girl!
You will have enough and better food to eat." Despite this, I did
not let go of the bread. I still was not entirely convinced . . .

We walked several miles each morning and evening from our
camp at Birkenau to Auschwitz, where "Canada" was located.
On the way we encountered men working on the roads, or at the
railroad station. They dragged huge weights, harnessed to loaded
carts which they hauled with terrible efforts, or pushed wheelbarrows full of tar or rocks; *kapos* and Storm Troopers drove
them on, beating them, ill-using the mortally weary crowd in
bestial ways. The emaciated bodies of the wretched men were
covered with dirty, torn rags. The sight of these men always
depressed me in the same way. And even more when I thought
that—who knows?—perhaps my brother and father were also
suffering in this way.

I kept daydreaming of meeting Hilek unexpectedly; I did not
believe I would meet my elder brother Marek here. I knew from
friends, neighbors of ours from Nowolipie Street whom I had met
in Majdanek, that Marek had escaped from a transport by jumping from a window while the freight car was in motion, while
they were taking him to Majdanek. In the ghetto we had sometimes hidden at the home of these neighbors during sudden "campaigns," in a well-hidden room. After Marek had escorted us to
the bunker in Mila Street, he went back to Nowolipie Street for
food, and was trapped there by the siege, so he took shelter in the
neighbors' hiding place. But everyone had to leave it "voluntarily" when the Germans set fire to the houses in the street and the
fire started penetrating into the apartment . . . In the train—so my
neighbor told me—my brother helped the feeble, revived the

unconscious then decided, with several other bold spirits, to escape. Not until after the war did I learn further details from Marek himself; as he was jumping from the train, an SS bullet struck his shoulder; a peasant in a nearby village looked after him, and he stayed the night there. Later he managed to return to Warsaw, where he hid until the end of the war in the apartment of Mrs. Jozefa Bartosiewicz, a Polish lady; Mr. Strojwas contributed to his upkeep. I had been used to obeying and following Marek's example from childhood. In the ghetto he gave me lessons in French, he worked through the school syllabus with me from the third to sixth grades. Then he hired a private teacher for me. He paid for these lessons with what he earned in the ghetto: he gave injections and various medical remedies.

As I was walking to "Canada" that first day, with the piece of bread in my hand, a ragged man, emaciated as a skeleton, leaped towards me with hand outstretched. Without saying a word. His eyes rolled like those of an animal baited to death. I hesitated. Should I hand over the bread voluntarily? I had never imagined myself in a like situation. And I do not know whether I would have decided to make this improbable gesture, had not a comrade prodded me impatiently.

My fear of never eating my fill very soon proved completely groundless. As soon as I took off my striped prison uniform and leaned down to pick out a dress to wear while working from a pile of old clothes, I found all kinds of food scattered among the heaps of clothing. I grabbed literally everything that came to hand: bread, pieces of broken cakes, smoked meats, bacon—I stuffed myself greedily, without restraint. But almost at once, to my extreme surprise I realized I was replete and had even had too much to eat. Still, I could not control myself, though I looked for more select tidbits.

It was the custom in "Canada" for us to change our clothes for work—we could "dress up" in the most beautiful dresses, blouses or jerseys, in the finest and most elegant underwear—all left behind by murdered people. We could eat as much as we wanted—though we were forbidden to take anything back to the camp. Every evening, before returning to camp, we were put through three spot-checks. These were carried out by dead-drunk Storm Troopers: first in the barracks, wearing only knickers and vest; then before leaving "Canada," wearing our striped prison uniforms, and assembled for marching out to the highway; and for the third time in front of the camp gate. Anyone on whom was found the smallest trifle was beaten terribly, her hair cut off, and she was immediately thrown out of the labor gang. We trembled with agitation during these searches.

Even so, everyone smuggled things back into camp . . . There was not a single day on which we did not bring in something. I vied with the others in this respect. After all, the prisoners in the camp were dying of hunger and cold. So many good things, pillaged from our murdered brothers and sisters, the Jewish people from Hungary, were going to waste underfoot that—or so it seemed to me—it would rescue the entire camp from the torments of starvation, illness and dirt. How, then, was it possible to come back empty-handed from "Canada"?

Every day I put on a new pair of shoes at work, came back wearing them and gave them to comrades in the camp; in the mornings I went to work in old, shabby and rotten wooden clogs, which I threw into the trash can in "Canada." I often hobbled with difficulty in shoes too small for me and intended for companions; I would bring back pieces of scented soap or fine pieces of silken underwear in shoes that were too big, for they did not make us take our shoes off during the checks. We smuggled gloves, blouses, underwear on our stomachs, under the coarse striped camp chemise. I hid pieces of bread, cake, bacon under my own clothing as I held it during the searches, and returned with a beating heart thus loaded to my friends Celina and Polusia, who awaited me uneasily and impatiently right by the camp gate. Fortunately the SS did not catch me a single time.

But I was not able to smuggle anything out of "Canada" for Mrs. Prajsowa and Rozka. Both had been transferred to camp "a"; however, they continued working in the barracks and had the same "privileges" as before. I lost contact with them and did not find them again until later, under circumstances that were especially hard for me . . . I will come to this in due time.

Meanwhile, work was proceeding at full swing in "Canada." Loads of Jewish people from Hungary flowed without end into the gigantic death factory. There was never sufficient space on the ramp where they unloaded train after train, there was no room for the people and their luggage, for these condemned people were unaware of what lay in store, and brought everything they had of value with them. Great heaps of suitcases, bundles, trunks and packages overflowed the ramp, the barracks of "Canada," and the spaces between the barracks themselves. Enormous trucks, loaded to overflowing, brought these things to us from the ramp, while personal clothing and jewelry, which people took off at the moment before death, before entering the "bath," were brought directly from the crematorium.

Rich and poor, fat and thin, tall and short, old people and children . . . In this terrible clothing store, carefully packed or just opened food went to waste, as did unfinished remains of food, slightly tainted, moldy, along with still more tragic evidence of interrupted lives: babies' nipples, dolls, scraps, photographs, letters, private papers. I gazed at all this, and was overwhelmed by a weird sensation of terror, as though the entire world were being brought here to Auschwitz, to be cast naked and deprived of all its humanity into the crematorium furnaces that smoked by day and night.

Men working in "Canada," as we did, unloaded the trucks and kept the best things for themselves. Sometimes, these men chose a "mistress" from among the women (this was what they were called in camp language), to whom they gave various expensive oddments as proof of affection or as a reward for "love" (the huge piles of clothing gave ample opportunity for practicing this "love"). "Canada" obviously deprived people of all reason and acted on them like a narcotic. There is no other explanation for what happened.

Most often I worked outdoors, tearing up rags or old clothing, to make sure they did not get into the good things, sorted to be sent to Germany by the Nazis. But I usually tore up everything that came to hand, good as well as bad clothes, so that the Nazis had as little use of them as possible. Almost all women I worked with did the same, watching to make sure they were not observed by Storm Troopers prowling around the warehouses, gorged with food and mostly drunk. Sometimes they drunkenly importuned women prisoners. During our dinner break they very often forced us all into the shower baths in "Canada"; they enjoyed themselves and laughed uproariously.

Women "specialists" worked inside the barracks, sorting clothes and taking them to the disinfecting gas chambers built for the purpose in the "Canada" area. Then they made bundles of the clothing, which were stored in warehouses ready for dispatch. When trains arrived, everyone in "Canada" was mobilized into dragging and loading these bundles hastily into the freight cars.

The killing and pillaging went on all summer, until late fall.

During those several weeks when I worked in "Canada," I put on plenty of weight and regained my health and strength. I also helped various comrades and even chance acquaintances. I was by no means the only one to do this; I was simply following the example of most of the women in "Canada." I was much younger than they, so could not take advantage as they did of various opportunities. For instance, I never found any gold or jewelry, nor did I ever get anything from the men, whom I feared and instinctively avoided.

"Canada" had a far more depressing effect on me than on the grown-ups. I was now closer to mass extermination, could no longer delude myself, or stubbornly insist, "It is impossible." I began losing my faith in life, in its stability and value, and still more in the possibility of ever getting out of this hell. For hundreds of thousands of people were perishing—although (as people in the camp whispered) the Germans were face to face with ultimate defeat. I also lost my faith in people and what little respect I had left. I became brusque, sharp even with my closest friend Polusia. I was closed up in myself, taciturn, in a constant state of irritation. I could no longer find a common language with anyone; I considered talk senseless in the face of the baseness of the world we lived in, in the face of the unpunished crimes of which we were daily eyewitnesses, in the face of the prison indifference to everything that did not concern us directly. But despite my spiritual breakdown and despair, I never stopped smuggling things out of "Canada" for other people, not for a single day.

Fortunately Polusia too got into "Canada," though rather late, and now I could shun her with a clear conscience, break off a friendship of which I was no longer capable. While working in the pit of hell, I could not be friends with anyone. I could not endure myself, so how could I get along with others?

There was eating and drinking, women kept trying on new "outfits." On the way to work, we continued to pass close to the people from the transports, people brought here to be gassed, whose clothing we would be sorting in an hour or two. One day, as we were passing one such column of Jewish people from Hungary,* our labor gang halted for a while. During this short pause, I found myself close to a young married couple; the mother was holding an infant in her arms. It was crying; the father glanced at his watch, then at a straw basket from which a baby's bottle projected. He asked his neighbors, then us, the "locals," whether it was far to the labor camp and the barracks of the Jewish settlement in Birkenau, as it was almost the baby's feeding time. They had only a few dozen yards to go, the last few dozen yards to the gas chambers, to their "eternal" settlement. No one answered his question. What could be said to the condemned?

Finally "Canada" came to an end . . . It was partly liquidated and our labor gang disbanded. In the fall of 1944, the transports began decreasing, became less and less frequent, then finally stopped entirely. From time to time a load of people arrived for gassing—mostly Jewish people brought here after "selections" in

---

*Hungarian Jews were being transported en masse to Birkenau in mid-May, 1944; the estimated number of persons deported was 400,000.—Ed.

other camps or ghettos. The Soviet army was moving ahead, the
Nazis erasing evidence of their crimes.

Slowly the piles of luggage were put in order and cleared
away; the last freight cars of loot were dispatched to Germany.
The warehouses of "Canada" were clean, quiet, empty. The
women roamed idly around from place to place; there was no
longer any work . . . and nothing to eat either.

We expected to be transferred any day—and something a good
deal worse. We had to expect that the SS would do away with us
too, before the Russians arrived. Thus the liquidation of "Canada" could mean death for us. Death shortly before liberation.
Each one of us feared this terribly . . .

Our previous hunger and uneasiness returned.

Yet ever fresh and more comforting news was circulating in
the camp, of the situation at the front, of the expulsion of the
Germans from Poland. It was not easy to distinguish between
invention or lies, and the truth, in these rumors, but after various
changes in the camp, the violent ups-and-downs in the moods of
the Storm Troopers themselves, it was felt that the end of the
Third Reich was at hand, and this in turn heightened our terror of
death. Even when "Canada" was working at top speed, the Nazis
gassed men from the *Sonderkommando*.* They gassed those who
rebelled against the Storm Troopers in the crematorium in the
local disinfection chamber.

These incidents caused wild panic and terror in "Canada,"
though at the same time, the news of the revolt of the *Sonderkommando* against the SS filled us with admiration and pride.

At the same time, a rumor circulated among us that the head of
the crematorium, a German NCO, had himself been gassed,
which meant that a like fate awaited us. We did not know why
the SS should sentence one of themselves in this way.

---

*Jews of the *Sonderkommando* employed in the Auschwitz crematoria and
burning pits were liquidated every few months, or more frequently; in October
1944 there was an insurrection in the *Sonderkommando,* which at that time
numbered 1200 men (on account of the speeding up of the extermination
campaign)—almost all died.—Ed.

The SS sometimes had human reactions too. When all the food was gone, some of the women and a group of young girls asked our chief and obtained from him food from the last packages intended for dispatch to Germany. He was especially kind to us children, would often eye us sadly, call us to him and hand out various goodies—walnuts, chocolate, dried fruit.

Finally the "reduction" we had been waiting for with such terror came. One evening after work, the Hitlerites assembled us in "Canada," and began carrying out a "selection." Some women begged and prayed to be left in this labor gang. But it was useless. There were no more transports for the gas chambers, therefore such a large labor gang was not required. But instead of rejoicing at this fact . . . the prisoners regretted losing their "good" jobs!

They crowded us into a locked, walled block in camp "a" just as they had done at the start of my sojourn in Auschwitz during quarantine 18 months earlier . . . The terrible suffering began again, though now it was even worse, because we were no longer used to it. In addition, our fate was hanging in the balance, dependent on the final decision of the camp authorities.They kept us in isolation for several days and nights in the locked hut, watching that we make no contact with the rest of the camp. We even went to the lavatories guarded by a room overseer. We were given very little food, and that irregularly, sometimes once in several days . . . The crowd and stench worsened the atmosphere still further, which was like that of a death cell. Hunger cramped our bowels, though we were spared because all of us had put on weight during the last weeks in "Canada"; at least we had something to grow lean on . . .

I did not often think of the likelihood of death. Generally, I did not wonder what would become of us. But I could not endure the immediate present—being locked up. I kept looking for some way to escape, to make contact with the outer world.

Once I got away from a group with which I was being led from the barracks to the lavatory. I crept back into camp "b," to Celina. I knew very well that if they caught me on this trip, I would pay for it with my life. However, I felt sure that once I was with Celina, I would be spared. Celina knew many block and room overseers, who exercised influence in the camp. Who knew whether they would be able to get me out of the prison? The thought that Celina would welcome me with open arms, and give me bread, added to my courage. I overcame many difficulties and risks on the way, finally reaching the hut out of breath and winded. I ran over to the familiar bunk and . . .

Celina was talking to a friend. She saw me standing there, impatiently waiting for her to come to me. Yet she did not interrupt her talking. I was in a hurry, I had to get back as quickly as possible, before the *kapos* started looking for me. All the prisoners who had friends among the women sacked from "Canada" were worried about their fate, and did what they could to throw food or something to drink through holes in the wall. Each one would have been only too happy if a friend of hers succeeded in an undertaking like my visit to Celina, but Celina paid me no attention. When I tried to interrupt, shyly explaining I had only a little time and would like to say a few words to her, she shrugged, as much as to say she was occupied by something more important, that I was bothering her! Nor did she change this aloof attitude even when I, trembling with indignation and misery, tears in my eyes, ran out of the hut.

Going back and creeping into the section "a" prison block was really terrible! I returned there like a whipped dog. Even death did not seem as terrible to me as what had happened.

Finally, the scales of our destiny tipped towards life. For reasons unknown to us, the camp authorities decided to keep us alive and return us to the various huts and jobs. For the time being, danger had moved away—and meanwhile, the news from the Eastern front was ever better . . .

The fall of 1944 was drawing to a close. The Nazis began dismantling the crematoria. Each morning, as all the labor gangs passed through the crematoria yards on their way to work, each of us took a lump of wood to get rid of somewhere far off, in the fields. How cheerfully and jauntily we carried this wood, though it was very heavy. We breathed deeply with relief at the sight of the empty, extinguished crematoria. But this did not in the least increase our hopes of survival. The SS could shoot us at the last moment before their defeat. We briskly rejected this terrifying thought . . . The Russians were advancing rapidly, the Nazis could not make it in time . . . after all, they had to save their own skins.

My next and last labor gang in Auschwitz was the Potato Unit. First we dug ditches for storing winter supplies of potatoes, then we unloaded potatoes from freight cars. Once again, we spent entire days outdoors, in the frequent fall rains. Our shovels were heavy and awkward, for pounds of mud clung to them. Our feet and the wheelbarrows full of potatoes sank into the wet, churned mud. The SS and *kapos* drove us on, and beat us with their horsewhips if we slowed down at all. Men, lean as skeletons, labored the same as we. The air raid alarms were our only respite; then the Nazis fled to the shelters, forgetting us and the potatoes. We bartered smuggled potatoes for bread or soup, and sometimes cooked them on ashes in the block; or fellow prisoners who had access to a fire might cook them for us, in exchange for half the portion. If the worst came to the worst, we ate the potatoes raw.

The "organization" of potatoes, like every kind of illegal activity in Auschwitz, required great skill and was very dangerous. Every evening after work in the labor gang, an old Storm Trooper, as bad-tempered as the devil himself, searched us thoroughly for contraband. He poked us all—men and women—with a thick stick he used for walking. And he nearly always found some daredevil . . . So, every day, summary executions took place. Yet the suffering of victims beaten until the blood flowed, into insensibility, to death—did not frighten the rest of us from smuggling potatoes into the camp. We merely tried to improve ways of hiding them from the eyes of our executioners. We hid potatoes in our boots, under clothes, on our persons—wherever possible. I usually carried mine in an aluminum canteen from which I ate the soup we obtained at noon. I used to put five or six potatoes into this canteen, replace the lid and hold it normally in my hand, as though it were empty. Fortunately, it never occurred to the Storm Troopers to look inside the utensil. Various monograms and Stars of David were engraved on these canteens: previously they had belonged to Jewish people from the Lodz ghetto, gassed that fall in Auschwitz. These were large and very useful canteens, which we used instead of canvas bags. I bought myself one for a ration of bread. It was very convenient, especially in the Potato Unit.

One August evening, even before they assigned me to the Potato Unit, and soon after they released us from isolation, a large-scale roll call took place in camp "a." All the women from other sectors of the camp assembled from every corner of Birkenau. And this was the occasion on which I again met my previous good friends Mrs. Prajsowa and Rozka. The SS brought us together to watch them hang the runner Mala, in the center of the square, for escaping in the uniform of an overseer. After a few weeks, Mala was caught by the Nazis and brought back to Auschwitz. Mala was a pretty young Jewish girl from Belgium. We used to see her every morning and evening; she stood at the camp gate when we left for work and when we came back; she used to note down the gangs leaving, and their destination. We also used to see her when she came to our block overseers with instructions or orders from the camp HQ. On these occasions she often warned us of a forthcoming "selection," disciplinary actions or a "visit" from Dr. Mengele; as a camp runner she was the first to hear of everything. So we were all heartily glad when Mala succeeded in escaping. But now she was standing at the gallows, surrounded by Storm Troopers. The camp commandant made a speech to the prisoners on this "occasion." But before she finished, Mala cut her own veins and struck a Storm Trooper in the face as he hurled himself upon her. Savagely ill-treated, she was taken to the crematorium on a stretcher . . . The story of this courageous girl, her life and her death, was for a long time the topic of conversation in the camp. Mala became a legend to us, a symbol of heroism.

Mrs. Prajsowa and Rozka looked after me from the start. They asked me to their hut, gave me a bowl of camp soup, and invited me to come and sleep in their bunk. I gladly accepted, as my bunk was very crowded, and I had nothing with which to cover myself. My sleeping in their block was somewhat risky for them, and for me too. But they paid no heed, and treated me just like a daughter and a sister. I too was ready to take any risk, as long as I could stay with these true and sincere friends. They were indignant at Celina's behavior, and I was very sorry that when I had been working in "Canada," I had no opportunity to help them, and show my gratitude. But I had not even known where they were . . . So now I was all the more eager to bring Mrs. Prajsowa potatoes in my famous canteen. Mrs. Prajsowa made potato cakes for the three of us: any remaining potatoes she bartered for a ration of bread. So we lived together several months, helping each other and cementing still further the bonds of our friendship.

One night, Mrs. Prajsowa was substituting for the night watch in her block, and was secretly cooking some soup for us and for several sick prisoners, when she burned her hand with boiling water in her haste and fear of the block overseer. There was no help for it—she had to go to the sick bay. Rozka and I had warned her dozens of times to be careful. But she refused even to listen. Not for one moment did she stop taking risks in order to help others in misfortune—it was a sacred duty to her.

Now we began onerous daily trips to visit Mrs. Prajsowa in the sick bay. We economized in bread, bartered soup for it, and smuggled it into the sick bay. True to her principles, Mrs. Prajsowa shared these gifts with her neighbors, much to our indignation. We dared not protest aloud, however.

Mrs. Prajsowa looked dreadful: her face was as pale as the face of a corpse, contorted with a grimace of pain. The burns refused to heal, and her stay in the sick bay looked as if it might be a long one. It was very sad and unpleasant for us without her maternal care. Hunger made itself felt. Hurrying to the hospital, squeezing through crevices or gaps in fences, the gates and past sentries at the camp crossroads exhausted our nerves and our strength.

Once it so happened that we got stuck on the way back from the hospital between one camp and the other . . . It was late, both gates had already been shut . . . We were trapped. All that was wanting was a Storm Trooper or sentry to come along. That would have been the end of us! Usually we crept into the camp from the sick bay and back by furtively joining groups of prisoners being escorted to work or to the hospital by a *kapo*. Sometimes they were groups of men, at other times women. This time not a living soul could be seen. We had left the sick bay sector through a hole in the fence, but now we were stuck in the middle of a crosswalk between the camps, enclosed by the barbed wire fences of both. We could neither go on nor retreat—it was as though we were in a trap.

Meanwhile dusk had fallen and night was coming. Our teeth chattering, trembling, we feverishly considered our situation. It was hopeless. All we could do was crouch behind a pile of stones and wait for whatever happened next. If a Storm Trooper saw us, we would die before we could open our mouths to explain. But the night covered us with its merciful darkness, and the pile of stones hid us from the eyes of sentries. Towards morning we joined a *Sonderkommand* labor gang which went to the sick bay daily to remove dead bodies for cremating.

The next day we visited Mrs. Prajsowa again, but we were much more careful, nor did we tell the sick woman of our adventure until she had recovered.

Seeing the inevitably approaching end of the Third Reich in the winter of 1944–1945, the Nazis carried on a quiet but systematic evacuation and gradual liquidation of the camp. Every few weeks they sent transports of several hundred people away to other labor camps, deep inside Germany. Some women volunteered to go, deluding themselves into thinking they would be better off in a new place than in Auschwitz. But most tried all manner of ways to avoid leaving, in the fear that it would be even worse in other Nazi camps. Especially as the Russians were already not far off, and the hope of speedy liberation grew increasingly bright. However, none of us really knew whether it was better to leave or to stay. The greatest temptation was provided by the rations of food distributed for the journey: bread and a piece of sausage, like the white bread and milk formerly promised in the "children's block," and the various wonders supposedly awaiting women in Dr. Mengele's "experimental" block.

I was never tempted by these Hitlerite "benefits." I was never greedy for "better" conditions or "bigger" rations of food. On the contrary, I always sensed the real purpose behind these noble, kindly gestures. I dreaded the transports to Germany as a burned child dreads fire. I escaped them by jumping out of the barracks windows and hiding in the lavatories; I did the same when Dr. Mengele roamed the camp, choosing his experimental "rabbits" from the blocks. I had come to Auschwitz from Majdanek full of illusory hopes, but had jumped out of a frying pan into a fire . . . Everywhere was equally vile and dangerous, in the clutches of these bandits and criminals. I preferred to stay in Auschwitz, where at least I knew every hole and corner, and all the dangerous traps.

Camp "a" grew noticeably emptier; after the departure of numerous transports to Germany, the Nazis transferred all the remaining prisoners to barracks in fields B II b and c (formerly they had kept thousands of gypsy families in camp "c," then they had gassed and cremated them, like the Jews). Once again I was separated from my friends, Mrs. Prajsowa and Rozka; both were transferred to B II b some weeks earlier than my block was.

Now, however, Celina's block was close to my barracks. Celina apologized to me, and tried to make up for her previous behavior. I visited her every evening. I had to forgive her, as I was lonely and depressed by parting from Mrs. Prajsowa and Rozka. Besides, Celina treated me as in the past with great affection. She sneaked me soup, or bread and jam, while I gave her potatoes I acquired. Sometimes I stayed all night with her; she slept in comfort, alone on a bunk, with an adequate supply of blankets.

During this time I made friends with several 18-year-old girls from Bendzin; we worked together in the potato labor gang. After a few weeks they transferred our gang to B II b, where I at once sought out Mrs. Prajsowa and Rozka. I used to go back to my hut for roll call and to collect my bread ration; I spent the rest of the time after work, evenings and entire nights with Mrs. Prajsowa. Everyone thought I was a close relative of theirs . . . Celina was transferred with her entire block to camp "c," which was separated from our camp by electrified barbed wire. I often talked with her across this wire, especially since her hut was very near the fence.

I regard fair-haired Alvira, a *kapo* in the potato labor gangs, among those who contributed to my survival in the camp.

Alvira's father was German, her mother Jewish, which was why Alvira had been brought to Auschwitz. She was something over thirty, tall and graceful. Her eyebrows and lashes looked entirely white against the background of her red face. She was not pretty, nor even likable. Without knowing why, I always had the idea that handsome people are good, understanding and generous. Consequently I was often disappointed. All the same, pretty faces still attracted me, and awoke friendly feelings in me. *Kapo* Alvira proved to contradict this naive theory of mine. She was exceptionally kind to me and to several other children in the labor gang.

Right at the start, seeing how helplessly I was digging and that I could barely lift the heavy shovel, she asked how old I was. I did not hide the truth from her. "Fourteen?" she repeated in surprise and sorrow. "I have left a little daughter at home . . ." she added after a moment, but so indistinctly that I hardly understood her.

At the word "home" I felt bitterness overwhelm me. I envied this red-faced, ugly Alvira, who spoke German as well as the overseers, for having somewhere a home, a family, a little daughter to whom she would return when the war ended. But where should I go, to whom would I return if I managed to survive this hell? Who in this world would be waiting for me? Who would rejoice at my return?

"I have no home, nobody anywhere," I said aloud, though in a choked voice. And I looked defiantly at her red face which I disliked so much, and which now seemed to me still uglier and repulsive. I wanted the *kapo* to realize that despite everything, her situation was far better than ours. And I was not at all ashamed of my envy. Suddenly, Alvira's eyes filled with tears. She did not shout at me, as I had expected; she embraced me fondly, and kissed my brow . . .

In this way we became friends, an unexpected friendship but a sincere and deeply human one. From that time on, Alvira assigned me to lighter work, and often protected me from other *kapos* and the SS.

The potato bunker contained a room with central heating and special basins for pickling vegetables, cabbage, turnip, carrots, etc. Work in this warm pickling room was much easier than work outdoors, and in addition it was possible to eat one's fill of vegetables, and to smuggle a few of them out to the camp for "sale" in the evenings. A few dozen young girls worked here. They washed the floor, scrubbed the empty basins, then filled them with sliced cabbage or turnip, pressing the vegetables down at the order of a Storm Trooper with their feet on which they had clean rubber overshoes. Alvira, who supervised the group of women working outdoors, managed to get me a place in the pickling room. This was real salvation for me. In exchange for smuggled potatoes or pickled cabbage, I was able to buy a woolen dress and a good winter coat from women in the clothing section, also stout leather shoes and even blacking to clean them with. So once again things began going well for me. I walked about replete, decently dressed, clean and warm; my new comrades in the pickling room took a liking to me and as I was one of the youngest, they surrounded me with care and attention. Every day we washed from head to toe in a bucket of hot water which a stoker brought from the boiler house—in a corner blocked by planks, taking turns to ensure that no Storm Troopers caught us at this forbidden bath. We also washed our underwear, and dried it on the radiators. All this, needless to say, did not occur without fear and continual risk . . . The stoker from the boiler house, who rendered us various services, was a German, a political prisoner. He had been in Auschwitz since the foundation of the camp, and had been transferred here from another concentration camp in the Reich; he had been suffering in this way since 1933, from the moment Hitler came to power. This German cooked tasty potato soup for us, and was always ready to help us. We felt a liking, gratitude and respect for him. "He's a German, yet he is suffering as we are," we sometimes said to one another. "This means that Germans are not all alike. They are not all 'like that.'"

Yet I could not understand why some Germans were "like that" and others not; why some preyed on people, persecuted and killed them, while other Germans endured persecution.

New Year 1945 was approaching, the sixth year of the war and Nazi rule, the sixth year of our tragedy and suffering. We came to the conclusion, from the many very varied changes in the camp, that the end was near. News of the defeat of Germany reached the camp; sometimes the Storm Troopers themselves spoke of it. People were no longer put to death in the gas chambers. The crematoria were partly dismantled.

Our canvas patches with the Star of David were now changed for numbers of red squares, which had hitherto only been worn by Aryan women and political prisoners. This was meant to indicate that they had not imprisoned us for being Jewish. So they reckoned Jews as political criminals, who threatened the existence of the Third Reich. I became a political criminal, a dangerous enemy of Hitler's regime, at the age of 14.

At this time, or perhaps a little earlier, a Red Cross delegation visited Auschwitz, the "labor camp." The SS prepared feverishly for this inspection during several weeks. They bustled about so as to bring the camp into some sort of "acceptable" state. They ordered us to "spring clean" the huts, bunks and outdoors around the blocks. Everywhere was painted, whitewashed, polished. The death camp authorities wanted to prove to the Red Cross delegation that Auschwitz was a model and completely innocent labor camp in which prisoners of war lived and worked in suitable conditions . . . Finally the long-awaited delegation arrived.

An indescribably tense atmosphere, which seemed loaded with electricity, prevailed in the camp. When the Storm Troopers conducted the delegates from "another world" around the camp— lying to them about the purpose of various camp installations, barracks, kitchens and our appearance, which was not very reminiscent of the appearance of human beings—a deathly hush descended around them, which the prisoners were ordered to maintain on pain of death. But suddenly, in the sick bay, the silence exploded like a bursting balloon. The woman in charge of the sick bay, a Polish doctor, paid for her courage immediately after the delegates departed by torture in the Gestapo dungeons in Auschwitz. People said she died with outstanding heroism, and she certainly knew what awaited her when she told the Red Cross delegates the whole horrible truth about the Auschwitz tortures.

This woman doctor, like the runner Mala, became the personification of human dignity and courage to us.

On January 1, 1945, I had an accident; it led to my hand becoming useless, but had it not been for a fortunate coincidence, I would have lost my life . . .

On account of the New Year holiday we only worked till noon. We came back from work by daylight for the first time in many months, and this was why I decided to take advantage of the opportunity to talk to Celina through the barbed wire and hear how she was getting on. The weather was fine, dry and not very frosty. I was in a kind of unusually happy mood, looking hopefully at the future. As I had survived it all this far, what more had I to fear? I ate a bowl of soup Mrs. Prajsowa gave me and went towards the barbed wire with Rozka. Mrs. Prajsowa tried to prevent us: "You should not go wandering off," she grumbled. But we laughed at her constant "groundless" fears for us. A large number of prisoners were wandering about outdoors, many of them talking loudly at a distance with friends or relatives in camp "c." Such conversations between women prisoners were allowed, in principle.

Fine, white snow was sparkling beautifully in the rays of the winter sun. This snowy whiteness and the light dazzled me. I began calling loudly "Celina! Celina!"

There was no reply from the other side. Not discouraged, I called still louder, more insistently: "Celina! Celina! Celina!"

The sentry on the watchtower must have been bored and waiting for some excuse to amuse himself. I was standing at the barbed wire, comparatively close to him, and his eye happened to fall on me . . . He aimed and before anyone could notice and warn me, a bullet struck. The sentry was probably aiming at my heart, but missed and hit my arm.

At first I did not understand what had happened . . . I felt a strange warmth on my arm and almost simultaneously heard the noise of a shot very close; only then did the pain in my hand and fingers start, and spread throughout my body. I saw Rozka running away, and realized someone had fired at me . . . and I rushed after Rozka, stumbling time and again, then getting up, while fiery red spots danced before my eyes. My hand hurt so that I would gladly have torn it off. My head was throbbing like a mill; I thought, "So much suffering, so much suffering and now, just before it all ends I am going to die and will not live to see the end." I wanted to stay alive at any price, though it seemed that life might leave me at any moment. Don't fall! Don't close your eyes! Don't turn pale! Don't die! No, don't die! I will endure any torture, even the worst, as long as I don't die! Blood was flowing from the sleeve of my coat, making its way down my thick winter clothing, recently bought for smuggled potatoes—and it was escaping from me faster than I from the sentry's field of vision.

I dragged myself to the sick bay after Rozka. The sick bay at this time was in our sector, not far from the place where this new misfortune happened to me. But the way to the sick bay seemed endless. I knew nothing, could barely move in a dense blur, following Rozka blindly . . . The pain of my hand and the fear I was going to die from the shot gave me strength. Rozka was crying loudly as she led me, bleeding, into the hospital.

Meanwhile all the other women had run away from the barbed wire and taken refuge, terrified, in their blocks. A few minutes later our sector and the neighboring sector knew and were talking about my misfortune. I became celebrated again . . .

But for the time being I could not get help: the sick-bay nurses were on holiday—it was the New Year after all! . . . In any case, the sick bay merely served for assembling sick and weak prisoners; from there they were sent to the gas chambers. Now, with the gas chambers not functioning, or largely dismantled, the sick died in the hospital in their plank beds, while the block overseers and their "staffs," the alleged nurses and the room overseers, stole and shared their soup and bread rations . . . And Rozka and I hurried in unexpectedly . . . To make matters worse it was a holiday, when they had time off! What nonsense! To come to the sick bay for assistance, help, sympathy!

"Help her, help her," Rozka implored, running from one nurse to another.

Finally someone deigned to listen. She bandaged my wound with dry paper, without even washing my shoulder or arm. She merely said loudly to Rozka that I was lucky the bullet had come out, as could be seen by the two holes in my arm—otherwise, things would have looked very bad for me . . . I was half naked and half conscious. They told me to lie down on a bare mattress, without even giving me a single blanket to cover myself with; the plank bed was narrow and dirty, standing in a dark corner of the hut. They brutally drove Rozka away as she watched in stupefaction, holding my blood-stained clothes in her hand.

Once again I was left alone and suffering among strangers, indifferent people, on a cold, hard bed, convinced I would either die of my wounds or that the first Hitlerite doctor who chanced along would kill me off.

I had overheard a great deal in the camp about such incidents, but had never dreamed anything of the sort would happen to me. My presentiments, the instincts by which I had guided myself all the time in the camp, and even earlier, in the ghetto, had let me down entirely . . . I had felt good all day, my heart had been so light when I left Mrs. Prajsowa to see Celina!

All night long I felt like howling with pain, and did not close my eyes for a moment. The pain attacked my entire left side.

The next day, and for the succeeding days, I lay in a fever, shivering with cold. None of the nurses or room overseers came near me. The blood in which I was soaked had dried to form smelly stains on my blouse and body.

Like the other patients, I was only given a little turnip soup once a day, still worse and thinner than the usual camp soup. My wounds swelled with pus, lice crawled over them . . . In the meantime, I had to pretend I was not seriously ill, for seriously ill patients were killed off in the sick bay. From the moment when I realized I was not going to die of my wounds, I began looking forward hopefully to the day when I would be able to move my hand freely. But my hand was still stiff and completely dead. I could neither open nor close it, nor move my wrist and elbow.

In the evenings Mrs. Prajsowa and Rozka crept in to see me. The tearful Mrs. Prajsowa brought a bowl of soup made of smuggled potatoes; she offered me her blanket. She kept lamenting my misfortune, saying over and over, "Ai, ai, why did you go wandering around those wires? I asked you never to go there."

They often drove Mrs. Prajsowa away with prods and beatings. But she, that tall and fine-looking woman, radiant with maternal goodness and nobility, endured the brutality of the room overseers in silence, meekly, with bowed head, but she kept coming back to the sick bay. How grateful I was to her! How ashamed I was, and how I regretted not heeding her warnings! Mrs. Prajsowa laundered my blood-stained clothing; it awaited my return to the hut.

My comrades in the potato labor gang decided to bribe a sick-bay orderly with cigarettes to discharge me as soon as possible; I found this out when I was unexpectedly summoned to her little room, where I saw Madzia, one of my friends from the labor gang. The very sight of Madzia, a likable girl, slender as a young pine tree, with her bright face and lively looks, filled me with comfort. However, I was not discharged from the sick bay; not because the bribe for the room orderly (a Jewish woman from Hungary, and an unusually bad person) proved too small, but because my condition was worse than my comrades and the room orderly supposed. When—in the presence of the room orderly—a nurse took off the paper bandage which Rozka had obtained for me by crying on January 1, I felt such terrible pains around my shoulder blade that I almost jumped out of my skin and uttered a loud shriek. The nurse was surprised and examined my wounds closely: the bullet proved to be still lodged in my shoulder. There could be no question of discharging me from the hospital . . .

An SS doctor was expected to make an inspection of the hospital any day—this was the head doctor of the sick bay, who had

not made an appearance here for a very long time. I was afraid
that when this doctor saw my useless arm and learned I had a
bullet in my shoulder, he would shoot me, as had been the practice for years.

Finally he arrived. Our block overseer had been bustling
around the hut since early morning. She screamed and hit people,
scolding the room orderlies for untidiness in the block and on the
beds. The room orderlies hastily tried to make up the many ar-
rears, quarreled with one another and of course vented their rage
on the patients.

Then the head doctor stepped into our hut. The block overseer,
stiffly erect, walked beside him as he passed around, making
remarks and comments to her on the way from one patient to the
next, and bed to bed. At one moment he pointed to my bed, and
asked what was the matter with me. I need not describe the terror
with which I saw him approaching, stern and supercilious. He
listened to the block orderly's explanation without interrupting
her. I gazed into his face with the utmost tension. What looked
like a faint glimmer of curiosity appeared on it. He ordered the
bandage taken off, and had me moved to the center of the hut,
nearer the light, and here, as he inspected my wounds, he inquired about the circumstances of the injury. I described what
had happened in my own way, half in German, half in Yiddish,
as when I had explained to Hössler at the "selection" why I could
not part from Hela. And now, as then, I realized that my fear of
this "Superman" had evaporated. He heard me out, then repri-
manded the block overseer for letting me lie so long in dirty linen
with dried blood on my body. I could hardly believe my own
ears. But the act of that sentry did not make the doctor indignant;
nor did my suffering move him in the least.

The block overseer cringed, casting me looks full of hate that
boded revenge. The doctor told her sharply to wash me, change
my linen and send me to the hospital in the men's camp at once,
where they would remove the bullet in the operating theater.
Announcing this, the doctor left the sick bay. In spite of everything I was worried; one Nazi inspects the sick in the name of

order and discipline, but another with the same principles in mind puts people to death. Both carry out their functions precisely and faultlessly . . . But in my position I had to consider the changes in the camp brought about by the approach of the battle line (barely three weeks now stood between us and freedom).

The Nazi's orders were carried out scrupulously: washed, wearing a thin silk chemise, shivering with cold on the stretcher, after many vexations, prods and the like (the room and block overseers relished their vengeance), I finally arrived, half-dead, in the men's camp.

The operating theater there generally served the Nazis for various experimental "scientific" operations on prisoners: they brought in children, especially twins, for this purpose. Prisoners were rarely operated on, and those who were, were mainly Aryans. The German *kapo* had me placed on a table in a small waiting room and handed over papers and details regarding me to the orderly on duty, then went away. The orderly, a man in his twenties, made a sympathetic impression. His blue eyes seemed to be looking at me kindly. He certainly guessed I was afraid, and after a while said in German, "The doctor will be here right away—she is a woman, and has a kind heart."

Then he asked what was the matter. His kind voice and the tranquillity of the waiting room acted soothingly. I told him of the New Year incident, mingling Polish words with German; I thought the orderly was a German Jew . . .

"Where are you from?" he suddenly asked in pure Polish, and at once he became more intimate, still more deserving of my confidence.

He explained to me, in some embarrassment, that if he could not make out where a person was from, he usually began speaking in German. Before the doctor came, we managed to tell each other how old we were (he was 24, I 15), and our names (his was Abram).

The doctor, a Russian woman in her forties, seemed much less likable than I had expected. She spoke German badly, with a Russian accent. She was brisk and matter-of-fact, asked me a number of brief questions about the incident, examined me, then made the same diagnosis as the SS doctor: the bullet must be removed from my shoulder at once, then the severed nerve must be rejoined. Two operations! Seeing my depression, the Russian woman smiled for the first time: it will not hurt, she assured me, and then your recovery will be fast . . .

"Shall I be able to move my hand as before?" I ventured to ask.

The doctor sighed: first it would have to undergo special massage, radiation . . . "In Auschwitz?" I thought in despair. I kept looking at her imploringly, but she told me nothing more.

Pain and fever numbed my despair. I stopped wondering what would happen to my hand. I was afraid of more definite, closer danger. This time—the operations.

In the small room where the orderly placed me, women who were recovering from operations were lying singly on bunks: they were Aryans. It was comparatively clean and cozy for a camp hospital. The atmosphere was tranquil and pleasant enough, compared with the noise and crowds in the blocks. The two nurses, elderly Polish women, did not swear at or humiliate the patients. They behaved towards us with something like respect, rarely met with in the camp, although they did not show us any affection or special concern. They were not bad-tempered, but neither were they kind. They carried out their duties mechanically, indifferently, like automatons. But I preferred this to the behavior of the orderlies and nurses in other blocks of the hospital. I thanked God that I had at last found a place in this terrifying Auschwitz where calm and respect for other people prevailed!

The next evening two Jewish doctors came to examine me; one was a surgeon from Lodz, the other came from Greece; it was they who were to operate on me. Abram came in with them. During the examination he stood beside the bed and listened attentively to the doctors' counsel . . . I was very grateful to him for being there, and for his interest in me, almost like that of a brother.

In the view of the doctors, I had been exceptionally lucky: the bullet had passed within a few millimeters of my heart and spine without even injuring a bone . . . It had only injured a nerve called the radialis.

The surgeon stuck a needle in my arm, from the palm upwards. I felt nothing. My hand was dead, as if it did not belong to me. Only pus oozed out of the wounds, and blisters formed around them.

The doctor applied a proper dressing of real bandages, then both left. Abram glanced back at me from the door, and his look embarrassed me, though I did not know why. I turned to the wall, covered my face with the blanket so as not to see anyone, or let anyone see me . . . I heard only the sound of departing footsteps. Then my thoughts began wandering, so many changes, so many new people, and the strange look of the orderly, the operation awaiting me tomorrow . . . I finally sank into a heavy, agitated sleep.

They did not remove the bullet the next day. The pain decreased slightly, but I could do nothing with my hand, not even comb my hair or wash myself. There were washbasins and water taps in the hut, but I unfortunately could not get out of bed. I had a high fever all the time before the operation. Famine was as bad here as in the rest of the camp. The same repulsive turnip soup. It seemed even nastier than usual on account of my fever. I could not endure its smell. I ate only the ration of dry bread and sometimes drank a little chamomile. Yet I felt better here than anywhere else in the camp. I had a little peace here. And something else: the kindness of Abram.

I kept waiting for him to come in, and when he did and our eyes met for an instant, my heart beat with joy; at the same time I was overcome by a kind of shame, as though someone had caught me in a disgraceful act. In addition, I quite soon realized that Abram—though there were no reasons for it—was no longer showing his concern for me as clearly as at first. He joked and talked to the other patients, asked them how they were, or said "Good morning" and "Goodbye" to them. But he did not come near me for the next few days, only glanced fleetingly in the direction of my bed, and then our glances met, which was all I was waiting for.

But I decided not to be the first to speak. I regretted Abram's indifference, especially as his eyes denied it.

I was angry with myself too, for being concerned with such a trifle at a time when I was in danger of being crippled. By this time I knew I would never be able to move my left hand properly. A cripple at the age of 15! Surely that was cause for sorrow? Yet here I was, looking for more troubles for myself! Abram avoiding me? Was that worth worrying about!

I kept telling myself this all the time, but it did not help. When I caught his fleeting glance upon me, I was permeated by a strange, unknown, indescribable sensation.

Abram's behavior even drew the attention of one of the nurses: "What's this, are you angry with the girl, that you avoid her so?" she asked him point-blank, smiling and indicating me.

I thought I would sink into the ground for shame.

"Do I have to talk to all the patients?" snapped Abram crossly.

He said something more, but I was not listening any longer; I hated him then, I was humiliated and angry. I almost burst into tears. But he loitered around the room in embarrassment until he finally went out.

Abram's friend Samek was a barber in the men's camp. I met him on the second day after my arrival in the hospital. His job enabled him to move freely in the camp area, and he frequently visited us. He knew everyone in the block, and came over to me immediately to inquire—in the Auschwitz manner—whether by chance I knew anything of his relatives, friends or acquaintances. My conversation with Samek began, as usual, with questions: where was I from, how, why? Then it turned out that I had been working in the potato labor gang with a girl cousin of Samek, and had lived in the same barracks as she. Samek was glad to hear of his cousin, but I was close to tears, suddenly remembering my comrades, their unsuccessful attempt to get me out of the sick-bay, Mrs. Prajsowa, Rozka and Celina. Something stabbed me in the heart, especially at the recollection of Celina, since it was directly connected with my mishap.

Samek was some years older than Abram, and much taller; he too came from Poland. He had already been in prison a few years, like Abram. They stayed together and made friends, they together "organized" the obtaining of food.

Samek brought me a comb and hand-mirror, and sat down confidentially on my bed: "Look at yourself," he said jokingly, "and comb your hair."

It was easy enough to say "Comb your hair," but how could I, with one hand? For the first time since being injured I saw my face in the mirror, flushed with fever, cheeks burning, eyes glittering. My hair was terribly disheveled, tangled, very thick. I gave him back the mirror, then tried to tidy my hair with my one good hand. Still smiling with tolerant superiority, Samek took the comb from me and, with the air of a grown-up teaching a helpless child how to use a comb, set about combing my hair.

I did not protest, though I was much abashed, and thought Samek was being intrusive. But I was afraid of offending him. At one moment I felt that Samek's hand, slowly and carefully stroking my hair, was trembling. His cheeks were flushed and his eyes unnaturally bright. I was suddenly overcome with disgust for this man. I moved my head several times to shake his hand off, but he pretended not to notice. Then I lost control of my anger, and flung myself on the bed, groaning with pain, for I hurt my shoulder. I pulled the blanket up under my chin and shut my eyes, telling Samek that my wound hurt and I wanted to rest. Only then, willy-nilly, did he rise from the bed and loiter out of the hut, cheerfully saying goodbye to the nurses.

I was pleased to get rid of him and, fastening my eyes upon the door, began daydreaming of Abram.

Sometimes both the men appeared in our hut together. Samek at once came over to me, while Abram fidgeted around the room, talking to patients and nurses louder than usual, glancing furtively in our direction from time to time. Then I would pretend to be enjoying Samek's visit, would say something to him in a lively manner—to be revenged on Abram, and to demonstrate to him that I did not care about his favors, and that other people did not avoid me, on the contrary . . .

One day Samek brought me a plate of hot soup and placed it in triumph on my cupboard. He was certain I would joyfully accept his gift, but my disappointment at the sight of Samek instead of Abram in the hut doorway made me feel hostile towards this soup and its donor . . . Besides, I was furious with Samek for continually treating me with his confidential and self-assured smirk like a little girl, with whom he could do as he chose. He took my resistance and my dislike for his company—because of his own pride—as mere childish sulks and whims. I disliked him still more. So, when he came in with the soup, proud of his supposed generosity, I almost trembled with indignation. That he should start feeding me was the last straw.

As Samek and Abram had been in the camp for some time, in quite good jobs, they had many acquaintances among "influential people" and so managed not badly for themselves, "organizing" better food, clothing, etc. Everyone in the hospital knew this, which was why people tried to keep on good terms with them . . . But I never let myself be guided in friendship by such considerations. On the contrary. And I did not want to take advantage of the help of these men under any circumstances, and vowed never to accept food from them.

"I will not eat your soup," I said rudely, "take it away!"

Samek laughed; he knew how hungry I was. He believed me to be teasing him, wanting him to plead with me and insist. Finally he left the hut, still joking and wishing me "Good appetite!" In the evening he took away the untouched soup, offended. After that he never again tried to offer me anything. He kept visiting, but began to treat me differently, more seriously, with greater reserve and respect.

Abram had witnessed the entire incident over the soup.

One evening, as Samek was talking to me, seated on the edge

of my plank bed, the air-raid siren sounded and the lights in the hut were switched off. Soviet aircraft were circling overhead, rockets and searchlights of the approaching Soviet artillery brightened the darkness from time to time. This had been happening more and more often in the evenings and at night, sometimes by day. Each time hope was renewed in our hearts . . .

When it became dark in the hut, Samek moved closer, while I instantly jumped away to the far side of the bed. I tried to go on talking to him in an unconstrained manner, but he kept silent. "Mind, you will crowd the wall out," was all he said, and began moving over again. Panic gripped me, the more so as the air raid promised to be a long one. What was it I feared from Samek, really? I did not fully understand, but I felt something was not right; Samek kept silent, breathing loudly and brokenly, he was acting differently.

When the alarm went off, Abram had been in an opposite corner of the room. Then, suddenly, as though he instinctively wanted to help me, he moved uncertainly towards my bed. Would he finally come over, or not? On the way he exchanged a few words with one of the patients, stopped by another, and finally halted at our side. He addressed Samek in an everyday manner, as though reluctantly, pointing at something through the window. Both started talking about the war—and Samek spared me his companionship. I suspected Abram of doing this on purpose, and was glad.

Finally, the two doctors who had examined me several times before took me to the operating table; Abram assisted them with the instruments. The surgeon made jokes and tried—as did his colleague from Greece—to soothe me; he anesthetized the swollen and sore places where the bullet was lodged. In reality the operation was not as terrible as I had expected—just as the doctor had assured me. But when they brought me back from the "torture chamber" to my bed, I felt like crying with weakness and agitation. I so longed for someone's affection and care! I dared not appeal to the patients or nurses, they were all somehow dry and indifferent. I turned my face to the wall. After a time I heard someone's cautious, timid footsteps. It was Abram. I pretended to be asleep, I held my breath. Then he leaned over me and whispered: "Are you asleep?"

I did not reply, or even move.

"I know you are not asleep," he said. "Does your arm hurt?"

I clenched my teeth and eyelids, so as not to betray my sudden joy.

"Why don't you speak; are you angry with me? I know you are not asleep."

I turned to him and said defiantly: "Why should I be angry with some orderly or other? Do I have to talk to all the orderlies?"

I felt immediate relief; I had paid him back.

He did not take offense, but got my point, smiled and sat down beside me on the bed. We said nothing, but looked into one another's eyes. Those were marvelous moments. Then Abram put his face close to mine, and I heard something I had already guessed: that he had been avoiding me deliberately, because even after the *kapo* had left us alone in the waiting room, he decided he ought to keep away from me; here, in the camp, there was no place for such feelings . . .

I read in Abram's eyes that this was the whole truth. How could I resent his previous behavior? He let my hand go from his big, strong palm and took a little object, wrapped in cotton wool, from his pocket: "Guess what this is?" he asked, half in joke, half in earnest.

He unwrapped the cotton wool and showed me a small spikey piece of metal covered with congealed blood. It was the bullet they had removed that day from my shoulder. He carefully wrapped it up again and put it back in his pocket: "A souvenir," he whispered, then rose, adding, "Sleep, it will do you good," and left the hut.

I tried in vain to fall asleep. I kept going over and over each one of Abram's words, and each time I relived my joy, a profound joy such as I had never known before. Now the world looked entirely different, it was exciting, attractive, full of beautiful surprises; suffering and unhappiness were less threatening, further away, avoidable. Whenever I closed my eyes the figure of Abram appeared in the doorway; he was of medium height, with a kind and thoughtful face, his expression one of energy and determination which inspired liking and trust. Abram's movements were easy, rapid and decisive. His youthfulness and awareness of his own power shone from him; it was this that attracted me so, and which seemed something unbelievable in this camp. In his presence, even when he was moving about the hut without coming over to me, I felt safe. When he was beside me, sitting and talking, I had the impression that there was no evil from which he would not protect me.

The doctors told me that I would have to undergo another operation to join my severed nerve. They assured me it would not hurt, but they could not undertake it yet because pus blisters had reappeared around the wounds, and we must wait to get rid of them. My stay at the hospital thus promised to be an extended one. When I asked the doctors whether I would be able to move my hand and fingers after the second operation, they replied—as the Russian woman doctor had done: "Probably—but only after massage, exercise, etc." There was no question of any such treatment in Auschwitz, while to be crippled—especially for a Jewish girl—was the equivalent of a death sentence.

Fortunately, it was already January 1945; the frequent Soviet air raids and ever-stronger echoes of the victorious progress of the Soviet forces enabled us to believe that the end of the war was at hand.

Abram was sitting at the foot of my bed, leaning against the wall, telling me in a low and intent voice of his home, his mother, father, and brothers. He came from Krosniewice, a little town near Kutno in Central Poland. Up to the outbreak of the war, he worked in a factory in Lodz. In 1939, he was sent to prison, then

to the concentration camp at Bereza Kartuska, for belonging to
the Communist Party. He had already been through numerous
experiences in very different concentration camps in Germany
and Poland. In Auschwitz he belonged to a secret anti-Fascist
movement. He was well informed of everything that was going
on, far more accurately and better than I. All in all, I seemed an
ignorant little child beside Abram, and was very proud that he
favored me thus with his confidence. Listening to what Abram
had been through, I felt like his accomplice. When he stopped
speaking, I in turn longed to tell him everything about myself . . .

Meanwhile, the lights in the hut had been turned on and off
several times on account of the alarms: then they were turned off
for the night, as always at this time. But nobody prevented
Abram from sitting by me, no one interrupted our talk. No one
was interested in us at that time, nor did anyone interfere. The
other women were asleep in their bunks, the Nazis kept running
to the air-raid shelters, preoccupied only with their own safety,
and the nurses had gone to bed.

Abram went out of the hut for a few minutes, then came back
on tiptoe so as not to awaken anyone: he carried a plate of soup
and two spoons, sat down beside me on the bed and declared
cordially, though in a joking tone: "If you don't want me to
starve to death beside you, take a spoon and eat with me."

There was no help for it, I had to obey despite my principles,
but I tried to eat slowly, and not to take full spoons. Abram
pretended not to notice this, but he lingered over eating. The soup
was excellent; I had not eaten anything so tasty for a long time.
Abram and his friend did their own cooking. In addition, the
plate was a "real" one, wonderful in comparison with the bat-
tered and rusty tin bowl I used, or my canteen!

When Abram pressed my hand on leaving and finally said
"Goodnight," it was beginning to turn gray outside. We hardly
slept during that night and the many following; not until dawn
did Abram leave, and even then I had the impression that we had
not been able to tell one another anything.

From that first night which we talked through, life for me was transformed into a happy, waking dream. Everyone around at once realized we were in love. Apparently they only needed to look at us. Abram took care of me as a mother a sick child, brought me water for washing every morning, managed to get me a piece of scented soap and a bath towel. He often helped me dry myself and comb my hair if time allowed, as it was hard for me to manage with one hand. We rarely talked in the daytime, because he had to work, though he watched over me all the time. He took offense and was cross when I kept on refusing to accept food from him. We had many squabbles on this subject, but finally Abram broke down my scruples with his affection and powers of persuasion.

The nights belonged to us. We spent them in endless talks. Thanks to Abram, everything I said about my life regained its former, or an even greater, glow and charm. Nor did I find it hard to summon up, without the slightest resistance, even tiny and unimportant happenings from my memory. Abram heard them all with equal interest. I talked openly and frankly about everything, just as I really thought and felt.

We talked in whispers to avoid awakening the sleepers. The time passed with incredible speed. Abram leaned his head on his hands, watching and listening without interruption. It was as if I were telling him exceptionally startling and interesting things.

I wanted him to know my mother, father, brothers—at least from what I told him. My friends from the ghetto, too: Piniek Zborowski, who was the most popular boy in the group of my playmates in the yard, but who always teased me, and sometimes made me cry; Marian Kokiet, a funny fat boy who was the best student in our secret study course; little Sewek Zajnderos of Nowolipie Street, who wrote such beautiful verses . . . My girl-friends, especially Erna Zajdman and Elusia Geszychter, daughter of the woman dentist in whose apartment we had lived on Muranowska Street. I liked to sit by the bed of the paralyzed Dr. Geszychter and listen to her amusing little tales of a childhood and youth spent in Russia, and of her medical practice in Poland. I used to like watching Elusia peel soft, frozen potatoes, cutting them very fine and carefully, so nothing was wasted, then place them gravely and intently in a pan of water, set it on the little stove, which was difficult to light (damp wood was cheaper and easier to get). In silence I admired how quickly and skillfully, with what enthusiasm and art she prepared thickening for the soup with a decagram of butter and pinches of the flour she bought daily in a little shop nearby. Before the soup was cooked, Elusia lifted the lid, plunged a spoon in and took a little sip; she relished this long-awaited, one and only meal of the day; she licked the spoon thoroughly, covered the pan in order to start tasting again a moment later. When the soup was ready, Elusia poured out platefuls for her mother and herself; both ate greedily and with such relish that looking at them, I developed a raging appetite, though I was replete and ate tastier food at home . . . The ceremony of cooking and eating never changed, except that the faces of Elusia and Dr. Geszychter became paler and more earthen daily, and their stomachs swelled up with this barren potato soup . . .

The Nazis drowned Erna and her family in a bunker on Nalewki Street during the April insurrection. I almost shared her fate, as I had stayed with them for several days shortly before the siege of the ghetto, and barely managed to return to my mother at the last minute, when we crossed from Nowolipie Street to Mila Street. Elusia, her elder brother and sister went to the *Umschlag* voluntarily, as they were literally starving to death in the ghetto, and the *Judenrat* promised those Jews who volunteered for the journey a loaf of bread and kilogram of jam . . . The Gestapo shot the paralyzed Dr. Geszychter in her bed. Piniek Zborowski and all his family (his uncle was chairman of the house committee at 7 Muranowska Street) perished in Treblinka, to which he was taken after the Mila Street "selection." Piniek's father, who was in his forties, was shot still earlier in a ghetto street by the Nazis; I learned this after the "encirclement" in Mila Street. I met Sewek in Majdanek. Later I heard he was gassed there, along with a large group of children "selected" from our transport.

All these dead, murdered friends, childhood playmates in the Warsaw ghetto, now lived only in my memory.

My wounds slowly healed, but my hand was still powerless. Day by day it grew thinner, leaner and covered with sores. Once I said to Abram: "Why do you need me, what sort of a wife will I make after the war with a hand like this? Would it not have been better if that sentry had killed me?"

Abram tenderly took my injured hand and covered it with kisses: "How can you say that?" he cried angrily. "You don't have the right even to think such a thing."

This helped me. But I was still dreading the second operation, mostly because they would afterwards send me back to the women's camp, and I would have to part from Abram. But I hoped that he and I would greet freedom and a new life together.

Samek continued visiting me. Now he behaved towards me more like a friend or brother. He knew, as did the doctors, that Abram and I were in love. In addition to Samek and the two doctors who were taking care of me (and tried to discourage Abram on the pretext that "this was neither the time nor the place" for affairs of this kind, my health did not permit it, and so on), I was also visited by little twins, boys aged about six or eight; the Nazis were keeping them here for "scientific and experimental" purposes. They were from Czechoslovakia. I grew very fond of them. These orphaned children began treating Abram and me as their parents.

In the end, it turned out that the operation on my severed nerve was not recommended in view of my exhausted condition and the lack of proper medicines and vitamins . . . I was glad of it. I persuaded myself and all my friends that the war would soon be over—after all, the Russians were almost at the camp gate—and when the war was over I would submit to the operation immediately . . .

One morning, some men brought a new patient into our hut. They were accompanied by a Jewish doctor whom I had never before seen in the hospital, but whom the nurses and patients evidently knew well, for they greeted him very cordially when he came in.

"He will come over to me right away," I thought resentfully, "and start asking questions: what's the matter with me, where am I from, how old I am, how long have I been in the camp, whether I happen to know or have seen this, that or the other prisoner in the women's camp." I was used to this sort of questioning. I heard the doctor say to the nurse, "From Warsaw, is she?" and he immediately approached my bed. Ignoring my impudent look, he told me he was from Warsaw too, and he mentioned his name. At the sound of it, I sat up in bed, startled and excited. He was the doctor from Mila Street, who had recommended my brother Marek to his patients in the ghetto, for injections and various medical treatments.

Of course he remembered Marek very well, and what was more he had met Hilek here, in Auschwitz, even lived in the same hut with him, slept in the same bunk.

"Where is Hilek?" I cried, wild with joy.

But the doctor did not answer me directly. He said slowly and prosily that Hilek had worked very hard, grown thin, his health failed him, and that they no longer lived in the same barracks . . .

"What has happened to Hilek, what is he doing now?" I interrupted.

"Now?" the doctor echoed, as though not understanding my impatience; then he suddenly recalled: "He is not here any longer."

What did "not here any longer" mean? That Hilek was no longer in the block? Where had they taken him? The doctor must know, after all, they slept in the same bunk! Surely he could not mean that Hilek was dead?

But the doctor did not deny it. He merely corrected himself in a way that was kindly yet ruthless at the same time, and said that Hilek had not died a natural death, but had been taken to the gas chambers after a "selection."

I stopped listening. I stopped seeing. Perhaps it was the fever, but it seemed to me that Hilek was standing beside me, by my plank bed. Just as I remembered him best: tall, handsome, a 20-year-old boy with thick black hair. He once dressed up as a witch to frighten me when I refused to eat my dinner; he had taken me to school in the mornings, holding me all the time by the back of my coat collar, like a puppy . . . And he often left me in the middle of the street to gape at some new model car . . . so that I was late for lessons through his fault . . . His quiet wedding to Hela, their great love during the ghetto's most tragic days, before its final liquidation . . . His sufferings at the hands of Storm Troopers at the *Umschlag* . . . No water, the torture of thirst . . . Hilek told us then that if he lived through the war, then at the greatest festivities or holidays he would drink all the toasts in plain cold water, not in any wine, even the most costly! Water! He did not live to see the day . . . He is no longer here, and will never drink any toasts.

My face, swollen with crying, alarmed Abram when he came into the hut. His presence acted soothingly upon me, though this time I could not calm myself for a long time.

The Warsaw doctor visited me several times, paid me unpleasant compliments, brought me various tidbits such as ersatz honey, milk, etc. I immediately gave them away to my neighbors. Later he learned of my affection for Abram, and tried to disparage him in my eyes. I was indignant. Abram simply could not bear that doctor.

Three weeks passed from the day when they had brought me on the stretcher to the hospital. The last ten days of January 1945, were at hand. Everyone already knew that in the approaching days, the Nazi torture camp at Auschwitz would disintegrate under Soviet pressure, with a carefully worked-out "extermination plan." How would this happen, what would it be like, how would the ferocious animals act in their death agony? Innumerable rumors, guesses and wild fancies circulated on this topic.

Late one night I was awakened by movements in the hut. I was surprised to find the lights on, while sick reports, documents, identity papers were strewn all over the floor . . . The nurses and patients were scuttling around the hut, talking loudly, agitated and excited. Now and again, people I did not know rushed in, spoke rapidly to the window, then disappeared again. Before I knew what was happening, I saw Abram standing by my bed. He was dressed for a journey. A sinister presentiment seized me.

"They are evacuating the camp," said Abram. "I have to leave with the first transport. They are already assembling for departure . . ."

I lay as though turned to stone. Abram leaned over, kissed my lips, my eyes, my cheeks, then slipped into my hand a little mascot, a tiny pocketknife and a little silver chain with a heart, which he had made out of a cigarette case and engraved with his initials a few days earlier.

When Abram left, I realized I was more alone than ever, and completely helpless on account of my injury. The prisoners were putting on their thickest, warmest things; they whispered to one another in corners . . .

But I still lay there, desperate and helpless, wearing only the thin silk chemise in which they had brought me from the women's camp. What was I to wear? Outside was the January frost; I had no dress, not even any shoes. The Nazis would take away all the living, fit people, but would shoot the sick and helpless on the spot! They had done so in all the other camps they had been forced to evacuate before the approach of the Soviet armies . . . I could not expect any help. Each of my fellow prisoners was entirely absorbed in her own preparations and fear of an uncertain fate. My fate did not concern anybody. I myself lacked the fortitude to think of it. Involuntarily I listened to the louder conversations that were going on, and decided that nobody knew anything. The only certain thing appeared to be the approach of the Red Army.

I did not expect to see Abram again that night. When the door creaked, I did not even look around.

The nurses and patients rushed up to him, bombarded him with questions: had the transport come back? Had they stopped that evacuation? When he replied that he had simply run away from the marching column, they were disappointed and cross. He could not rest—as he later told me—because I had been left without clothes, helpless, thrown on my own resources. He was afraid the SS would kill me.

"Don't worry about me; they are not going to look for escapers now," he concluded.

But I was not at all worried; as long as we were together, nothing bad could happen either to him or me. I had gained the firm conviction that the Russians would liberate us before the Nazis had time to carry out evacuation of the camp.

Abram brought me an entire "traveling outfit," and helped me dress. When I was dressed from top to toe I no longer looked like a sick, injured or crippled person. Abram's blue jacket, thrown over a woolen dress, a man's thick topcoat and long warm trousers which he acquired for me somewhere, and his own leather boots, strong and hobnailed—all masked my thinness very well. He pulled on gloves he had found for me in the operating theater. They were white surgical gloves . . . And he kept telling me to repeat his address in Krosniewice, where we were to meet after the war . . . He wanted me to learn it by heart.

"You won't forget? Tell me you will not forget," he kept asking.

"No," I replied, "never."

From early morning we had been awaiting the order to evacuate the women's camp, but it did not arrive until late afternoon. So I ate my dinner of soup with Abram, and we spent nearly all that day together. Before they took me and the other women

away, Samek came to say goodbye to us. As the time for parting
drew nearer, Abram's depression and agitation increased. He
even gave voice to doubts whether we should ever meet again;
the general belief was that the Nazis were prepared to dispose of
their victims at the last moment . . . On the other hand, I was in
good spirits, calm and self-confident, as always when I was with
Abram.

When I left that little hospital hut to join a group of patients
and local nurses, before marching out to the women's camp,
Abram slipped into the pocket of my topcoat a cube of ersatz
honey, a little bottle of milk and a pack of cigarettes; he and
Samek watched me from the distance. I did not feel bad, nor was
it hard for me to walk down the Auschwitz highroad in the direction of the women's camp in the group of prisoners escorted by
SS. I could feel Abram's loving gaze upon me, the touch of his
hand, his kisses on my face.

Panic, similar to the panic of the night before in the hospital,
prevailed in the camp. The cold, hunger, uneasiness were indescribable. I could not find any of my previous friends, acquaintances or comrades; they had been taken away in earlier
transports, supposedly to somewhere in the heart of Germany.

Evening came. The women's camp (no longer B II b) bordered
on the electrified barbed wire of the men's camp. Wandering
alone in a crowd of unknown, agitated and excited prisoners,
stumbling in the snow, I dragged myself almost half-conscious,
to these wires, in the hope that one of the men would send my
greetings to Abram, or call him over for a moment.

When I was in the vicinity of the hospital barracks, terrifying
whistles from all sides resounded for the evening roll call or
assembly. I wanted to turn back, when I saw someone's impatient hands wrenching at the frame of a frozen window of a hut
close to the barbed wire. I did not even realize that it was the

barracks in which I had been a patient . . . I stood there uncertainly, waiting, not knowing why, though it was risky. Then the window opened wide, out jumped Abram, he ran swiftly to the fence and called in my direction through the wires, so that I heard him despite all the whistling: "Keep going! Don't forget! Don't forget!" and he waved his hand, then ran full-tilt round the barracks.

I never saw him again . . .

But that same evening, before the huge column moved off, an unknown woman prisoner sought me out, asking everyone for "Halina with an injured hand." I gratefully and tenderly accepted from her a half loaf of bread, the last proof of Abram's concern.

It was late at night when they took us away from Auschwitz.* Red and yellow tongues of flame, and blue clouds of smoke stood out against the white background of snow; the Hitlerites were burning the evidence of their crimes. For the march we received a can of very salty preserved meat and half a loaf of bread.

We had been waiting so many months, weeks, days for the Russians to come—but now that they were approaching, now that the sounds of battle were so close, we were forced to leave.

As before, the Nazis herded us along with brutality and cruelty. We marched all that night and day, and several following days and nights, without respite. Anyone whose strength ebbed, fell; anyone who slowed down was shot. We were forbidden to look around. They left behind corpses of men and women with their skulls shot in, lying on the icy road. Time and again, the sound of a shot pierced the air. We trudged past deserted spots, fields, villages, little towns. Flight was almost impossible, because we were guarded by Storm Troopers armed from top to toe, and also because our striped prison uniform and camp clothing with marks in oil paint would have betrayed us at once . . . The area was inhabited mainly by *Volksdeutsche,* or by Polish people who were scared to death and brutally terrorized by the Nazis.

---

*Evacuation of the Auschwitz concentration camp was ordered on January 17, 1945; on January 18, a total of 22,465 men and women left the camp; on the following day around 3,530 left. Evacuated by the SS, the camp was taken by the Soviet forces on January 22.—Ed.

I could no longer feel my feet for cold and exhaustion. I kept slipping, and could hardly drag along Abram's hobnailed boots. As a result of my long stay in the hospital, I had gotten out of the practice of walking. I did not know any of the women walking beside me, and no one came to my aid. I fell more and more behind, and soon found myself in the next to last ranks of the column. Slowly I began losing all awareness of reality. The frost, sleepiness and weakness acted like a narcotic. The last ranks did not have a moment's respite, for they constantly had to keep up with those in front, leveling out the distance. I drank the milk Abram had given me, but the milk only intensified my thirst. From time to time I stooped with difficulty to gather a little snow; I rubbed my face with it, put it in my mouth—anything, so as not to fall asleep forever.

No end to this infernal march was in sight. They drove us on, continually promising a halt, a rest. Another mile, they said—a few more steps. We had nothing to eat or drink but snow. The frost increased, the road became as smooth and slippery as glass; acrobatic feats were necessary so as not to twist one's ankle, especially in my hobnailed boots. At one point, my supplies of energy gave out, and so did my capacity for controlling my muscles. I felt I could not take another step. At the same moment, I heard a familiar voice calling in German: "Hey, you, what are you doing here?" Someone's strong arm took mine. I did not immediately look at the face of the woman who had saved me. When I came to, I was not able at first to remember where I had seen that red face before. Not until I saw her pale blue eyes, cordial and sympathetic, did my doubts vanish; it was Alvira! The *kapo* from the potato labor gang. She was curious to know what had happened to me. Leaning my whole weight upon her, I told her everything that had occurred. She drew me to her still more strongly, and almost staggered under my weight. She herself was slender and quite frail, ailing, wiping the sweat from her forehead, but she did not leave me, and suffered with me almost all that day, until late evening, when the SS finally allowed us a halt. Next day we walked together until noon, when I happened to meet Celina and a whole crowd of my friends from Auschwitz, during a very brief halt in some town or other; Alvira handed me over to Celina. I never saw Alvira again. I do not know what became of her. To a large degree I owe her my life—had it not been for her, I would have been shot by the SS during that march.

From now on, Celina was with me all the time, until the end of the war. I no longer felt alone, strange and useless to anyone in that huge crowd of herded prisoners. By myself I could not have coped with the march, nor later, in the camps in Germany. I could not even have opened the can of meat obtained in Auschwitz, nor the ersatz honey, which melted in the pocket of my topcoat, and Celina had to cut it out with a little knife borrowed from some woman or other. Once again she and I ate together, sharing bread, honey, and preserved meat. Celina surreptitiously took the cigarettes—Abram's present—from me, lest the SS see, and smoked them all, with her friends. I was a little vexed with her for such recklessness, and thought we should have kept them, as they would be useful to barter for food in the camp where they would assuredly shut us up . . . But I did not say so, for fear that Celina would take offense and I would be alone again.

The further we were from Auschwitz, the more often the SS allowed us to rest, usually in roadside stables where we could hardly find room to move; quarrels and fights broke out in the inconceivable crowding . . . Many women died of exhaustion, others began discarding heavier garments, even throwing away the cans of meat, to make the march easier. Although Celina was very tired, she picked up cast-off food from the road, and stowed it in her bag; she once found a handful of sugar in a handkerchief . . .

At the end of our endurance, we finally reached the place where open freight cars were awaiting us; packed tight, we set off for the remainder of the journey. This journey—my third—differed from the previous ones in that now we had air to breathe, but we suffered agonies of cold. The train dragged along, slowed and stopped in sidings to let pass military trains retreating from the Eastern front, transports with evacuated German civilians. How very different Hitler's soldiers looked now, compared to those I had seen in 1939, arrogant, self-assured, invading the ruins of Warsaw!

Now the cans of meat and the bread Celina had collected saved us from starvation. For it was not until we were in the freight car that hunger began making itself felt. Earlier, during the march, sleepless, breathless, exhausted—we did not feel hungry at all, we wanted nothing but a drink of water and to rest a while.

But our frugal supplies soon came to an end . . . Then, whenever they allowed us to get out and relieve ourselves around the freight cars, we would collect snow in empty meat cans. As long as the sugar in our handkerchief lasted, Celina sprinkled it with snow and we found this unusual ice cream delicious.

Although real fights took place in the freight car for every inch of space, the two armed sentries arranged a comfortable bed for themselves; we were not allowed to move in that direction under pain of being shot. They took some Jewish woman or other as companion. She lay beside one or the other of them by day and night. The other women gazed at her with hatred and contempt, but they envied her that space on the floor. She, pleased with her privileges, looked down on us.

Early one morning the train stopped at a railroad station, and the unloading of the "goods" began. We read the name *Ravensbrück* in large black letters: we had heard of the terrible conditions in this camp at Auschwitz. Now we were to experience them ourselves . . .

All day long we waited in an empty space behind barbed wire, until the Hitlerites found us accommodation. Late that evening they herded us into a shed where we fell, half-conscious with exhaustion, on the dirty muddy ground, and sank into deep sleep. The next day we obtained a little watery camp soup; people spilled it over themselves in the pushing, while Ravensbrück *kapos* and "important" people from Auschwitz who sought to gain power here, too, snatched utensils away from the starving women, hit us over the heads and shoulders. To lack a bowl in the camp was almost equivalent to death by starvation.

Towards evening, roll call was held in front of the shed. They counted us systematically several times, after which they ordered us, threatening dire punishment, to hand over all jewelry, knives, forks, spoons—absolutely everything we had brought from Auschwitz. A search! However, we had already been warned. I was trembling with fright, though I had nothing of any value on me; all the same, I regretted having the chain, little heart and the penknife-mascot Abram had given me before we parted. Was it worth risking my life for such trifles? Would not Abram have advised me instantly to dispose of the things, had he known I might perish on account of them? Yet I hesitated, so difficult was it to decide.

"Better hand them over," Celina advised in a whisper.

I was about to throw my souvenirs on the heap growing on the ground before us, when I thought that perhaps I would never see Abram again, and I did not move. After all, they wanted genuine jewelry, gold, precious stones—I tried to convince myself and Celina, agitated by the sight of the Storm Troopers prowling around . . .

After the search and roll call, the SS divided us into groups, then herded us to the various blocks. Celina and I, along with a crowd of some hundreds, were directed to the "disciplinary block," as there was still a little space there; we spent some ten days and nights on the floor of this small hut, locked in and separated from the remainder of the camp. The "permanent" tenants of the *Strafblok*—murderers, prostitutes, scum of the underworld—ill-treated us incessantly, drenching us with buckets of dirty water, cursing and abusing us; they stole our frugal camp rations of food. In the crowding, it was hard to protect ourselves from being pushed and shoved, and in addition lice crept under my bandages and penetrated my festering wounds. Lying on the dirty floor, trampled underfoot, I returned in imagination to the hospital barracks at Auschwitz. Now it appeared a paradise, something almost unreal, and soon these memories ceased to move me.

Outside on the roof the snow was melting, the water poured
noisily down the gutters, cornices and walls. It was February.
People were already saying that Soviet and Anglo-American
troops had entered the Reich. While awaiting their final victory,
we spent long days delousing ourselves, fighting and quarreling
over a scrap of floor space. We were given food—watery soup—
once a day: irregularly, once in several days, a piece of bread
(one fifth of a loaf). They let us out once a day for roll call, and
sometimes during the day a few of us managed to get outdoors to
relieve ourselves. However, they did not make us work . . .

One sunny afternoon in mid-February, a roll call was unexpectedly taken in the yard; the SS counted us, then took some
women, in pairs, outside, beyond the walls.

The further we went from the *Strafblok,* the lighter my head
became. Under SS escort, they loaded us at the railroad station
into a train—a passenger train! Each couple obtained a whole
loaf and piece of sausage. The doors slammed and the train
moved off, whistling shrilly, as though indignant that it, a re-
spectable German passenger train, was having to carry Jewish
women . . .

Where to now?

But when it came to the point, we did not care. The great thing
was that we each had bread; a whole, uncut loaf! Proof they were
not herding us to death. And we could eat our fill. Surprised and
delighted, we sat on benches in the capacious, light and warmed
compartments. Outside the windows—splendid, wide windows—
moved the landscape . . . Only the lice, encouraged by the pleasant warmth, started attacking us with renewed vigor. Had it not
been for them, we would have been traveling like genuine pas-
sengers in a passenger train.

The train often stopped at various stations for shorter or longer
periods. We furtively observed the German world through the windows, watched the people, and saw how Germans behaved in their
Fatherland . . . Neat farms, well-kept manor houses, pretty houses,
beautiful scenery, people at work, life proceeding calmly . . . Nothing here spoke of the German barbarity we knew from the ghetto

and camps! Yet here too, when we looked more closely at their life, we could sense an atmosphere of tension, their fear of expected defeat. Because of the air raids, towns and houses in the country were blacked out. Silent groups of people stood at the railroad stations. The walls of houses and buildings were plastered with notices warning citizens of the Reich to beware of the Red Enemy: "The Red Enemy is approaching. The Enemy will be revenged!" they cried hysterically. These notices pleased us, and we prayed fervently that the "red enemy," our saviors, would arrive as soon as possible.

Towards morning we reached the little town of Neustadt-Glewe. A large, round clock in the railroad station showed the hour of five. It was a clean little town, sleeping peacefully at this hour, and it made a favorable impression.

The SS herded us down quiet roads amidst woods, under a large escort. The camp at Neustadt had presumably been established only recently, as we had never heard of it. Perhaps it lacked the notoriety of Auschwitz, Majdanek, Ravensbrück and Buchenwald, but it soon proved no less terrible.

It was not large, and did not look threatening at first sight. The few wooden barracks were occupied by Polish women, brought here after the Warsaw insurrection, and Ukrainian women. They worked many hours a day in a nearby aircraft factory, concealed in the woods. Not far from the camp was an airfield, with huts in which German airmen were billeted opposite the camp's barbed wire. When we entered the camp area, the SS went away, leaving us along the walls of the empty, locked huts; our surprise at there being no introductory registration or search began changing into uneasiness as our wait lasted until evening. Then the permanent residents of the camp came back from work. After roll call they received their usual food ration: one-fifth of a loaf, and some coffee (a bitter, dark fluid), then were dismissed into the barracks to rest and eat in their bunks. But we received nothing to eat, neither that day nor during the following days . . . Obviously the camp kitchen and supply department were not prepared for such a large transport of prisoners! The "local" inhabitants of the

camp, the Polish women deported here after the Warsaw insurrection, often shared their bread, soup or coffee with us, though
they were dying of starvation themselves. But there were less of
them than of us and besides, they were working in a factory, so
they had to keep up their strength.

We slept on narrow, rotten and shaky bunks, two to each: a
Storm Trooper locked the hut and turned off the light. The windows were closely sealed by shutters. That black, overcrowded
hell echoed and thundered with quarrels and shouting. Buckets
for excrement stood in a little passage by the exit. There were not
enough. By dawn, the whole floor was awash with urine and
feces. We carried the filth about the hut on our feet; the stench
made people faint. Trips to the buckets in that unbelievable
crowd and the closely packed bunks were accompanied by the
cursing of women we woke. Sometimes the old bunks fell apart
with a bang, injuring the sleepers.

Nights in Neustadt were an inferno, but days were no better.
After the many-hour roll call before dawn, some of the former
Auschwitz prisoners were taken away to perform various kinds
of work, while some remained in the camp. Torture by hunger
started. We drank nothing but water, creeping for it in washrooms that were guarded by women sentries armed with sticks—
our fellow prisoners who volunteered for the work. If by chance
some lucky woman managed to steal a turnip or beetroot from a pile
of vegetables near the camp kitchen, envy awoke in our hearts,
even though the Hitlerites punished us severely—sometimes by
death—for stealing. Many women lost their lives here for a
stolen beetroot or turnip. We were told to be patient, until the
additional kitchens and appropriate utensils arrived.

For the time being we were collapsing from hunger. The
weaker of us died during roll calls, in the huts, outdoors. I could
not stand on my feet, and dragged myself with difficulty up and
down from the upper berth. To make matters worse, Celina
caught cold and had a fever, but I could not help her in any way.
I could only stroke her head, put my hand to her fevered brow,
and comfort her with words. But even talking required more and

more effort. There was a roaring noise in my head, black dots whirled before my eyes, the least movement made my heart thump heavily. I had convulsions, there was such an agonizing pain in my stomach that I could get to sleep neither by day nor night. I had never before suffered such torment. I had not even imagined that it existed. During the ten days of this monstrous famine we were not always allowed to lie on our bunks; time and again a *kapo* rushed in and forced us to perform various tasks with her whip or stick: cleaning, carrying packages about, and so on . . . Sometimes then I would think of religious fasts, especially those connected with the holiday of Yom Kippur, when people voluntarily honor God by fasting. But I vowed that if I survived the war and had something to eat, I would never make myself fast. Vowing this, I deliberately and with relish declared revenge on that God we had believed in at the home of my parents, but who had deserted us all in our misery and who, here in the Nazi extermination camps, had proved to be an invention of fraudulent priests who ordered us to love and respect Him, and fear His justice!

I still do not know how I survived to the tenth day of the fast; finally they gave each of us a quarter-liter of hot, thin and un-salted soup with bits of turnip and potato peelings floating in it. On the evening of the same day we received one fifth of a loaf. What good fortune! At least, for those who had survived. I ate my ration of bread immediately. I never learned how to econo-mize, or keep food in my bag . . . I jeered spitefully at those who cut their bread into paper-thin, almost transparent slices, and ate them slowly, by installments, a slice every few hours, like a dose of life-preserving medicine . . . I laughed when these provident women were robbed, later in the night!

I was in no danger of being robbed. My everlastingly hungry stomach was the safest hiding place.

After a while, the SS assigned a group of us former Auschwitz prisoners to work in the aircraft factory; we stayed in the same block, and were able to obtain the same food rations as before. The rest of the prisoners were transferred to other huts where conditions were worse in every respect: for instance, a loaf was distributed not among five persons, but among ten.

I hid my useless hand in the big sleeve of my man's topcoat, and Celina and I found ourselves among those working. For twelve hours, during either the day or the night shift, I inserted screws into parts of aircraft. I did it all with my right hand, managing for myself fairly well, using my left hand for holding the material. At noon we obtained a half-liter of good thick soup—but it was the only and basic meal of the day.

The deafening roar and noise of the machines, the enormous gloomy workshops, the merciless cold of the factory walls, the strict discipline and labor beyond our strength in neverending fear of the foremen who, with a crowd of youths from the *Hitlerjugend*, drove us on without respite, continually increasing the standards of productivity, hiding my injury from them—these were not easy to bear. The air-raid alarms, during which the Nazi specialists, foremen and our overseers crowded into the shelters, gave us some respite. The air-raids came more and more often, and lasted longer. But we were seized by an ever-increasing fear that we might die by bombs intended for our enemies.

The previous Auschwitz "elite," some ex–block overseers and a former *Lagerkapo* (a woman *Volksdeutsch*) occupied several bunks with the best straw mattresses and blankets in the barracks. In Neustadt they did not perform such "important" functions as in Auschwitz, but they had certain privileges here too; they did not have to work, they obtained more soup, and the thickest at that, they could go to the washrooms and toilets when they chose. Although they no longer ruled us, they found plenty of opportunities to ill-treat and torture us with impunity. So they continued to be dangerous and threatening to us Jewish prisoners.

"Calendar" spring had come to the world; its mild, warmish breath penetrated into the camp too. Along with it came fresh news of victories over fascism. The names of German towns and localities captured by the Red Army were spoken of, people talked of fighting near Berlin, of the Germans' panic-stricken flight . . .

Work in the aircraft factory became impossible for me any longer. "I don't care if it is a block with no bunks, one-tenth of a loaf, watery soup, but not this terrible suffering in the factory," I thought.

One day I did not go to work; they sent a prisoner from the non-working block, and transferred me to her place. Celina remained in the factory some weeks longer. Then she too had to stop working, from exhaustion.

In Auschwitz, a similar block of "non-workers" would long since have ceased to exist. Its inhabitants would have been taken to the gas chambers. However, there were no crematoria in Neustadt-Glewe; "selections" were not held—the prisoners simply died of hunger, disease, starvation. Sometimes they were shot "as an example" if they developed a taste for turnips or beetroots from the kitchen . . .

A very narrow corridor ran along the block, with small rooms holding only two or three army beds on both sides; the toilets and washroom were in the center; in a word, it was a hut with "conveniences" . . . But I could not at any price find myself a regular sleeping place in any of the little rooms. There were no bunks. Every square inch of floor, every cubic inch of air was already "allotted." Every newcomer inspired dislike, even hatred, in the tenants of the barracks who were already there. When I tried to get into one of the rooms, I was thrown out, scratched and kicked by the wooden clogs of Auschwitz. I was all bruises. The barracks became somewhat less crowded during the daytime, when a number of women were distributed throughout the camp, or went voluntarily to work in the hope of acquiring a piece of turnip, a potato or beetroot in the kitchen area. But when the time came for distributing soup and bread, the barracks once again turned into a crowded beehive.

I and the others who were too feeble to fight for a place in the rooms had to spend the nights in the passage. I lay on the dirty floor, which was covered with excrement overflowing from the blocked-up lavatories. I leaned against a wall without even taking off my topcoat, merely removing my shoes, which I stowed, camp-fashion, under my head. Frequently, women coming or going to the lavatories jogged or trampled on me. Fortunately they were in stockings, but even their stockings, stinking and soaked with excrement, left wet and hideous traces on my face and arms. I loathed myself, I felt like a crushed, repulsive worm! What would my mother have said, had she lived to see her child so ill-treated? I wept silently out of sheer despair and humiliation. Surely I had never before been so helpless in the face of indignity. Towards morning, when the Storm Trooper unlocked the hut door, the throng of pushing women flung me outdoors like a bundle of rags. It was wet, dark and cold in the big roll call area, but at least I could breathe fresh air. Immediately afterwards my terrible hunger pangs started.

When Celina stopped working in the factory and was transferred to a neighboring hut for "unproductive" prisoners, my situation during the day greatly improved. Celina at once found herself a "good" place on the floor—there were no bunks—near a window. The room was occupied by former Auschwitz "celebrities"—ex–block overseers and ex-*kapos;* it was at least possible to move around in comparative freedom.

So every day after roll call I went to visit Celina and we sat through the day together, until evening; I often slept with my head on her lap, as I had done once on my mother's lap. We passed the time mostly in delousing ourselves and killing the lice; they crept freely over the walls and floor. Prisoners told one another of their past lives when they were free and when they were in camps. They commented on political news and rumors, told their dreams, predictions and omens. I confided in Celina my love for Abram; I could not resist the inner need I felt to talk about him. I believed then that we would meet again. I couldn't foresee that before I was liberated from the hands of our murderers, Abram would regain his liberty and shortly thereafter would die of typhus.

Celina was now wearing the jacket Abram gave me before leaving Auschwitz. Her own clothing was already very ragged. Celina's friendship was my only support here. Celina helped me by pushing a way through the camp crowds, protecting me in lines for food rations, combing my hair with a thick comb she got in exchange for some bread. She took great care to see that lice did not get into my hair . . . Sometimes we both crept into the washroom, where we bathed from head to toe. Celina knew how to overcome obstacles in the camp which I thought were insurmountable. She did not ponder over things, she had fewer scruples, less reluctance than I in the struggle for food. Celina was always able to wheedle something from one of her Auschwitz friends who had a job in the kitchen, and whom I knew from the Mila Street bunker—a little soup or raw vegetables, even a bit of ersatz coffee. But I avoided this woman for I was ashamed of my misery and did not want her to read my face, that I was hungry and was appealing to her pity. Bread was not distributed during roll call, but groups of ten women were counted off inside the hut, and they were given one whole loaf between them. The prisoners shared the loaf themselves, quarreling and fighting. Rations for each were measured by a piece of string, carefully and attentively, before the loaf was sliced into ten very minute portions . . . Sometimes the loaf was moldy in places. To which of the ten famished women would this inedible slice fall?

We often bartered one or two portions of bread for a turnip. True, the turnip was not as tasty or desirable as bread, but there was a good deal more of it. Celina cut it into thin slices, spread margarine on them. From time to time we acquired a lump of this grease, the size of a sugarcube—and sprinkled the "sandwiches" with "coffee." We regaled ourselves with this tidbit, vowing never to forget it when the war was over and we were free. Somehow I never could bring myself to swallow raw potatoes, even during the periods of greatest famine—they just would not go down my throat.

Celina took charge of our provisions. She liked planning how much and when we should eat. She divided the ration between herself and me, putting the rest away in her bag and swearing solemnly not to touch it before the appointed time. But after a few minutes she would peep greedily into the bag and meekly cancel her previous decision . . . And I always agreed to this joyfully.

The days grew longer, April was ending . . . None of the predicted dates had brought us liberty yet. The prophetic dreams and omens supposed to mark the end of our slavery had not come to pass. Our superstition had betrayed us, while famine continued to grip our intestines, the lice devouring us and our strength ebbing. Savage Nazi discipline ruled the camp; the Storm Troopers had not changed a bit. I thought with envy of those who had remained in Auschwitz—they were probably already free.

Shortly before our liberation, the Nazis distributed food packages which the International Red Cross had long ago sent for us prisoners. One cardboard package to five women. They contained wonderful things: canned meat, powdered milk, butter, genuine coffee and so on. An incredible bustle prevailed in the camp, with people running about, squabbling, bartering, stealing, sharing the treasures, fights . . . Nor did this pass without people wondering and philosophically speculating what this sudden SS favor could mean.

Celina and I devoured our share of the package that same day, as well as the camp bread and soup. All we needed to complete the bliss was water, to moisten our throats, dry from the banquet. But the Red Cross had failed to include water in their packages—not foreseeing that even water would be short in the Nazi camps. In the evening I parted from Celina as usual to go back to my hut for the night, really replete for the first time in many months. I was no longer sleeping in the passage near the lavatory, but on the floor in one of the rooms, covered with a blanket. A group of Polish women I met by chance had taken me in. When I told them of my life in the ghetto and camps, they were touched and henceforth took good care of me. That night, on account of what had happened, or perhaps as a result of the coffee beans from the Red Cross package—I could not close my eyes.

After the feast which we owed to the Red Cross, hunger returned to torment us still more during the following days; our appetites were sharpened by recalling the tidbits—the mere recollection caused our stomachs to contract, and saliva to flow into our mouths.

Celina decided to sell Abram's jacket to a girl working in the kitchen, for a bowl of soup. Everyone liked that blue jacket; it often attracted the attention of those who were not hungry and not obsessed with the thought of food. The offer was tempting, but from the start I did not even want to hear of it. We would eat the soup within five minutes and be hungry again; to me the jacket was a valuable souvenir. "Besides," I urged Celina, "you have to wear something." But she tried to persuade me that this was no time for sentiment, that the weather was getting warmer and she could do without the jacket. In the end I gave way, overcome with hunger. I sat down behind the barracks; Celina hurried to the kitchen and came back with a concealed bowl of thick, hot soup. We ate it with two spoons borrowed especially for the purpose—taking a spoonful by turn—trembling with fear lest any of the starving women see us. The bottom of the bowl very soon appeared. Celina left the licking of the bowl to me, as a reward for losing the jacket. But of course the soup did not by any means satisfy us.

It was one of the last days in April. I was lying exhausted on the floor beside Celina, in her hut, when the blazing rockets that announced an air raid began flaring. Recently the Hitlerites had stopped using the warning sirens. Instead they signaled "our" air raids by rockets. The Storm Troopers ran in their usual confusion to the shelters. We, as always, did not move. Then a woman at the window noticed white sheets of paper floating lazily down, like snowflakes, dropped from the Soviet airplanes. Leaflets! They fell gently on the hut roofs, on the ground beyond the camp wires, in the area occupied by German airmen. When the alarm ended, we ran outdoors excitedly. Through the fence we could see airmen picking up and reading the leaflets in gloomy silence. The Storm Troopers ran all over the camp, shouting furiously that no one was to dare touch these leaflets on pain of death. But some women had already managed to pick up and hide a few, and the news immediately spread around the camp that it was an ultimatum to the Nazis, written in several languages. The ultimatum stated that if the Germans in this region did not lay down their arms within the next three days, the entire area would be totally bombed and razed to the ground . . .

Three days! This meant until May 2. Either freedom or we would perish along with our executioners. We had no doubt whatsoever that the threat contained in the ultimatum would be carried out.

Our fate was to be decided within three days!

Nothing altered in the camp. The same roll calls morning and evening, the counting, the marches out to work, distribution of soup and moldy bread, locking the huts and unlocking them at dawn. Each night I lay down to sleep with the hope that in the morning the hated Storm Trooper would not unlock the door of the hut, that he would not herd us out with blows and curses. But every day he appeared punctually to do his duty . . . We lived in a state of intense excitement, agitated, terrified; once we believed that the Nazis were quietly moving out, but we were driven to distraction by the thought they would blow the entire camp up. Who knew what might come into their heads in the last hours before final defeat? We awaited May 2 with fear and impatience.

It proved a rainy, cloudy day, reminiscent of fall. They kept us at roll call much longer than usual. Meanwhile it became completely light. The Storm Troopers and overseers carried out their usual functions, preserving a stiff and threatening attitude, but they did not give the order for work. What was happening? Do not dismiss! Stay where you are!—these were the orders repeated time after time. Could it be that they were wondering what to do with us? To send us to work or not? Finally everyone without exception was ordered back into the huts. Here we were again locked in. This was something out of the ordinary; we were never locked in the huts during the day.

Just as long as they do not shoot us here, we said to each other lying on the ground without thinking any more of hunger or lice. Despite the strict orders, a few daring women peeped furtively out of the windows.

At first, nothing happened in the camp to confirm our hopes or fears. Not until later, around noon, did large trucks loaded with food drive in (it soon turned out that the Nazis had brought the food from Ravensbrück, which was already in Soviet hands). The Storm Troopers took some dozen of the stronger women, mostly Ukrainians, to unload the products. The food was carried into the stores of our camp, near the kitchen. The nervous tension increased still more when, in the afternoon, we noticed the German overseers and the SS in civilian clothes. Meanwhile soup was being distributed in some of the huts. But they did not take any soup kettles to other blocks.

The confusion was intensified. Bolder and more enterprising prisoners began jumping out of the hut windows and joining the women unloading food at the stores; they snatched whole packages, which they threw to their friends through the hut windows . . . Or they hid food under their skirts and fled back to the huts. The Nazis saw this going on, but no one fired a shot, which encouraged the rest of the women.

I was standing all the time by a wall, close to the window, watching in amazement the indescribable confusion around the trucks and admiring the bold actions of our women. The camp commandant himself, the terror of the entire camp, master of life and death, appeared in the center of the roll call area. He was dead drunk. He staggered ludicrously, and began to make a speech, even though he could hardly stand upright—he soothed us concerning the change in situation which was not their "fault," and almost apologized for not being able to take us somewhere further away from the approaching "enemy." Within a few hours, the "enemy" would enter Neustadt-Glewe and they, the Germans, would have to retreat and leave us behind, alas. "Try and keep calm, for panic at such times is dangerous," he thoughtfully advised us. "You need not fight over the food, there are enough supplies in the kitchen stores . . . There are also Red Cross packages and other food, enough for everyone; there is clothing too. The most important thing is to maintain order. Maintain order!" he shouted hoarsely.

Nobody was listening. As he spoke of the approaching enemy, a feeling of freedom overwhelmed everyone. But as long as the commandant stood yelling into the loudspeaker, as long as Storm Troopers and overseers were roaming around the camp—even though they were now in civilian clothes—I could not believe this was freedom!

Unbelievable chaos and pushing was going on in front of the kitchen. Women trampled each other underfoot, women in the crowd who wanted to get into the food stores were pushed and shoved. The formidable Storm Trooper who daily locked and unlocked the huts, the same Storm Trooper before whom we had trembled with fear, was now mildly trying to persuade prisoners not to cause such confusion: *"Bitte schön, liebe Frauen, gehen sie hinein,"* he said, politely inviting them into the hut. No one paid any attention to his airs and graces. He was pushed contemptuously aside like some bothersome intruder. This scene was capable of providing a great deal of satisfaction.

Dusk was falling when the Nazis got into a truck, and—after delivering a final salvo into the crowd at the store—they departed, leaving the camp gate open. They had time to kill one woman and wound several others.

I did not stir from my place at the window. I had been standing there almost since morning, and although I could plainly see everything, I felt no particular joy or emotion. I was simply curious to see what would happen next.

Celina had jumped out of the window with others while the commandant was making his speech, and now came back, out of breath, to unload her acquired food on the floor. She put a piece of bread into my mouth, crying joyfully, "Take it, eat as much as you want, remember how you used to dream of slicing a whole loaf?!"

Yet I did not eat very much . . . Somehow, after the first greedy mouthfuls, I could not swallow the food. I was almost amazed at myself looking at this big loaf. To have bread, yet not want to eat it!

I took up my position at the window again; women were running out of the barracks to see whether the overseers and SS were coming back, or whether by chance other Nazis were coming to replace them. Then, from the direction of the highway, came a powerful chorus. The women who had hitherto been sitting on the floor, entirely absorbed in opening cans of food, immediately dropped them and ran out to see for themselves what was the cause of this joyous ovation.

Some troops were arriving. But they were not Germans. The entire camp poured out of the huts to greet them. A few minutes later a tank rolled through the gate, followed by Soviet troops.

I did not stir from the window; I wanted to rejoice feverishly like the others at our miraculous liberation. But I could not.

Finally, Celina dragged me away from the window and took me to a comfortable, clean hut outside the camp, where German airmen had been living. We lodged two or three to a room. After many years I was again lying in a soft, warm bed, undressed, with my shoes under the bed—not under my head! All the same, I could not fall asleep that night. I was afraid. I had the idea that the Nazis would come back at any moment. They were still lurking in the forest and now, under cover of darkness, would recapture the camp, attack the airmen's hut and shoot us all for daring to occupy beds intended for the "supermen" . . . And the night was by no means tranquil. Shots, explosions, the sound of numerous footsteps did not cease for a moment. It was said in the camp that it was the Russians exploding shells thrown away on the roads by the retreating Germans—but I kept jumping with fright at every explosion.

The next morning was a sunny May day. I went out into the open air with Celina. On the highway we were greeted by a mild breeze, carrying from afar the sound of a song sung by marching troops. Only then did I take a deep breath and know that at last, at last, we were free.

The first free song I heard on German soil was the Russian "Fishing by the river . . ."

To this day, the song sounds to me as grand as any elevated, magnificent hymn, and always arouses in me the same emotions.

Conclusion

I spent my childhood in the shelters of burning Warsaw, within the walls of the Warsaw ghetto, behind the barbed wire of Majdanek, Auschwitz, Ravensbrück and Neustadt-Glewe.

Of our entire family, only Marek and I survived. I met him after the war in miraculous circumstances such as occur only in the dreams of women prisoners—on a Warsaw street, the first day of my return from the Neustadt-Glewe camp, in June 1945.

Marek was riding a bicycle, and I was walking along in torn sandals, on my way to see the Jewish committee in the Praga district of Warsaw. Suddenly Celina, beside me, cried, "Look, that man on the bicycle looks like Marek!" I glanced around, not expecting anything, for Celina kept finding resemblances to relatives or friends and . . . I did catch sight of my brother. I cried at the top of my voice "Marek!" He looked around in surprise, immediately jumped off his bicycle and ran up to me. In the middle of the street, surrounded by a crowd of interested and touched people, we threw ourselves into one another's embrace. But after a moment Marek moved away a little, looked at me closely, and began asking me my name, my mother's first name, what had happened to her? He did not believe it was me . . .

While still in the camp, I decided that if I lived to see liberation, I would write down everything I saw, heard and experienced. But when the longed-for end of the war and of our sufferings came, I was absorbed by problems of a new reality. I was 15 and in ecstasy over my youthful freedom. And my new life, with its joys and everyday cares, did not let me sit down to this work for any length of time.

But everything, down to the most minute details, remained unerased and fresh in my memory, as though it had happened yesterday . . . I am haunted at night by ghastly dreams, nightmares of persecution. Often in my sleep I seek hiding places and refuges, I am fleeing with my mother or a crowd of women prisoners from Nazi bandits who are on our track.

When my first son was born, I thought, with how much suffering does a man buy his entry into the world; and with how much ease did the barbarians kill millions of people. When I, with pride and emotion, like all young mothers, looked at the mouth of my child, wide-open, greedily seeking nourishment, I recalled with horror the thousands of unfortunate mothers in the ghetto who had nothing with which to feed their starving infants.

So it is that always, involuntarily, at almost every step, scenes, memories and comparisons with those other days are mixed with my present life . . .

Now, as my life flows in a normal and settled way, the recollections of the past have suddenly acquired a sort of new force. This happened as a result of the alarming news of fascism being reborn in the world and rumors of the introduction of resolutions to prevent the further prosecution of Nazi crimes. Yielding to this inner force, I set about writing down my memories. At first it seemed to me I would never achieve the task. I have a husband and children, I keep a home, and it is rare that an ordinary housewife takes pen in hand to communicate her story to others. More than once I have cried over the work, living once again through the misfortunes and tragedies of my nearest and dearest, gassed or dead in extermination camps. During the work I was upset by any sound in the house, by someone's laughter, by a cheerful light conversation, even by the sound of music. I sometimes burst out at my children and husband for no reason. I know it was unjust, unfair, but I could not control myself; I was still breathing the infested air around the crematoria. I am sure that when my children grow up and read this, they will understand and forgive my seemingly unfair attitude.

The number tattooed on my left arm—personal evidence from Auschwitz—today attracts the attention of many people. For some, it is an incomprehensible and strange mark, for others it is a painful souvenir of the cruel times of Nazism, while for me it is a kind of certificate of maturity, from a period in which I experienced life and the world in their naked forms, a desperate struggle for a piece of bread, a breath of air and a little space, from a period in which I learned to distinguish between truth and falsehood, between manifestations of human feeling and animal instincts, between goodness, nobility and evil baseness. I got out of that hell thanks to the victory of the Red Army. I was 15 at the time.

Fortunately, not every owner of a certificate of maturity of this type pays for it through the loss of family and childhood, through daily association with death, through a store of terrible experiences and incidents. Yet such was the lot of thousands of Jewish children, hounded down and murdered by Nazis.

I wish through this book to express my most fervent desire that similar crimes never be repeated anywhere on this earth.

Hertzliya, 1964–1965

Epilogue

Journey into the Past, Poland 1986

[More than forty years after the events described in this book, the author returned for the first time to her native Warsaw and the camps where she and her family were imprisoned. In these excerpts from her account of that journey, she revisits familiar places in Warsaw and grieves for the lost world of her childhood, and, as she walks over the ground in the Majdanek and Auschwitz camps, she recalls once again her mother and other family members and friends who died there, and is nearly overcome by a profound sense of loss. She recovers herself by telling her story to researchers in the historical department of the Auschwitz museum, who painstakingly recorded her testimony. —Ed.]

June 12, 1986

Two days have gone by in Warsaw. How unusual it is, familiar and strange, near—and so far! The Saxon Gardens, Cracow Boulevard, New World Street, Jerusalem Avenue, the Tomb of the Unknown Soldier. A warm sunny day with misty brightness. Poles walk along the streets, stand at bus stations, lead their children, speaking Polish. Everyone speaks only Polish. I inhale the sight of the houses, the city, the air, the memories. Memories surround me; I touch them, they attach themselves to each step of mine, to each thought and feeling. Tears appear from behind my eyelids, choke in my throat. But here, at the entrance to the Saxon Gardens the tears are different. They are the tears of my early childhood.

A refreshing coolness, gray pavements, dark walls of multicolored houses, gray sky and sun that warms but does not burn. Everything is just as I was used to, the climate that I grew up in, a natural part of me. Suddenly there descends on me that feeling, the most genuine and true one, the one from before the war, before the Germans came. Suddenly, as if someone erased years, an eternity of time. I am here. I was always here. Here I was born. Here my father was born, my grandfather and his grandfather. They taught me to walk, to speak, to feel, to understand. I could have lived out my years here as my parents and their parents did.

I stand here, after forty years, in the middle of the street in the early morning hours, thinking, crying. Yes, this is it. It's here!

Here they brought me by the hand to this garden, played with me, taught me, pointed out things. From here we used to run away from a sudden storm, through these same streets, between the walls of these buildings. It's true. I'm once again walking along these same pavements and paths. Alone. They are no longer in these houses. They no longer walk along here, even though I feel and hear their footsteps, their steps that are silenced, their voices, their laughter, their warnings. Under these skies, not shining but warm, I can actually touch and feel their presence that no longer exists. Their presence is that which touches and presses on the fountains of my tears. How clear and natural is the rhythm of them both here in the Warsaw street! I would like to be here forever, to feel them beside me from "then." I cannot get enough of this feeling, of the scene of the past in the moment that goes by in the present, in the Jewish Polishness of my country, in the midst of crowds of Poles who know nothing of my existence, not from then—and not now. I do not belong to them; I am not one of them. But nevertheless those skies, the pleasant air, not burning, the grayness of the walls and the pavements, they are not less mine, they are inside me, they are me. Whoever denies this does not yearn for it anymore. Therefore many of us do not want to encounter this anymore, to see and to feel once more because it hurts and greatly disturbs us. It is very painful.

It is good to feel this pain, to feel these tears through my eyelids, in my throat, on my cheeks, to breathe in the smell of the air and the street—to feel around me the presence that is no more, the sight of the places where they moved, were active. They have remained here forever, and I, as it were, have raised myself up to faraway places and have changed to become someone else entirely, someone without tears, without roots, without my real self. Even so, I have returned for a moment. I am once again in Warsaw, with myself as I was, among my family who are no longer alive, in the places where I lived in their midst, walking on their remains, on their ashes and on mine. I wonder at my memories, at my yearnings that go down deep, at the tears that flow of themselves without my being able to keep them back. And I say to myself: I am in Warsaw, I am in Warsaw . . . I am here. It is unbelievable. It's hard to grasp who I actually am and what I have been doing in another place up to now. But it is actually here that I understand and know everything most precisely.

I will know the rest for myself today in Treblinka . . . in a few hours in Treblinka. How many answers will I find there! I will not light candles, nor will I pray. I will not run away from the memories, from the stories, from reading them or writing about them. I will not release myself from the obligations by lighting a candle or mumbling a prayer. I will not flee to God who in this inferno revealed once and for all his nonexistence in such a decisive and unequivocal way.

June 13, 1986

. . . We returned a few minutes ago from the former Yeshivah of the Lublin Scholars—today a medical school. I don't know why, but during the whole time I wanted to cry, and after all I'm not religious. But I thought about the Hasidim who had studied there once. It seemed that I saw their faces, their figures in the long black shiny kapotes; I heard their voices, their footsteps and screams of the fear of death when the German soldiers arrived in trucks and stood before that wonderful building, ran wildly up the steps and snatched them all away in order to murder every last one of them. Not one of them is left today! We have come from far away after so many years, and now in the same hall that served as a synagogue for them and their families Polish students sit and listen to learned lectures on the human body and its care—for I don't know how many times we realize that they are no longer here! The beautiful yeshivah building that they built is still standing, the marks of the mezuzot that were torn from the doorposts are still there. Our traces are there, because we were also there—and Poland is there, this street exists, everything is in its place as before and goes on but without them and without us. Even those Jews who are there are not what they were then. . . .

June 15, 1986

I haven't written about Majdanek, but the visit there will never be erased from my memory.

I was finally there. I cried my heart out for all those years. I've never cried like that. I sat on the ground before the gas chamber and screamed to the heavens. After that I got up, straightened up and went inside. Darkness and a strange suffocation pervaded, tension and the silence of the murder and death that raged there and which now sleep together with the ashes of the victims in the mildew of the black beams, in an emptiness heavy with the weight of their endless suffering, permeated with the sighs of their dying. I went into every one of the barracks, one after the other. There was darkness inside, emptiness, hell—as in graves, like the inside of open graves where Death lives like a spider hidden in a dark corner. With a strong confident step my shoes stamped loudly on the wooden floor. I went farther and deeper inside as if I wanted to wake someone up, to scatter the desolation, to defy Death and expel him, to turn him out from "then" also. I felt within myself the power of my freedom, the strength of my life and my agony until everything seemed possible to me there and then. I wanted to blow something very human into all this and to conquer the nightmare, to show that I existed and that I control my fate with all the strength of my humanity, my pain and my terrible anger. This was together with the decision to breathe life into all those death-covered buildings and their shadows. For I am one of the tortured and the murdered here, a spirit that wanders between earth and sky, between the endless pain, depression and tears. I am one of that pile of thousands of corpses walking around on earth, moving, talking, screaming, dreaming, whispering and reminding. My steps strike the floors of the black mildew-covered barracks. My dear ones and my family must hear them in space, must absorb the mad echo that brings the message of life.

I walk here after forty years, carry them on my back, in my eyes, in my thoughts and in my blood. On this ground, by this path, they carried us to the fields of slaughter. The same sky spread above us when they dragged us here, separated us, undressed us, tortured us.

Today everyone knows that this abyss is called Majdanek. We didn't know the name then, and in the first moments we were happy that we were not taken to Treblinka, notorious even from the days of the ghetto. Now everyone knows, but no one can imagine what we felt, what we thought and what each of us said to his neighbor when we arrived here then, when they threw us from the cattle cars overloaded to suffocation, in order to pack us together behind barbed wire, to torture and murder us.

My heart turns over inside me with all these thoughts and memories and above all with the longing for those who were taken from me forever in this place. It seems to me that I stand here with them. My beautiful young mother smiles at me in spite of her terrible weariness, she holds me to her in her big woolen tweed coat and comforts me. She points to the barracks beyond

the fence and to the people in the striped clothing pulling wheelbarrows. "They won't kill us," she says, "we are young and
healthy, we will work at farming and survive, we will be lucky to
be liberated." It seems that I see her, that I feel the warmth of her
body through her wide coat. I hug her. She is here. Sorrow en-
gulfs me, an abyss of helplessness, exactly as then, and a terrible
anger because I am alive and well and standing again on this
path—and she is not here and she will never be! I am free but
completely helpless in the face of that disaster, as I was then in
those days as a small persecuted girl. I cannot change anything,
only scream to the heavens without shame or inhibition—until
my last breath.

A group of tourists passed me as I sat on the side of the road,
and the museum guard called to me: "Who did you lose here that
you are crying like that?" His voice rings in my ears, it reaches
me from another world, from the land of the living; but I am with
the image of my mother who was murdered here, with her
shadow in an empty void, and perhaps also with my own death.

What could I have answered him? They continue on their way
and I remain with my ghosts. I cannot contain it all, endure it all.
I don't want to accept the reality at all. I only want to lie on this
ground, to cover my eyes and to scream through the terrible tears
which froze around me then and suddenly flow from me like
boiling lava. It's good that no one sees my face covered with my
hands. After that I got up. I went into the gas chamber where I
was held then, an eternity ago, for a whole night and from where
I went out the next morning because by chance they had run out
of gas. People listened to the explanations of the guide spoken in
many languages. I pushed myself forward in among them rudely
and wildly. I stopped the guide in the midst of his words without
apologizing and without his permission. I stood in that chamber
as if it belonged only to me and I began to tell what happened
there to us, how we felt, where we were brought from and under
what conditions. I forced myself into someone else's words, into
their souls and their consciousness, without their asking me or
agreeing to listen. The burning torrent within me turned into a

fountain of words drenched with tears and pain. Everyone wept. I heard loud breathing, the rustle of handkerchiefs. I myself did not look at anyone. Before my eyes I could only see what I had been telling about in great agitation. I did not cry. I did not speak out of desperation. On the contrary. Everything was normal for me during all those horrible years; and so was it now also when I suddenly found myself once again in this place in the gas chamber. So I just told the story. But it sounded as if it were the voice of all those who had been there with me then. You could see it in those gathered around me who listened to me attentively. . . .

June 17, 1986

I would like to be at home already, but not less would I like to be here forever. I myself don't know what I want. I long for solitude, to run along the barracks and on the ashes of the camp, with my own fantasies, my thoughts and my feelings, to keep away from the rest of the people in the group and not to listen to the statistical explanations of the different guides. For me to be here means to feel the intensity of terror, of death and also of my own life, the eternity of my love and my longings. I don't want partners or witnesses to this. No, no! This is not a sightseeing tour. This is not Poland and not Israel. For me it was and still is the Holocaust—its great crushing weight which gives to everything in life a different meaning, a meaning which few people today have come to grips with. I am torn apart by the tension, the anger, the pain, the tremendous amount of endless explanations. I cannot find a place for myself within me. One part of me is torn inside and wants to escape far away from myself, to run to the winds, to choke Death with my bare hands; another part which is attached to Life restrains the first part. Both parts drag me after them, no one knows where. They crush my arms, shatter my brain. These feelings, thoughts and endless memories. There is no end!

Tomorrow I will go to Auschwitz. Auschwitz! My sister-in-law, Hela, me, everyone—how will I stand it? How much time

will the next eternity of the union of life and death take? the
futility of them both? They rouse earthquakes, volcanic eruptions
in my body, release all the feelings and memories. I am after all a
human being, a human being, important and yet insignificant at
the same time. Important because of that same madness that was
carried out on my generation, on me. Tomorrow I will go through
the gate of that madness or of its still-burning remnants as a
grown-up and free person. I will go to Auschwitz tomorrow,
which in a way I have never left. I did not have to come here to
prove this. Nevertheless it will seem different when I find myself
on the grounds of the camp itself. I am already losing my equilib-
rium today as I think about it. Tomorrow I will be myself to the
fullest, in my terrible completeness; nothing of me will be missing, no detail will be covered or blurred. Auschwitz will be attached to my personality physically, which to a great extent was
formed there, then.

But what does it matter? Who cares about this terrible fact that
I grew up there and that my personality was formed there? Who
can tell how it will be and what will be in a few hours? What did
I know when they brought me and Hela in the cattle cars from
Majdanek? . . .

The last few meters stretch out endlessly. We are arriving in
Auschwitz. I want to run away or go somewhere—to go and hear
the screaming quiet of Auschwitz in 1986. My head is pressed to
the window. I absorb the view and can hardly believe it. We
travelled this way then too; squeezed together in that nightmare
train. I didn't see anything on that day until they took me off at
the station. Today I am 56 years old—then I was 13. It seems to
me that I am now that same helpless, hunted girl, a young girl–
old woman. Such fantasies pass through my head! What shall I
do? How shall I push together the past with the present?

I cannot possibly be a tourist in the death camps where I was
tortured for years. I became familiar with all the corners of Hell,

down to the rock bottom, and I died a thousand deaths. I don't mean only my life and my sufferings.

We get off the bus. I am the first to run forward. I can't wait. I must prove that it is here, that I am really here. I must convince myself that I was once that same miserable Jewish prisoner condemned beforehand because of my origin. I was a child not needed even for terrible strenuous hard labor. It is hard to believe and hard to free myself from the intensity of the terror from then. Others do not experience this; they can't even imagine it!

I recognize the gate, the barracks, the entrance to the camp. I explain to our guide that I was here. He denies it vehemently. "No, this is Auschwitz; you were in Birkenau . . ." "But I went to work every day from here, to 'Canada'; they sorted out the clothes of the murdered people there." The guide becomes silent and admits: "We're standing exactly beside the barracks of 'Canada.' " I guessed, just as an animal smells. I identified the place immediately, after so many years!

I was tense, like a place set with mines about to explode. I couldn't walk around, visit the different places. I asked the guide to accompany me to the archives or to the museum administration. I felt that I had to tell them, to pass on what had happened then, things they don't know about. They couldn't know all the details that I know and remember.

We went into one of the old barracks as free people in Auschwitz—as in a fairy tale. The guide introduced me and left. I wanted to talk, to tell so much. I thought I would be able to, that as usual I was strong and in control of myself. For years I have been telling different groups of youngsters about that period with no difficulty.

First the director of the history department listened to me. But he immediately called Helena, who researched the fate of children who had been in the camp. They were both surprised and excited at my unexpected and stormy appearance. At first they treated me with reserve. Were they in that way perhaps trying to protect themselves from the tension and my great agitation? In any case the urgency and flow of my explanations convinced them and held them spellbound. I suggested I read before them an article of mine connected with my stay in Auschwitz. Then they didn't refuse me. Helena asked if she could bring a tape recorder. Now the enthusiasm and tension was on their side. The director lost his composure and reservations. Time was pressing. They wanted to get as much done as possible. They wanted to hear my stories from the war, not only about Auschwitz. Suddenly everything came alive, intensified, stopped being statistics, history.

My voice stuck in my throat; I hadn't expected this. Once again I found myself physically in the barracks in Auschwitz. Through the windows I could see the same rows of barracks. I saw myself then and now. It turned out that this was beyond my strength. I couldn't go on. A convulsive crying stuck in my throat and wouldn't let me utter a sound. I tried quietly to get control of myself. I swallowed the tears in helplessness, but they choked me like a raging storm. Nothing like that had ever happened to me. I bit my lips. The director and Helena looked at me, fearing that all was lost. In that place everything took on such tangible meaning. Here the inferno took place, in and between these barracks of red bricks. They are looking at me through the window of this office. I am two people here, the one from the camp and the one who has come from across the sea after forty years, older and different, but burdened with the fate and weight of the trials of the first. Even now, when I write of this after a week, I can scarcely keep myself from throwing the notebook from my hand and collapsing on the bed in wild crying. The comfortable room and wonderful bed that my new friend from Cracow prepared for me in her warm home do not succeed in relieving this pain.

At first I spoke into the tape recorder of my impressions that I had written on the way, and then I began my story of those years. I had already regained control of myself. They stopped asking me questions. How could they know what to ask about the details of daily life in the camp? I soon found out that all these things were new and astounding to them, in spite of the fact that they were constantly delving into endless documents. They sat beside me listening attentively, shocked at the immensity of the horror and human pain that unfurled before them. I tried not to look at them and see the tears flowing from their eyes, down their cheeks and undisturbed onto the desk. They made me feel uncomfortable. From time to time they would wipe away a tear stealthily with their fingertips so that they could write. A mood of understanding was created between us as if we had known each other for years and were close.

Through the windows you could see green trees and different groups of visitors. People visit the camp like other interesting museums. They listen to explanations, which to my ears sound like pitiably weak echoes, even though they use words like terrible, awful, cruel, dreadful. Words, only words—empty. They cannot express what it really was like. But it cannot be otherwise. The guides are young.

The director and Helena greedily took in every word that came out of my mouth. Now and then just to spite, my voice failed me and I was forced to stop speaking in order to overcome my tears. Wild outbursts of pent-up crying interrupted my words. But fortunately only for a short time. I tried to swallow the tears in my throat, taking deep gulps as quickly as I could, and they waited for me patiently in the belief that my strength would return. They now found themselves in the same position in which the room we were sitting in enveloped me then.

After an hour or so I came back to reality. I stopped my story. I wanted to rejoin my group, to look at the camp, to go into the barracks.

My hosts jumped up from their places as if suddenly awakened from a deep dream, ready to fulfill my every wish. They began to phone immediately to find my friends. It wasn't difficult. Helena came with me. We found them in one of the barracks. A young woman with a quiet delicate voice was explaining to the people the conditions in which the prisoners were kept there. I looked at her, at the wooden bunks I knew so well—dark, gloomy, crowded and now empty. They are carved in my memory together with all that happened on them then. Once again it was so difficult to contain in my mind the present and the tremendously terrible past, the reality and the memories. Of course I will not begin to describe what I remembered and what I saw in those moments before my eyes. Nevertheless just one small detail, as it were, known today to everyone: roll call in the camp. Do people really know what roll call was then? I raised this question later before the director and Helena when I returned to their office after my group had left. (I stayed on in Auschwitz a few more hours to finish my story.) I clarified the small details to them, and they asked me not to forget them during recording.

Roll call in the camp—not a selection, not a transport to the gas chamber or death in another way.

Terrifying whistles reach into every corner of the camp and into the human soul. More than a thousand women squeezed into the block push wildly in a rush through the narrow door to get out of the barracks as fast as possible and to keep from being beaten. In each row five prisoners must stand, the distance between them being that of an outstretched arm. Fleeing in panic, confused by the whistles, the shouts and the fear, more than five assemble in each row. You have to move, run to another place, but no one wants to leave the place she was standing in. They know very well that to change your place sometimes means to decide your fate, to change it. And who would agree to that of her own free will? So arguments, fights, curses burst out. No woman wants to give in, nor does anyone want to stand in the first or the last row because it's cold at this hour and it's impossible to stand close to the one in front or in back of you and warm yourself up a little without those in charge noticing and beating you without mercy for it. You don't know which rows will be sent to easier work and which will be sent to that place from which there is no return. Maybe there will be a selection (that was always expected) and the place a prisoner stands can decide if she sticks out too much and will be taken to the gas chamber, or they could simply count and take away every tenth person.

Anything can happen, and who knows where it's safest? Why move, change your place? There are women who are beside a sister or a good friend in the camp and they want to stand to-

gether, to be together always, to help one another and share everything with each other, to get the portion of bread together.
Portions of bread are not cut equally, and the one who receives
two pieces joined together isn't sorry about the unequal measur-
ing. After all, each crumb is a treasure! Only the one in charge of
the block and her helpers decide in those disagreements with
beatings and severe punishments. Who can imagine today the
magnitude and importance of those daily problems connected only
to the prisoner count in the morning and evening? The fear of being
sent to another terrible camp, being separated from a relative, being
sent to the next world! Everything was arranged at the roll call!

The prisoners in the first and last rows were exposed constantly to the eyes of those cruel women in charge who tormented them for the smallest thing—for weakness, pallor, poor
dress or whatnot. To stand in the middle was safer and warmer,
although sometimes it was actually better to stand at the ends. It
was possible to get faster to the soup kettle, to get the bread ration
first, which we waited so longingly for. How many ambitious goals
and struggles were concentrated in this one detail of life in the death
camps! Do people understand this, do they know about it?

My group returned to Warsaw, and I remained in Auschwitz.
Helena put on the tape recorder, changed the cassette (the
fourth), and I continued telling my story from then without noticing the tears running down her cheeks onto the desk. In that way
we continued working. Suddenly I felt a great weakness come
over me; my heart began to pound quickly. I was ashamed to
admit that I didn't feel well. But I was forced to stop. I was afraid
I might faint. I apologized and asked her to stop the machine.
Helena brought me some tea and suggested we go outside for
some fresh air. She was very worried about me, but no less did
she want me to finish my story: "When will you have a chance to
be here again?"

She was right. It was important, but I couldn't continue. I was
afraid I would die in Auschwitz, once more, in the Auschwitz of
today. It was already quite late. All the office workers and those
on the grounds had already gone home. We were almost the only

ones left. We went outside. Rows of empty barracks in the red-
dish summer sun of the late afternoon. Buildings and barracks
that had once belonged to the headquarters of the Nazis who had
looked after the camp and ruled over us. There is an indescribable quiet. Even at this moment I cry in my pain over the memory of the many voices that were silenced here. What words can
describe the silence of Auschwitz today? I hear there the cries of
torture and death. I listen to them here again, after forty years.

I leaned on the rail at the entrance to one of the barracks. I
stretched out in enjoyment. I felt the increased pulse and the
incomprehensible awareness that I was in Auschwitz as a free
person, respected and cared for with warmth and appreciation.

The young Helena of the research department for children in
the camp, gentle and penetrating, sat at my feet on the step and
waited until I could calm down and regain my strength. Around us
were tall trees covered with green leaves and the chirping of birds.
A paradise within Hell. The last visitors passed by, here and there a
song was heard, the sounds of a cafeteria, a souvenir stand. Could I
have ever dreamed that I would one day be here as a tourist, walking freely between the barracks of the satanic rulers, walking along
the *Lagerstrasse*—the main thoroughfare in the camp meant for the
German superman—and not be killed for that? That I could warm
myself like this in the summer sun which was setting at the entrance
to their barracks? I was privileged to do so. And still I felt inside the
feeling of terror of those days. It was reflected through the tranquillity, the warmth and luxuriant greenery all around. It was visible
through every grain of earth on that ground.

Helena tells me that former prisoners say nothing grew here
and you didn't see birds then. Now there are so many of them.
Yes, that is true. Life and quiet have returned. Now free people
walk here and not the crowds that were hunted, tortured,
crammed together, poisoned. Not miserable prisoners, most of
them Jews, and others. Visitors from far and near arrive here to
delve into those events, to think about them, to lay wreaths, to
light a candle, to pray, to prove with their own eyes that the
nightmare did indeed happen in our world. Some even sing songs

of praise to God but of course they will not forget that this place is essentially the symbol of the existence of the Devil. And the most important thing is that they come here and remember.

The weakness and bad feeling pass. I feel better. Suddenly I think that I will not retell my stories and memoirs. It is enough. They cause me great stress and agitation, which weaken my health. How much can I stand? Until when? I said this aloud. Helena was shocked. "But madam, this is only a momentary weakness, it will pass, you will get stronger and continue! You must tell it, people don't know anything about it today!" She looked at me with a pleading look. "People must learn about this. It must not be forgotten!"

Time slipped away without mercy. I had to get the train back to Cracow in time. I gathered my strength and went back with Helena to her desk. I spoke slower, in a lower voice, but I did finish my story. Helena was full of satisfaction and appreciation.

We began the race to catch the train. It turned out that it was leaving the station in six minutes. Helena called her husband from home, and we rushed away from the living–dead barracks of the inferno–museum. There was not even enough time for any tears or reflections. Four minutes before it left I jumped onto the train. That's how I left Auschwitz for the second time in my life. Without outward tears. They remained stuck in my throat like a bubbling spring. They remained also in my zealous and seemingly tranquil voice on the cassette of the history department in the Auschwitz museum.

The testimony that I gave in the museum allowed me to relieve the tension and pain, saved me from certain breakdown caused by my renewed meeting with the sight of the camp. But in all modesty I am convinced that its value is far greater than this mere personal consideration.

June 23, 1986

I have not written since I left Auschwitz. I have simply been busy with other things, in other words—in coming back to the living.

My attention has now been taken up with real trips, not into the past, happy meetings with friends from the city of Rzeszow whom I met by way of a long correspondence in connection with my book published in Poland in 1967. . . .

I spent the last three days in Warsaw, the city of my birth. I visited the old Jewish cemetery on Okopowa Street, the Nozyk synagogue, the Jewish Theater where Polish actors speak Yiddish and present programs on Jewish subjects, on Jewish life that flowed in Poland for hundreds of years. Poetry, folklore and plays in Yiddish that show their life and works in those days before the war. Everything without them. How painful was it to see and hear!

We also visited the Polish Theater and saw a good English comedy. Lots of laughter and entertainment were often interrupted by flashes of the fresh reminder of Treblinka, Majdanek and Auschwitz. I also thought constantly of what would happen if I had sat in that auditorium on the "Aryan side" and suddenly a German military policeman came in, as then. I had already seen the green uniform, the boots and the helmet. I couldn't prevent these thoughts and comparisons from flitting through my mind.

I visited the Lazienki Park, the Belvedere Palace, the Palace in Wilanow, the Praga quarter, the old Prague of Warsaw! Eleven days in which to renew forty years passed by as if in a moment. . . .

We're flying home but in my mind and in my heart the memories of Poland and especially of Warsaw are so fresh. Every now and then I burst out in quiet weeping. I miss the streets of Warsaw and that part of myself that remained there and is not found anywhere else even though I have a home and family, even though they are waiting anxiously and impatiently. I'm very attached to them. I fear their questions: "Well, how was it in Poland? How did it go?" And I, instead of answering happily and enthusiastically, will burst out in tears, because it's not possible otherwise to describe such a journey into the past.

I still long for solitude to continue feeling the closeness of the places where I spent my childhood. The shadow of all my dear ones who perished there hovers over them. It's doubtful if someone will understand me and be tolerant. They will say of course that my nerves have been weakened from the burden of these difficult experiences that I was warned about so much before my trip.

Only now do I understand how much a person is attached to those places where there is a trace of the past, some remnant— ashes of his relatives, echoes of their footsteps, their customs, their now-silent voices. I didn't realize this enough beforehand. . . .

We will soon land. I will meet my family, and everything will continue as usual. The dream is over. So much has been left behind. It seems to me that I have shed one more of my identities, of the many that I have assumed in my life. I have come full circle. I have finished another chapter, but no doubt not the last one. Perhaps I will open another one.

My journey is at an end. They are waiting for me at the Ben Gurion Airport to take me home.

(translated by Elaine Morton)

Postscript

Berlin 1939–1989

[*After Mrs. Birenbaum's trip to Poland, her memoir became known in Germany through the efforts of several leaders of church groups for German young people, who translated portions of her memoir in order to share it with their members. A few years later, Mrs. Birenbaum's son, Jaacov Gilad, was involved in making the film* Because of That War *in Israel, about the problems of children of Holocaust survivors. This film won a number of awards and was widely shown in Europe. As Mrs. Birenbaum's talks to school groups continued, interest grew in having her entire memoir translated into German as well as in having her address a forthcoming conference in Germany organized by the Lutheran Church.*

The confluence of these two initiatives led to her making two trips to Berlin in 1989, the fiftieth anniversary of the Nazi invasion of Poland. She was first invited to the three-day "Kirchentages" *("Church days") conference, held in Berlin in June 1989. Part I consists of her thoughts while flying to Berlin, "Hitler's former capital," for the first time.—Ed.]*

221

Part I. Flying to Berlin

June 4, 1989

I am flying with my husband. I would not have dared to go by
myself this time, for the goal of our trip is Berlin. It is history
itself that is taking us to Hitler's former capital. But who in
today's dynamic present cares about that history? I am to appear
in front of Germans, I am going to tell them my own history and
theirs, which they created, their fathers and grandfathers. . . .

Actually, I only wanted to write about the fact that fifty years
ago the words *Berlin, Germans, Hitler* burst into my mind, were
engraved on my body and soul, became my fate—my life and my
death, as well as my eternal, many-varied, many-faceted today.
And also that of my descendants, born after the war, in Israel.
Then I was absolutely and irrevocably sentenced to death, along
with millions of my compatriots and like hundreds of thousands
of children who, in accordance with Hitler's "New Order," were
to be the first to die along with the sick, the weak, and the
elderly. I was totally meaningless dust, a miserable speck among
so many excellent, great, and mighty representatives of my na-
tion, which they simply decided to exterminate. I happened to
survive and, on the fiftieth anniversary of that nightmare, to be
invited by the Germans (not brought by force by the Gestapo) to
Berlin for a series of talks about those times. . . .

At this moment, here in this German airplane, I somehow do
not believe that such talks make sense. I am flying with this
outdated story to Berlin, where I would have been killed instantly
had I dared to venture onto its pavements then. Now at least no
one will arrest me, no one will shoot me for looking Jewish, no
one will demand to see my *Ausweis*—"Lebens recht!"—in other
words, a certificate that I have a temporary right to live. . . .
There is a certain satisfaction in this—the revenge of the ten-
year-old Jewish girl from Warsaw of 1939 that I was that September, when Hitler's armies started to bomb Polish cities and

villages, to murder, burn, and destroy—as well as of the sixty-year-old woman, now an Israeli from Hertzliya.

[*The* Kirchentages *conference in Berlin was attended by 140,000 people, mostly young people from Germany and other countries struggling for peace and against nuclear weapons testing and production, and racism. Mrs. Birenbaum was warmly welcomed, made a variety of appearances, radio and newspaper interviews, and met with and spoke to a variety of people and groups, often in churches and movie theaters (combined with a showing of* Because of That War*). Part II excerpts her relating of these experiences. Once again she is overwhelmed by the irony of her role and is unexpectedly moved by her reception.—Ed.]*

Part II. June 1989

In the movie theater Arsenal, after the showing of the film *Because of That War* in our honor, I said that all kinds of impossible things happen to me in my life. . . . I watched this film here in an unbelievable onslaught of emotions, which I could barely contain. Tears, pain, astonishment, the sudden realization of the meaning of my ordeals constricted my breast, tears choked my throat and burned my eyes. At no time and in no place did I feel as acutely the meaning of my salvation from Hitler's talons—from the ghetto, Majdanek, Auschwitz, from the gas chambers and the thousands of deaths that I then faced eye to eye and so close to whose thresholds I stood—as here, when I saw myself, my house in Hertzliya, my family, my sons and grandsons on the screen of a Berlin movie theater amidst a German audience! I, that small girl, who in September 1939 turned ten and upon whose ears the words *Berlin, Germans, Hitler, "Farfluchte Jude! Raus! Raus!"* pounded, penetrating my brain like a terrible venom and instantaneously becoming the whole and only meaning of life and death, mine and of those close to me, neighbors, countrymen, and thousands of people who surrounded me in a crowd as we were herded to tortures the world had never before seen—to extermination. I involuntarily recalled the words of a certain woman, a prisoner, when we were mired in mud at a many-hour-long roll call in Auschwitz, growing numb from cold, hunger, and exhaustion, no longer resembling humans, barely able to imagine that we had once been human or that somewhere on the face of the earth people still existed. In front of us, beyond the barbed wire, was the huge chimney of the crematorium, the pillar of fire, and the thick smoke of people being gassed and burned. We looked at them with horror. We were helpless, like those who, dumped from the cattle cars, waited, not aware of their fate as they stood in line for death. "You will see," the woman said then, "the world and life will come again, and books will be written about us and films about us will be shown. . . ." It was a daring dream, totally impossible—a prayer without any hope of fulfillment. That woman is no longer alive, nor are thousands of those who stood next to me in rows on the roll call field. And yet . . . Today I am in Berlin, in Hitler's former capital!

The film was shown a second time, and I was invited to a discussion in the movie theater Bali on *Friedenstage*, the Day of Peace. I spoke, among others, twice in Martin Luther's church, where Hitler prayed to a figure of Jesus with a classical, muscular build and a body with the measurements of a true, pure-blooded "Aryan." I talked about my experiences in the ghetto and death camps. I read my postwar works based on these memories—the poem about the spirit of my mother, who was gassed and cremated in Majdanek, which appeared to me again during that strange "trip into the past." Then I was a prisoner—condemned because I was Jewish and on top of that a child. Now I was a tourist of spirits and ghosts. . . .

With bowed heads, frozen with emotion, petrified by the power of this still-timely human horror and pain, suddenly crushed by its magnitude, which exuded from me, from my body, my voice, my words—they were listening to me. Germans, in 1989. . . .

The young people . . . and their educators in East Berlin listened to me with the greatest concentration, astonishment, and tension. I talked; they sat in a circle around me, cheerful at first, absorbed in themselves, their own affairs and problems. Fair faces, fair hair . . . As my story intensified, their seriousness and dread grew. Some wiped their tear-filled eyes, others dropped their heads down low. This lasted for more than two hours; I had transported them with me—there. They were with me—I felt this. They could barely leave, return to reality. . . .

Everywhere I was shown great attention, feeling, and above all gratitude that I had wanted to visit them at all after the immensity of evil that I had suffered at the hands of their countrymen. But this was not all. My crazy fate had yet to send me another incredible experience, this time in the form of a conversation with a certain woman, one of my many listeners in Martin Luther's church. She stared fixedly at me from the sidelines when everyone surrounded me in a tight circle, asking with emotion about various details, asking me to autograph my book for them. Finally she came up to me. Her eyes expressed warmth and trust. I suddenly felt close to her. She wanted to confide in me. I understood—I had indicated in my presentation how well I knew the pain of loss. She had lost her father. For many years she did not even know the circumstances of his death. But recently a common grave had been discovered—and the diary of the last several months of his life. A description of his thoughts and feelings—"like yours" . . . On May 5, 1945, the underground had executed him along with 20 other German soldiers. . . .

With a choked voice I finished my presentation by relating this meeting in the movie theater Arsenal after the showing of *Because of That War*, adding that *then* I had prayed for him and for all those soldiers to be killed, otherwise I would never see freedom—otherwise the whole world would be destroyed. But for that woman, it was her father, whom she loved and for whom she cried. Her father. That is war, hatred, racism! It is difficult to deal with everything, even after fifty years. For me and for them.

[By 1989, arrangements had been made for the first German translation of Hope Is the Last to Die *with the publisher Reiner Padligur Verlag in Hagen. In October 1989, Mrs. Birenbaum was invited by her publisher to the Book Fair in Frankfurt; she also visited Berlin and Hagen, spending two weeks filled with various appearances. In Part III she recalls several of her most memorable encounters from that trip.—Ed.]*

Part III. To Germany for the Second Time

October 1989

. . . And so once again two weeks in Germany and about thirty lectures and gatherings! . . . Until then I had known Germans only as a steel wall of implacable death. I had come to contend with them as a free person with memories from my reality, created then by their countrymen. To bring right up in front of their eyes the image of these experiences so that they, their children, and their grandchildren might taste them for a moment. But I was faced with ordinary people, shaken, moved, terrified—shamed. Thus was I requited. With shared tears . . .

In the church, a young woman walked up to me and asked with great agitation whether in the ghetto we knew about the conspiracy in Germany against Hitler. I said no, to which she responded, "and if you had known, could we feel less guilty today?" In saying this she looked pleadingly into my eyes as if searching for absolution in my response. . . . One woman confessed to me that her father had been a Nazi. One of the big ones . . . "How am I to live with this? What shall I say to my son when he reads your book? Why did he do this to me?" . . .

In Hagen we were staying with my publisher. Once after dinner we went with him, his wife, and their three young children for a walk in the woods. . . . I was walking through these woods which smelled of autumn and golden leaves, rocking their youngest son in his carriage so that he would stop crying. My head was roaring—I had not been intended to live because I was a Jewish child. Jewish infants were torn from their mothers and thrown into gas chambers, or the mothers along with them if they refused to part from them. But today—in spite of everything—today . . .

(translated by Dosia Freeman)

Halina Birenbaum, a writer, poet, and translator, lives in Israel, where she lectures and talks with young Israelis about the Holocaust. She has spoken to groups all over the world. Her reminiscences were the basis for the Polish documentary *Hope Dies Last* (1992), and her experiences provided the impetus for her son's involvement in the film *Because of That War* (1988). Her works have been published in Poland, Israel, Germany, and the United States.